THE MASCULINE MASQUERADE

The Masculine Masquerade

An exhibition organized by Helaine Posner and Andrew Perchuk

at the MIT List Visual Arts Center, Cambridge, Massachusetts.

January 21–March 26, 1995

Library of Congress Cataloging–in–Publication Data

The masculine masquerade: masculinity and representation/

    editors, Andrew Perchuk and Helaine Posner;

    essayists, Harry Brod . . . [et al.] ; general editor, Don McMahon;

artists, Matthew Barney . . . [et al.].

      Catalog of an exhibition at the MIT List Visual Arts Center,

    Jan. 21–Mar. 26, 1995.

      Includes bibliographical references.

      ISBN 0–262–16154–0 (hc)

      1. Masculinity (Psychology) in art—Exhibitions. 2. Art, Modern—

20th century—Exhibitions. I. Perchuk, Andrew. II. Posner, Helaine.

III. MIT List Visual Arts Center.

N8222.M38M38 1995

701' .03—dc20   94–24084

                         CIP

This book was printed and bound in Hong Kong.

Andrew Perchuk and Helaine Posner

Editors

THE MASCULINE MASQUERADE

Masculinity

and Representation

MIT List Visual Arts Center

Cambridge, Massachusetts

The MIT Press

Cambridge, Massachusetts

London, England

Essayists

Harry Brod

Steven Cohan

bell hooks

Michael Leininger

Glenn Ligon

Andrew Perchuk

Helaine Posner

Simon Watney

**General
Editor**

Donald McMahon

Artists

Matthew Barney

Tina Barney

Clegg & Guttmann

Graham Durward

Lyle Ashton Harris

Dale Kistemaker

Mary Kelly

Donald Moffett

Keith Piper

Charles Ray

Michael Yue Tong

Contents

Acknowledgments

List Visual Arts Center exhibitions do not shy from taking on testy topics. Our recent schedule, for example, has revisited previously unquestioned accounts of American history (*Storytelling Chairs; Our Bodice, Our Selves*), scrutinized the fragmentation of contemporary body identity (*Corporal Politics*), exposed the polemical potential of the decorative arts (*Subversive Crafts*), and plumbed the relationship between patterns of economic consumption and aesthetic simplification (*The Bathroom, the Kitchen, and The Aesthetics of Waste; A Process of Elimination*).

Noting a strange imbalance toward the feminine among recent gender projects in the arts, we decided to confront that most loaded of cultural constructs, masculinity. Paradoxically elusive by virtue of being so pervasive, and resistant by virtue of being assumed to be unconditional and universal, masculinity had proved a slippery target for investigators. Research soon revealed, however, a number of contemporary artists and writers, both male and female, for whom masculinity's poses, props, and guises presented a rich and virgin territory. For the initial suggestion we are grateful to George Wagner.

Project co-curators Helaine Posner and Andrew Perchuk have mined this rich cultural ore in a remarkably fruitful and cordial collaboration. They and I are deeply grateful to the eleven artists and five outside essayists who have contributed so distinctively to the exhibition and publication. The individual collectors Marc and Livia Straus, Scott Watson, and Ealan Wingate and the institutions that have lent works to this exhibition, The Whitney Museum of American Art; Museum of Fine Arts, Boston; New School for Social Research; and Newport Harbor Art Museum are to be commended for their enlightened generosity. Janet Borden, Inc., Sandra Gering Gallery, and Jack Tilton Gallery all provided loans and material with invaluable efficiency and goodwill.

General editor Donald McMahon's diligent and intelligent reading of the essays is evident throughout this publication. Michael Leininger gamely undertook the compilation of an extensive bibliography of masculinity in the arts which will become an important research tool in many fields. Adam Weinberg at the Whitney Museum and Jay Tobler at Barbara Gladstone Gallery made special efforts on behalf of the project and deserve extra and public thanks. Michael Kim, Naomi Urabe, and Jennifer Reil were early, dedicated, and skilled research assistants. Laura Hitchcock worked miracles transferring unruly texts to disk. And once again Judy Kohn and Jessica Ludwig of Kohn Cruikshank Inc. have designed a book whose elegance and intelligence is a fitting vehicle for its contents.

Generous and critical support to the exhibition was provided by the Andy Warhol Foundation for the Visual Arts and by the National Endowment for the Arts, establishing once again their respective commitments to serious and challenging themes and the artists who grapple with them. Roger Conover and Daniele Levine have made our collaboration with MIT Press both productive and pleasurable from the outset.

The List Visual Arts Center staff may be small in number but it is enormous in talent, professionalism and dedication. I am grateful every day for each one of them.

Katy Kline, Director

THE MASCULINE MASQUERADE

Masculinity
and Representation

Masculinity as Masquerade

Harry Brod

This volume and the exhibition it accompanies invite us to contemplate "the masculine masquerade," a phrase whose meaning deserves some scrutiny. It might mean that there are multiple masquerades, and we are to consider the masculine one. Or, it might mean that there are multiple masculinities, with one or more of them being a masquerade, and the other or others by implication not, with us being invited to consider that masculinity which *is* a masquerade. But I believe a much more radical invitation has been extended here. I believe that we are being invited to consider masculinity *itself*, in any and all of its forms, as a masquerade.

What does it mean to consider masculinity as a masquerade? To begin with, we should note that this idea flies in the face of deeply held beliefs about the nature of masculinity. The masculine self has traditionally been held to be inherently opposed to the kind of deceit and dissembling characteristic of the masquerade. Philosophers such as Plato and Rousseau have, for example, considered any sort of playacting or pretension to be corrupting of the masculine virtues. Hence, Plato banishes poetry from his ideal utopia, for its dramatic recitation requires one to pretend to be what one is not; and Rousseau, who follows Plato

here as in so much else, warns of the corrupting influences of theatrical artifice on the pure soul of the noble savage. Like the American cowboy, "real" men embody the primitive, unadorned, self-evident, natural truths of the world, not the effete pretenses of urban dandies twirling about at a masquerade ball. The masquerade was the province of the female, as it was so named in the psychoanalytic tradition, in Joan Riviere's 1929 essay "Womanliness as Masquerade."[1] According to the traditional view, only effeminate men would adopt a masquerade. To those who hold such a traditional view, the phrase "masculine masquerade" is an oxymoron, a contradiction in terms.

How and why, then, have we come so far from traditional views of masculinity, to the point where the idea of masculinity *as* masquerade can now be plausibly articulated? In order to answer this question, we must go back to the roots of the current challenges to and reconceptualizations of gender which emerged from the activism and scholarship of the 1960s and '70s.

The wedge used to open up the discussion about masculinity and femininity was the distinction drawn between sex and gender. Sex was shown to be biological, while gender was social; the one the product of nature, the other of nurture,

1.
Joan Riviere, "Womanliness as Masquerade," *International Journal of Psychoanalysis*, 1929. Reprinted in *Formations of Fantasy*, eds. Victor Burgin, James Donald, and Cora Kaplan (London: Methuen, 1986). Cited in Avery Gordon, "Masquerading in the Postmodern," *Cross Currents* (1990), 65–82. In "Masquerading as the American Male in the Fifties: *Picnic*, William Holden and the Spectacle of Masculinity in Hollywood Film" (in *Male Trouble*, eds. Constance Penley and Sharon Willis [Minneapolis: University of Minnesota Press, 1993], 203–32), Steven Cohan notes that essays by Stephen Heath, Mary Ann Doane, and John Fletcher take up "Riviere's case study, which originated the discussion" and "extend it to the problem of sexual representation in film" (229): Stephen Heath, "Joan Riviere and the Masquerade" in *Formations of Fantasy*; Mary Ann Doane, "Film and the Masquerade: Theorizing the Female Spectator," *Screen* 23, nos. 3–4 (1982), 74–88; and John Fletcher, "Versions of Masquerade", *Screen* 29, no. 3 (summer 1988), 43–69.

or culture. While the differences between male and female were held to be differences of sex, masculinity and femininity were understood as in the domain of gender. This distinction between biological sex and social gender was crucial for many reasons, not the least of which was that by opening up a space between nature and culture it created room and laid the conceptual foundation for rethinking our notions of masculinity and femininity. For part of what we usually mean when we call something "natural" is that it is a given phenomenon, fixed and constant. Attempting to change something of that order is like banging one's head against a brick wall. But if gender were social, then it is learned rather then permanently ingrained behavior. (A later, more technologically advanced and computer-literate generation would come to speak of "hardware" or "hard wiring" versus "software" or "programming".) And if learned, gender could—at least in principle—be unlearned, and changed.

Gender, from this point of view, is a role, not a biological condition. The concept of role, as used by social theorists, was taken from the theater, in which an actor's part was at one time indeed literally written on a roll and handed to him, to be unreeled as it was played. The core element in the concept of a role is that a role is separate and distinct from the person playing it. A role is a performance, an enactment of a persona different from that of the actor. To speak of a role is to invoke a distinction between the behavior exhibited and the "real" person behind or beneath the role, the agent *in* the role. Indeed, actors come to be criticized if critics feel that they are just "playing themselves" in their roles. We may say that an actor "becomes" his or her character, but we know that this is merely a figure of speech.

To speak the language of role, then, is to radically separate the person from the behavior. The concept of a "gender role" is thus more radical than most who use this now-common coinage often realize. For example, it means that believing gender roles to be natural is self-contradictory, for to speak the language of role is to invoke the distinction between nature and culture, to say precisely that what is being discussed is *not* natural but cultural. Further, most people conceptualize gender identity as part of one's true self. When people reach down to a core sense of themselves as masculine or feminine, they tend to believe that they have reached something essentially true about themselves. But to believe in the existence of gender as a role is to disavow the belief that one's gender *is* a part of one's essential self, because the conception of gender as a role entails the separation of one's gender from one's self.

As a consequence, the concept of gender as a role greatly undermined the theoretical foundations of traditional views on gender, which assumed continuity rather than rupture between biology and culture. As feminist theory moved further into the '70s and then into the '80s, however, gender role theory increasingly came to be seen by many feminist theorists as carrying with it its own set of highly problematic theoretical assumptions and propositions.

First of all, the theoretical framework of gender role theory within sociology— the field that has, together with psychology (or perhaps more accurately, social psychology), contributed most to the development of the theory—was, from the outset, saddled with the functionalist viewpoint it inherited from the classic sociological theorist most associated with role theory's development, Talcott Parsons. For Parsons, masculine and feminine gender roles were complementary, each working alongside the other (as long as the system functioned properly) to keep an integrated social structure moving along smoothly. To feminists, this presumption of the harmonious complementarity of roles was pernicious because it masked the fact that gender roles were in reality not relations of complementarity but rather relations of domination—specifically, male domination over women. The fundamental feminist insight was this: In naming gender, one is not simply naming a (sexual) division of labor; one is, rather, naming a system of power, further denoted variously as patriarchy, sexism, male dominance, and so on.

Even when stripped of functionalist assumptions about harmony and complementarity, the very concept of role seemed, to some, unable to do justice to the dimension of power that feminists argued should be central to any discussion of gender. As Judith Stacey and Barrie Thorne put it in an influential article:

The notion of "role" focuses attention on individuals more than on social structures, and implies that "the female role" and "the male role" are complementary (i.e. separate or different but equal). The terms are depoliticizing; they strip experience from its historical and political context and neglect questions of power and conflict. It is significant that sociologists do not speak of "class roles" or "race roles."[2]

The concepts of "the female role" and "the male role" were met with criticism from other quarters as well, because they imply the existence of a single norm for each gender, against which variations from that norm must be seen as devalued deviations. As scholars and activists became more aware of the need to understand differences within each gender as well as differences between the genders, role theory became untenable. Were one to remain within the framework of role

theory, it would be necessary to speak not of *the* female and male role, but of female and male *roles,* as they vary by class, race, ethnicity, sexual orientation, religion, age, appearance, region, mental and physical ability, and various other categories. But this multiplication of roles, while it represented an expansion of gender role theory, also served to undermine the explanatory power that had attracted many to role theory in the first place. The metaphor evoked by role theory, an image of society handing each of us a gender script that we are "socialized" to play out, seemed clear enough. But how could one now account for the many variations to the "script"? How and by whom are our parts assigned and modified in so many ways? By what means are the diverse scripts that each of us now plays (as, for example, gay, white, and male) interposed?

By the mid-'80s these critiques of role theory had reached ascendancy. In the late '80s and early '90s, an alternative conceptual framework emerged. While most would say that role theory was replaced or at least displaced from its dominant perch by a mode of theorizing derived from a different intellectual tradition, I would argue that the shift is better understood by saying that role theory was not so much abandoned as it was radicalized. The most precise way I know how to describe the transition from gender role theory to its successor is to say that role theory was *aufgehoben* in the Hegelian sense—that is, sublated and transcended. (Though I shall employ this Hegelian framework in what follows, I will then note a significant drawback to this methodology.) In a true dialectical reversal, the neglected element of the concept of role came to dominance over the previously privileged aspect, eventually negating the entire framework of role theory and bringing forth a new

2.
Judith Stacey and Barrie Thorne, "The Missing Feminist Revolution in Sociology," *Social Problems* 32, no. 4 (1985), 307.

3.
Judith Butler, *Gender Trouble: Feminism and the Subversion of Identity* (New York: Routledge, 1990).

4.
Judith Butler, *Subjects of Desire: Hegelian Reflections in Twentieth-Century France* (New York: Columbia University Press, 1987).

5.
Peter Osborne and Lynne Segal, "Gender as Performative: An Interview with Judith Butler," *Radical Philosophy* 67 (summer 1994), 32–39.

6.
John Stoltenberg, *Refusing to Be a Man: Essays on Sex and Justice* (Portland, Ore.: Breitenbush, 1989). This is not Butler's view. See "Gender as Performative" and Butler's most recent book, *Bodies That Matter: On the Discursive Limits of "Sex"* (New York: Routledge, 1993).

conception. To paraphrase another dialectician, the concept of role created its own gravedigger.

As we have seen, gender role theory, borrowing a metaphor from theater, described gender as a role performed from a script authored by society. But a role is more than a pre-scripted text reproduced on the stage; it is also an enactment, a performance crafted by an agent, who is independent of the role's textual givenness. This is the aspect of roles that has come to prominence in recent theorizing, finally supplanting the very role theory that gave it birth. For role theory is inseparable from the question it was created to answer. Is gender determined by nature or by nurture? Role theory resoundingly answers "nurture." More recent theories of gender as performance or enactment, however, see this entire debate as fundamentally miscast and misguided. Gender is here understood not as something we *are*, but rather as something we *do*. Gender is fundamentally a codified form of activity, a social practice, attaching itself to individuals as they internalize social structures, rather than an attribute or trait of individuals externalized to be writ large in society. As such, gender is a social relation practiced in social interactions, and therefore not reducible to "roles" inculcated by society and learned either on one's own or in the "separate spheres" of female and male "cultures," nor reducible to the unfolding of instinctive psychosexual "drives."

Judith Butler's *Gender Trouble: Feminism and the Subversion of Identity* was a groundbreaking articulation of the performative notion of gender.[3] Since I am writing from a Hegelian perspective, I should note that Butler herself has a Hegelian background. She published a book prior to *Gender Trouble* entitled *Subjects of Desire: Hegelian Reflections in Twentieth-Century France*.[4] In a recent interview, Butler refers to her Hegelianism and pointedly declines the interviewer's invitation to disavow a characterization of her work as dialectical.[5] Indeed, I would argue that the roots of the performative concept of gender lie in those aspects of Hegelian philosophy that used to be commonly called "process philosophy," in which what appear to be static facts are shown instead to be events or actions.

In its most radical form, the performative theory of gender even obliterates the fundamental distinction between sex and gender—the distinction that was, as we have seen, the sine qua non of contemporary feminist theory. The traditional view against which feminism rebelled held that the very fact of sex differences entailed the existence of gender differences. In this context, it was essential to separate sex from gender. An unqualified performative theory of gender, however, denies this distinction, but from the other side, as it were. It does not argue that there is at basis only sex, as the traditional view would have it, but that at basis there is only gender. This is a radical social constructionist view. It regards the very concepts of nature and natural or biological differences that might have grounded the division of the species into two sexes as nothing more than social, ideological constructs. John Stoltenberg's *Refusing to Be a Man: Essays on Sex and Justice* is the most fully articulated social constructionist view that focuses specifically on masculinity.[6] Again, in true dialectical fashion, as all the tenets implicit in a theory come to full articulation, the theory comes to contradict its own presuppositions.

It is but a small step from gender as performance to gender as masquerade.

Between them stands the metaphor of "masculinity as a mask," which appears as early as 1979, in Paul Hoch's prescient *White Hero, Black Beast: Racism, Sexism and the Mask of Masculinity*. Hoch uses Freudian psychoanalytic theory to argue that what is being masked and repressed to present the face of masculinity is an earlier more "feminine" anal eroticism, a repression also linked to the suppression of homosexuality. The masculine mask is worn in order to achieve a normative performance-oriented phallic heterosexual male sexuality:

When translated literally the word *masculinity* means mask *(for) anality*. In particular, *mas* is a shortened form of the Latin *masca* for mask (which is similar to the Arabic *maschara* for masked person). *Culus* is the classic Latin term for anus. In his remarkable paper "Character and Anal Eroticism" Freud showed how the repression of Anal Eroticism leads to the development of qualities of orderliness, parsimony, and tenacious obstinacy traditionally associated with the masculinity of the work ethic.[7]

There is, however, a crucial difference between the conceptualizations of gender as performance and gender as masquerade, for masquerade invokes a distinction between the artificial and the real. Behind the facade of the mask lies the *real* face, to be revealed when the masquerade is over. But it is precisely this image—of a truth concealed behind the fiction—that is rejected by performative gender theory, for which the performance is all there is. Our performance of gender is artifice, in the sense that it is created by us and is not "natural" but not implied in the sense that the artifice masks some other truth. Dissembling is not implied in the performance of gender. Insofar as the conceptualization of gender as masquerade invokes an image of a true, or real, person behind the performance, it is a step back in the direction of role theory, and may therefore best be understood, perhaps, as

occupying a position between gender role theory and performance theory, albeit much closer to performance theory in that continuum.

Nevertheless, the image of the masculine masquerade harks back to an aspect of early role theory in another troubling way as well: Insofar as it names a singular "masculinity" rather than a plurality of "masculinities," it seems to have inherited role theory's inattention to the importance of differences other than those of gender. It would be better to speak of "masculine masquerades" rather than "the masculine masquerade." The pluralized "masculinities," coined to reflect the significance of difference, has been an important development in contemporary theory, and is by now well-established usage. Indeed, five years have passed since Jeff Hearn observed that "masculinities . . . has now become the radical convention, if that is not a contradiction in terms."[8]

Tracing the development of gender theory as a dialectical unfolding of the conflicting of ideas inherent in its origins, as I have just done, may be—and, I hope, has been—an instructive strategy; nonetheless, the Hegelian method has a significant flaw, as I alluded to earlier. This method tells the story as one of a self-contained and self-referential internal unfolding of ideas. In so doing, it takes this flow of ideas out of its historical and political context, thereby distorting, if not actually falsifying the narrative. An accounting of that context is, then, necessary to rectify this deficiency.

All of the gender theories we have discussed arose at specific times and in particular places, a fact that must be accounted for. The various gender theories, as a group, may be seen as a developing line of reasoning which arose out of the U.S. postwar experience, specifically, in reaction to the profound but repressed cultural anxiety over gender identity in

7.
Paul Hoch, *White Hero, Black Beast: Racism, Sexism and the Mask of Masculinity* (London: Pluto, 1979), 96.

8.
Jeff Hearn, "Some Sociological Issues in Researching Men and Masculinities," Hallsworth Research Fellowship Working Paper No. 2 (Manchester, U.K.: University of Manchester, 1989). See also Harry Brod, ed., *The Making of Masculinities: The New Men's Studies* (Boston: Unwin Hyman, 1987; New York: Routledge, 1992), and Harry Brod and Michael Kaufman, eds., *Theorizing Masculinities* (Newbury Park, Calif.: Sage, 1994).

9.
For another fine analysis of how changes in men's consciousness in the '50s predated and precipitated the rise of feminist consciousness in the '60s, see Barbara Ehrenreich, *The Hearts of Men: American Dreams and the Flight from Commitment* (New York: Anchor/Doubleday, 1983).

10.
Steven Cohan, in Penley and Willis, *Male Trouble*, 221. Cohan cites Michael Malone, *Heroes of Eroes: Male Sexuality in the Movies* (New York: Dutton, 1979).

11.
Sherry B. Ortner, "Is Female to Male as Nature Is to Culture?" Michelle Zimbalist Rosaldo and Louise Lamphere, eds., *Woman, Culture, and Society* (Stanford, Calif.: Stanford University Press, 1974), 67–87.

12.
The field is currently best represented by the journal *masculinities: Interdisciplinary Studies on Gender,* edited by Michael Kimmel and published by The Guilford Press.

the 1950s. Steven Cohan sees a concern with masculinity as masquerade prefigured in certain Hollywood films of the 1950s and contends that those films were responding to widespread cultural anxieties about the erosion of masculine virility. Other analysts have argued that those anxieties were triggered by such developments as the replacement of the hardy entrepreneur by the faceless "organization man"; the rise of "effeminate beats" and other rebels who raised the threatening (to the established culture) specter of homosexuality; the increasing technologization of work; the entry of women into the workplace, which shattered the exclusivity of men's identities as breadwinners; and the technologization of war and the indecisiveness of the Cold War, both of which lessened men's equally crucial identities as warriors.[9] Cohan himself exposes the contradiction inherent in using the film medium to prop up traditional notions of masculinity, a contradiction central to our discussion of the problematic of presenting masculinity as a masquerade:

The cosmetic aspect of screen performance is crucial to the particular look of movie stars of both genders, although for men it runs against the grain of the traditional assumption that masculinity is the essential and spontaneous expression of maleness. As illustrated in Hitchcock's use of Kim Novak in *Vertigo,* which plays the artifice of her lavender blonde star image against her own Midwest (and brunette) origins, the appeal of a female actress usually gives her star image a cultural materiality inflected—through the tropes of clothes, voice, makeup, and hair—with specific references (even if faked) to class, age, and ethnic identity as the measure of her feminine authenticity. And as James Stewart illustrates in the same film, it is the comparative absence of those social references that inscribes the apparent invisibility and, hence, naturalness of his masculinity. That naturalness, however, is just another type of mask, since the actor is costumed, lit, made up—just like the actress.

For this reason, as Michael Malone observes, "acting itself is seen as tinged with unmanliness"; it is not a manly art like one of the professions or amateur sports precisely because "a real man" should not have to depend upon art for his virility. Screen acting in particular blows the cover of a "natural" man in its technical acknowledgment that gendered sexualities are constituted out of fakery and spectacle—out of what I have been calling "masquerade" and what Judith Butler terms "performance."[10]

Note the emphasis on the body as the site of the construction of gender in the above. This emphasis is characteristic of much recent work on gender, and brings us closer to understanding the particular significance of the present exhibition, to which I now turn.

In the three decades since the original publication of Sherry Ortner's much reprinted essay "Is Female to Male as Nature Is to Culture?", feminism has taken the following two propositions to heart: First, that the succinct analogy expressed in Ortner's title is a fundamental structural imperative of male domination, and, second, that it represents an orientation that must be drastically changed, because the idea of women as embodying the "natural" and men as symbolizing the "cultural" has been part and parcel of culture's devaluation of women.[11] Part of this project has been to demonstrate that women are as much makers of culture as men are. Unfortunately, it has taken longer for the necessary and corollary analyses to emerge on the other side of the gender gap, showing that men are as embedded in nature as women are. It has, in fact, taken the development in the last decade of a body of work constituting a field of critical studies of men and masculinities, a field sometimes (particularly in the United States) called "men's studies."[12] This field developed principally out of earlier critical perspectives, concepts, and methods developed by women's studies and gay studies, in conjunction with the women's movement and the gay liberation movement. Particularly as the latter has developed into queer theory and politics, its influence in destabilizing notions of masculinities has grown in significance.

Many of the recent studies of men and masculinities have emphasized the importance of understanding men as fully embodied beings—not as disembodied intellects, which men have often portrayed themselves as being in the Western philosophical tradition—and of seeing the male body as fully gendered. The theoretical concern with the male body also follows from identifiable historical trends. The technologization of work and war referred to earlier has diminished the importance of the male body as a productive or heroic figure and thereby undermined traditional male identities. These trends and the dynamics of advanced capitalism, which seeks ever-expanding markets, have turned the male body from a site of production to a site of consumption, as seen, for example, in the growth of the male fashion and cosmetics industries and the greater public display of the male body as a sexualized object. These are traditionally feminine positions. Not surprisingly, much of the present cultural anxiety about the erosion of masculinity (really, the erosion of patriarchy) focuses on the male body.

Most recently, a number of studies have focused on constructions and representations of male bodies in the mass media and other arenas. Exemplary works include Susan Jeffords, *Hard Bodies: Hollywood Masculinity in the Reagan Era;* Alan M. Klein, *Little Big Men: Bodybuilding Subculture and Gender Construction;* Yvonne Tasker, *Spectacular Bodies: Gender, Genre and the Action Cinema;* Paul Smith, *Clint Eastwood: A*

Cultural Production; and Barbara Melosh, *Engendering Culture: Manhood and Womanhood in New Deal Art and Theater.*[13]

As this exhibition and volume amply attest, an essential component of reaching new understandings of masculinities is to consider the work of artists who expressly take up questions of the materialities of masculinities and male bodies. I took care to pluralize the terms in the preceding sentence in order to emphasize the importance of difference in such reconsiderations of gender. For further discussion along these lines, see, for example, Kobena Mercer's and Isaac Julien's critique (in "Race, Sexual Politics and Black Masculinity: A Dossier") of what is probably the best-known body of such work today, the photographs of Robert Mapplethorpe. Mercer and Julien see Mapplethorpe's photos, particularly *Black Males*, as the highly problematic work of a white man who used sexualized black men's bodies to explore dimensions of maleness. For a discussion of masculinity that integrates race, class, and gender analyses, see Melissa Dabakis's "Douglas Tilden's *Mechanics Fountain:* Labor and the 'Crisis of Masculinity' in the 1890s."[14]

The Masculine Masquerade—the exhibition, not the concept—comes at a highly propitious moment and embodies important new critical perspectives on masculinities. It is certain to contribute to fundamental revisionings of masculinities.

13.
Susan Jeffords, *Hard Bodies: Hollywood Masculinity in the Reagan Era* (New Brunswick, N.J.: Rutgers University Press, 1994); Alan M. Klein, *Little Big Men: Bodybuilding Subculture and Gender Construction* (Albany, N.Y.: SUNY Press, 1993); Yvonne Tasker, *Spectacular Bodies: Gender, Genre and the Action Cinema* (New York: Routledge, 1993); Paul Smith, *Clint Eastwood: A Cultural Production* (Minneapolis: University of Minnesota Press, 1993); and Barbara Melosh, *Engendering Culture: Manhood and Womanhood in New Deal Art and Theater* (Washington, D.C.: Smithsonian Institution Press, 1991). The contrast with, for example, Joan Mellen's earlier *Big Bad Wolves: Masculinity in the American Film* (New York: Pantheon, 1977) is striking. For Mellen, the male "image" refers much more to the personality being projected than the body being displayed.

14.
Kobena Mercer and Isaac Julien, "Race, Sexual Politics and Black Masculinity: A Dossier," in Rowena Chapman and Jonathan Rutherford, eds., *Male Order: Unwrapping Masculinity* (London: Lawrence & Wishart, 1988); Melissa Dabakis, "Douglas Tilden's *Mechanics Fountain:* Labor and the 'Crisis of Masculinity' in the 1890s," *American Quarterly*, forthcoming. For a counterpoint to Mapplethorpe that is more concerned with men's self-presentation than with the photographer's gaze, see Daniel S. Kaufman, *To Be a Man: Visions of Self, Views from Within* (New York: Simon & Schuster, 1994).

Lyle Ashton Harris
Alexandra and Lyle, 1994
Unique Polaroid
24 × 20 in.
Collection of Alexandra Epps

The Masculine Masquerade:
Masculinity Represented in Recent Art

Helaine Posner

In his insightful essay on the Hollywood film *Picnic* (1955) starring William Holden, Steven Cohan focuses on the character of Hal, an egotistical drifter whose easy charm and physical strength, emphasized by the prominent display of his muscular bare chest, have a powerful effect on the women of a small Kansas town. Does the virile Hal embody "the cultural assumption that masculinity is the essential and spontaneous expression of maleness"? In other words, Is this man in his natural and authentic state?[1] As the story progresses, we see the "naturalness" of Hal's potent masculinity repeatedly called into question. His lying, his swagger, and his exhibitionism reveal both the inadequacy of his masculinity and the tremendous effort required to sustain his gender role. Cohan's point of view is quite clear, as the title of his essay—"Masquerading as the American Male in the Fifties"—indicates. The notion of the masquerade, as originally theorized in relation to the artificiality of femininity, actually applies to both genders and is manifested as a demanding and "ongoing performance" by men and women alike.[2]

An understanding of gender as historically variable and socially constructed is one that feminist theorists have long championed, supported in recent years by their colleagues in gay studies. From this perspective, to be constructed as a male means to perpetually exhibit a complex array of cultural codes that signal one's sexual identity and family, work, and social status. These signals are under constant scrutiny, certainly by women, but no less by other men who engage in a rigorous and unending regimen of "inter-male surveillance."[3] Mastering one's gender role is a strenuous endeavor, different, yet no more demanding, for the male than the female. Looking to the contemporary visual arts for representations of masculinity, we soon see that the creation of a strong and unconflicted masculine imagery is difficult, if not impossible, to achieve, which reflects the true complexity of establishing and sustaining a viable masculine identity.

On the other hand, viewed through the lens of psychoanalysis, as in the art historian Norman Bryson's brilliant study of the paintings of Géricault, the formation of masculinity and its discontents lies in the development of the positive Oedipus, or the young male's identification with the father. There is, however, an inherent contradiction within this model, for while impelled to identify with his father, the male must *not* be like the father in one highly critical respect: he may never possess the father's sexual power and privilege. According to

1.
Steven Cohan, "Masquerading as the American Male in the Fifties: *Picnic,* William Holden and the Spectacle of Masculinity in Hollywood Film," in *Male Trouble,* eds. Constance Penley and Sharon Willis (Minneapolis: University of Minnesota Press, 1993), 221.

2.
Cohan, 227.

3.
Norman Bryson, "Géricault and "Masculinity"," in *Visual Culture: Images and Interpretations,* eds. Norman Bryson, Michael Ann Holly, and Keith Moxey (Hanover, N.H., and London: University Press of New England, 1994), 231.

Bryson, "The crucial result is the experience of inauthenticity within the production of the masculine, that the male can never fully achieve phallic power, however great the exertion toward that end. However much the markers of the masculine proliferate, what subtends that proliferation is lack within the position of the masculine, the deficit at its very center."[4] The desire to identify (with the father, with other men), while very powerful, remains deeply problematic and forever incomplete.

   While masculinity is a personal narrative—which Freudians emphasize to the exclusion of gender's other, very real aspects—it is also, as feminists have argued persuasively, a social and political phenomenon. The male may, in practice, seek to resolve his sense of Oedipal inferiority by attaining status within the social order—thereby resolving the psychological within the social—compensating for private feelings of failure by active participation in the hierarchy. Access to patriarchal authority is not, of course, available to all males on an equal basis. Western society has an enormous investment in mainstream masculinity, typically defined as white, heterosexual, and dominant. This holds true both for those who possess power and those who seek the privileges associated with it. Until recently this standard definition remained largely unexamined. Man was posited as the generic human or universal against which all others are measured (and found lacking) which permitted men to remain blind to their own subjectivity. It has become evident that the conventional notion of mainstream masculinity, while societally sanctioned and rewarding to the few, has limited meaning in the lives of the majority of males and is, in fact, a repressive concept. As earlier studies of the construction of femininity have demonstrated, any attempt to understand

the male gender also requires an acknowledgment of its social diversity and an expansion of its traditional parameters, to include such important, and often overlooked, factors as race, class, ethnicity, and sexual orientation. The exhibition to which this book is a companion volume seeks to acknowledge precisely that diversity.

The selection of artists and choice of the works assembled in *The Masculine Masquerade* are the end product of a broad-based inquiry into contemporary representations of masculinities. It is our intention that this exhibition constitute an examination of the ways in which masculinity—and by extension, gender—is represented in our culture. Recognizing the impossibility of encompassing such a vast subject in a single exhibition, we have structured this project around specific male archetypes, as a means of generating a dialogue on specific issues. Our areas of investigation include: postwar American boyhood experience, the father-and-son relationship, heterosexual identity and practice, gay male identity, athletics as an arena of male expression, male fantasy and eroticism, the military and issues of aggression, white-collar authority and privilege, and the narratives of cultural difference surrounding Asian American and African American male identity.

In her recent installation, *Gloria Patri* (pp.112–13), Mary Kelly focuses on the themes of heroism and war, as means of investigating the psychological structure of masculinity. Set against the background of the Persian Gulf War, Kelly explores the identification of both men and women with the masculine ideal of mastery, most evident in the hierarchical and paternal order of the military, and the failure of the ambivalent individual to

4.
Bryson, 244.

attain this ideal. The use of macho language and reference to physical display in *Gloria Patri* may constitute another version of the masquerade, a show of intimidation that serves to mask both the individual and the collective lack of mastery. These frustrated energies often find their deadly outlet in war.

Gloria Patri consists of over thirty polished-aluminum shields, trophies, and disks arranged on the wall in three imposing tiers. It is a glistening—and intimidating—spectacle that refers to two of the outward signs of masculine glory and pride: the sports trophy and the military medal. Hybrid montages screen-printed on the disks variously depict the insignia of the army, air force, and ROTC, among others. Six of the trophies are topped by male figures, each holding a letter of the word *Gloria*. At the base of each trophy is etched a statement made on television by an American soldier during the Gulf War. From the astonishingly naive "not enough gees and gollies to describe it" to the starkly bellicose command to "cut it off and kill it," these transcribed sound bites illustrate the insecurity at the center of the pathological masculinity that Kelly sees as characteristic of the military mindset. Five short narratives, written by the artist and etched on aluminum shields, tell confessional tales of such everyday challenges as fishing for trout, a turn at bat, the birth of a son, boyhood rebellion, and a physical workout. In each case, the adventure, competition, or crisis at hand throws the narrator into despair, as he (or possibly she) valiantly tries and poignantly fails to measure up to the task. As the narrators reveal their precarious relationship to a role of mastery, we are reminded of Bryson's postulate of inauthenticity at the core of masculine identity. Our would-be heroes will never personify the "virtues" of the powerful fighting force that engen-

ders patriotic zeal and public adulation. In *Gloria Patri,* Mary Kelly has deftly examined a locus of predominantly male activity and revealed the vulnerability beneath its hard and polished surface.

Like Mary Kelly, Michael Clegg and Martin Guttmann turn their attention to the construction of a highly overdetermined and socially sanctioned male role, in this case the corporate executive, who they depict in a series of formal photographic portraits. These men—white, heterosexual, and aggressively capitalist—embody our definition of mainstream masculinity. Using a circumscribed set of codes pertaining to dress, pose, gesture, and expression, Clegg & Guttmann have produced a contemporary equivalent of seventeenth-century Dutch group portraiture, which signified the patriarchy's attainment of a comfortable, bourgeois social status. Both the history of art and the annual corporate report have provided source material for the artists' analysis of "the way power organizes itself as imagery."[5] While the portrait painter and the commercial photographer typically provide the patron with an idealized version of reality, it is a version of reality nonetheless; in pointed contrast, fiction and artifice pervade every aspect of Clegg & Guttmann's formidable life-sized portraits.

When they began their collaboration in 1980, Clegg & Guttmann hired actors to pose as corporate brass, as for example in *Executives of the Steel Industry vs. Executives of the Textile Industry.* Ironically, these skillfully simulated portraits of the powerful led to actual commissions of group portraits, such as *The Financiers* (p.106) and *The Assembly of Deans.* The artists retained the right to determine the final version of each portrait, resulting in both accepted and rejected commissions. Clegg & Guttmann regularly manipulate

5.
Clegg & Guttmann quoted in Mary Ann Staniszewski, "Dressed for Success," *Afterimage,* September 1989, 25.

the image to include false or montaged backgrounds and often combine several individual portraits to create a single picture. In their photographs, anonymous well-groomed men wear the prescribed white shirt, tie, and dark business suit, pose rigidly against a darkened interior, and stare expressionlessly under the intense glare of the lights. Occasionally, a woman adopts these conventions and succeeds in effacing herself in a traditionally male role. As established by the artists and accepted by the subjects, these tightly defined parameters serve to virtually erase personal identity in favor of producing emblems of authority. As in the military, the attitude and attire adopted by this elite provide a protective camouflage, while simultaneously exerting a considerable degree of intimidation. There appears to be nothing at all natural in either the production of white-collar male privilege or in its representation by the artists. Ostensibly critiquing corporate culture when they began their enterprise in the early eighties, Clegg & Guttmann's photographs increasingly collude with it to reinforce one of the most consciously constructed manifestations of the masculine masquerade.

The photographer Tina Barney takes us into the private world of the white, upper-middle-class power brokers who (in theory) populate Clegg & Guttmann's corporate realm. In place of the deliberately stiff formality of that team's posed portraits, Barney makes large-scale color images, resembling snapshots, of family and friends at leisure. She is, in fact, an insider, opening a window onto the discreet and tasteful lives of the wealthy WASPs who inhabit her social sphere. Barney depicts the everyday activities that take place within the luxurious homes and exclusive playgrounds of the privileged. A highly domesticated, socially and

psychologically repressed version of the patriarchy prevails in this calm realm, with conventional marriage serving as its facilitating factor.

Although they may appear to be candid shots, Barney's photographs are actually quite carefully composed to achieve the most harmonious effects of color, light, and spatial organization. Often multiple exposures are required to gain the desired results. *John's Den* (p.104) is a view into the well-appointed, oddly feminine interior (floral draperies, plush red brocade sofa, vase of pink lilies) inhabited by the conservatively attired, *Barron's*-reading John and his two school-aged sons. In the hushed atmosphere of this elegant setting, with its view of New York from above, we can imagine male privilege passing smoothly from father to son. In *The Boys* (p.105), Barney depicts three blond boys, identically dressed in white slacks, polo shirts and double-breasted blue blazers, attending a garden party. In this world, the effortless manners of the bourgeoisie are repeated without visible strain. However, one questions the naturalness of a milieu in which boys are dressed as miniature captains of industry. Barney's private realm may, in fact, be as highly codified as Clegg & Guttmann's public sphere. The upper-middle-class is America's iconic class, representing the status for which many strive. Money is, of course, a prerequisite, but one must also possess the gloss of culture, education, and style to gain acceptance. The apparent ease of patrilineal succession is, perhaps, not as effortlessly achieved as it would seem at first glance. Throughout Barney's work, intimations of boredom, isolation, lack of emotional connection, and anxiety multiply, suggesting the real difficulties of meeting the outward demands of class and resulting in the psychological strains that threaten to disturb an otherwise placid surface.

Graham Durward turns to the intimate ground of the male body, specifically the performance of its phallic function, in an unapologetic yet ironic representation of macho. Drawing on the formal vocabulary of Minimalism, Durward often absents the body, leaving behind only its emissions to declare its power and its presence. *Snow Drift* (p.107) is a mound of artificial snow that would seem to have been urinated on and then encased (enshrined) in a large glass box. Durward's physical marking of male territory is a demonstration of both the little boy's supposed anatomical superiority over the little girl, and the adult male's tendency to dominate through gross display. In *Black Emanation,* Durward shot narrow streams of ink across a big black-velvet triptych, in imitation of ejaculation, and autographed the faked trajectory of semen. In this wry work, the artist simultaneously emulates and parodies the heroics of Jackson Pollock's Abstract Expressionist "drip" paintings of the fifties, and the more recent grandiose posturing of Julian Schnabel's black-velvet paintings of the early eighties. (For a fuller discussion of Pollock's drip paintings, see Andrew Perchuk's essay in this volume.) But in spite of the artist's monumental, if self-mocking, efforts to assert his phallic masculinity, Durward shows this "to be an ultimately inauthentic, failed, and ridiculous pose."[6]

Although Charles Ray does not believe his sculpture fits within the framework of an exhibition examining the social construction of masculinity, it is difficult to ignore the emphasis on American maleness in his work. In his utterly banal *Self-Portrait* (p.118), Ray challenges the notions of identity and anonymity in his representation of the artist as a regular guy or "everyman." *Self-Portrait* is a mannequin of Ray; dressed in nondescript suburban mall attire, he is "inconspicuous and the essence of ordinary."[7] However, this is an oddly unnerving sculpture—while absolutely specific, it is also curiously vague. Here is the artist as a department-store dummy, a nearly identical yet dubious double. However, if one begins to scrutinize this replica of Ray in an attempt to elicit some sense of the self, he seems to disappear; his public image as an "average Joe" turns out to be an ingenious disguise. In an elaborate game of conceptual hide and seek, the artist asserts his physical being, then slowly fades from view. Ray's persona as the normal male is a form of camouflage. He blends with the background, lacking ego, personality, or definition.

According to the artist, a reading of his sculpture which focuses on masculine identity "destroys the enchantment of the work." Although *enchantment* is not the first word to come to mind in approaching Ray's prosaic mannequins, the word's darker connotations may well be apt. In another of his mannequin sculptures, titled *Oh! Charley, Charley, Charley . . . ,* eight nude Charles Rays engage in a sex orgy. What magic has conjured up this masturbatory fantasy, hovering as it does at the dizzying heights of male narcissism? In children's fairy tales the enchantments of witches turn princes into frogs, to be released only by the princess's kiss. In this tale, no princess need arrive to break the spell; our remarkably un-self-conscious and thoroughly self-involved prince would never even notice. Even multiplied eight times and exposed in flagrante delicto, "Charley" remains a strangely elusive and rather pale imitation of manhood.

The artists Dale Kistemaker and Michael Yue Tong investigate the psychology of boyhood experience within the context of two very different cultures—midwestern

6.
Andrew Perchuk, "Graham Durward," *Artforum,* April 1993, 99.

7.
Bruce Ferguson, *Charles Ray* (Malmö, Sweden: Rooseum—Center for Contemporary Art, 1994), 19.

America during the postwar period, and China after the Cultural Revolution. In the intimate space of *His Bedroom* (pp.110–11), Kistemaker returns to some of the most treasured artifacts of his youth—items that retain, in his words, "intense personal meaning." In this austere space, furnished only with a stylized twin bed and night table mounted by an illuminated globe, slides of "Plasticville," a toy village invented by the artist as a child, are projected on the wall. Kistemaker's miniature universe centers on the traditional boyhood preoccupation with the building of toy trains and model buildings and imitates the adult role of man as empire builder. Also appearing in slides (projected on the bed) are the artist's report cards, pages from autograph books, and childhood drawings of such subjects as a schooner and rocket ships. The sounds of a model train and children at play are heard in the background.

As in the village he created in his childhood, this installation is a blend of Kistemaker's dreams and his reality. It is an earnest look at the acculturation of an American boy, examining the codes of male behavior expected and values taught at school and at play, the violence implied in boy's verbal taunts, and the desire for escape into a safer fantasy land. Seen from the perspective of an adult, "these stereotypes of a make-believe world in which everyone was content and everything was in its place become charged with a sense of wonder and loss."[8] "Plasticville" is America during the postwar period, an era dominated by the 1950s' rhetoric of optimism, the virtues of progress, the triumph of democracy and capitalism, and the remaking of the world in our own image—a peculiarly male vision of success. Kistemaker's work speaks directly to the loss of innocence both on the individual and the national level, as revealed through the eyes of a

pre-adolescent boy facing the difficult process of gender socialization.

In his achingly personal, yet historically distanced sculpture, Michael Yue Tong explores traditional Chinese family and social relations, which are based on patriarchal authority and filial duty, and fulfilled, in part, by the ancient practice of ancestor worship. According to the Confucian philosophers, the rules of hierarchical behavior were codified in the "three bonds," wherein the leader dominates his subjects, the father rules his sons, and the husband controls his wife. The status conferred upon the man of the family, therefore, parallels the absolute authority of the ruler over his subjects. The observance of these time-honored values was disrupted in China during the Cultural Revolution and, for the artist and his parents, further diffused by the challenges of cross-cultural negotiation engendered by their relocation to the United States. Tong's work is a thoughtful study of the formation of a masculine identity forged within China's highly structured, male-dominated society, the psychological effects of his dislocation from that culture, and the eventual collapse of its system of values.

Tong's *Red Sky at Morning* (p.119) commemorates an actual event, the ritual performed by the artist's father and uncles at his grandfather's gravesite to ensure the honor and well-being of their ancestor. The ceremony was laden with political significance, as the site had been neglected and later damaged during the Cultural Revolution, when ancestor worship was condemned as an antirevolutionary activity. Tong recreated the original wooden coffin in steel, and lined this sculpture with black-and-white photographs documenting the ritual in which he participated as a young boy. This sturdy yet poignant shrine signifies the

8.
Andy Grundberg, in a wall text written for Dale Kistemaker's *His Bedroom*, exhibited at The Friends of Photography, Ansel Adams Center, San Francisco, 1994.

artist's affirmation of his ancestry, acknowledging both his male elder's attempts to respectfully reclaim their past and his own efforts to build a bridge across a cultural and historical divide. The endurance of patriarchal power and filial obligation was sorely tested during Tong's adolescence in America. The *Father Altar* chronicles the history of the artist's abuse at the hands of his father through the metaphorical presence of Chairman Mao. This political patriarch, whose image occupies the altar, becomes Tong's surrogate father in the installation's audiotaped account of the artist's formative years. It is a classic study of a father's violent attempts to reinforce an old paternal order in a new world, whose standards of success he is unable to meet, and of the son's Oedipal struggle to conform to and ultimately distinguish himself from his father's failed masculinity.

The British artist Keith Piper turns our attention to representations of masculinity within the public sphere. He focuses on the emblematic space of the boxing ring and on the public personas of two heavyweight icons, Muhammed Ali and Mike Tyson, in a video-installation interrogating black masculinity as a "social identity in crisis."[9] Ali and Tyson are examined within the context of the shifting cultural and political terrain of the sixties and the eighties. In Piper's view, these powerful black athletes represent two very different types of hero, but nevertheless each meets a regrettable fate. Muhammed Ali personifies the smart, verbal, politically active champion of the sixties who knowingly provokes the white establishment with his renegade stance. Mike Tyson typifies the invincible fighting machine, all brute force and no nonsense; he is the professional prize-fighter of the eighties who gets the job

done and collects the purse. In *Another Step into the Arena* (pp.116–17), Piper orchestrates a dynamic video blend of fast-paced imagery, saturated color, assaultive sound, and journalistic text to illustrate the downfall of these diverse exemplars of hypermasculinity; Ali, due to the punishing effects of his years as a fighter, and Tyson, due to imprisonment for his unregulated acts of violence. The artist's deft use of video underscores the media's exploitation of these fallen heroes.

Piper is alert to the pervasive antagonism against black men in our culture but also acknowledges the ambivalent nature of their response to a white-supremacist society. The artist reasons that the "scarcity of work about ourselves by heterosexual Black men is in my opinion, the difficulty we have in looking at ourselves without blinking. This comes from the fact of being at one and the same, victim and victimizer, torn between opposing and contradictory forces. It comes from the sense of one's self as the site over which numerous macro-global contests of territory are being played out," a site subject to the projection of society's fears and frustrations.[10] The black male cultural icons that Piper sets in his sights, from Ali and Tyson to Malcolm X and Martin Luther King, are all prominent national figures who challenged the white male power structure and were destroyed or else self-destructed. For Piper, they symbolize the precarious and turbulent state of black masculinity in our culture.

Both Keith Piper and Matthew Barney recognize in sports an illuminating metaphor for certain aspects of male behavior. For Piper, as we have seen, they serve as a stage on which certain social and political dramas are played out. For Barney, too, athletics becomes "an intensely personal form of theater."[11]

9.
Kobena Mercer, "Engendered Species," *Artforum* (summer 1992), 74.

10.
Keith Piper, *Step into the Arena: Notes on Black Masculinity and the Contest of Territory* (Rochdale, Eng.: Rochdale Art Gallery, 1991), 7.

11.
Marc Selwyn, "Matthew Barney Personal Best," *Flash Art*, October 1991, 133.

12.
Scott Watson, *Felix Gonzales-Torres Donald Moffett: Strange Ways Here We Come* (Vancouver, B.C.: Fine Arts Gallery, The University of British Columbia, 1990), 15.

The videotaped image of the artist's muscular, seminude body engaged in demanding tests of physical endurance in works such as *Field Dressing (orifill)* and *MILEHIGH Threshold: FLIGHT with the ANAL SADISTIC WARRIOR* has always suggested an underlying eroticism. Barney's ongoing gender performances in the strenuous roles of the freeclimber, bodybuilder, or football player tap into a psychologically charged male realm where sports, hero worship, voyeurism, sexuality, and unconscious urges seem to meld.

The subliminal undercurrent of male sexual desire present in Barney's earlier sculpture, performance, and video-installation works is gloriously released in the unbridled sexual energy of the cavorting satyrs in *Drawing Restraint 7* (pp.102–3). In this case, we are the voyeurs, gazing up at the sylvan fantasy unfolding on three video monitors positioned over our heads. These half-human, half-goat creatures of Greek mythology appear to be emissaries from the id—spinning, pursuing, or wrestling in a feverish state, but not without a tinge of humor (how else would one describe two satyrs struggling in the backseat of a limousine driving through the tunnels of New York?). Barney's impulse-driven, homoerotic satyrs—although they are not quite human—arouse our passions. In this acutely visceral work, Barney, who has before appeared in his work as an accomplished athlete and, occasionally, as a drag queen, here dispenses with the conventional codes of sexual and gender identity and affirms the polymorphous nature of erotic yearning.

The artist Donald Moffett unabashedly rejects our culture's traditional definition of masculinity as an exclusively heterosexual construct. Drawing on his wit, intelligence, and highly developed formal sensibility, Moffett asserts his sexual and social consciousness in a body of work that both seduces and provokes. He brings his interests as an AIDS activist and skills as a graphic designer to bear on his art, creating a positive representation of homosexual identity and desire. Whereas Matthew Barney remains free-floating and self-absorbed in his sexuality, Moffett delivers his message loud and clear. He is dedicated to making the homosexual body visible in our culture and to voicing his opinions about a range of private and public concerns, including the expression of desire, promotion of safer sex, wider availability of current treatments for AIDS, and greater governmental commitment to AIDS research. He promotes his weighty agenda with a light touch, focusing on the body, particularly its orifices, as the site of sexual pleasure and suggesting a greater openness, regardless of one's object choice, to the body's erotic potential.

Each work in Moffett's series of marbleized bowling balls sports a single large drill hole, framed with the words "choke," "glory," or "mon amour" in luscious gold lettering (p.115). These banal objects are elegantly transformed into funny, sexy signs for anal intercourse, the focus of homosexual desire as well as trepidation as the location of HIV transmission. They are works that "refuse guilt," proclaiming the artist's closely allied goals of homosexual assertion and social action.[12]

Moffett's *Sutured Snowman* (p.114), covered with pristine white floral appliqués marred by red floral "scars," is a poignant and poetic metaphor for a wounded masculinity. Slightly bowed, the snowman wears his wounds as a badge of the pain he has endured due, in part, to the devastation of the gay community as a result of the AIDS epidemic. Moreover, this snowman's battered state visibly manifests the sense of inadequacy and failure we have noted at the core of masculinity—a condition that most often remains masked. Moffett here provides a courageous and moving symbol for this psychic loss, with implications for all men.

Lyle Ashton Harris explodes all conventional gender and racial categories in a series of seductive photographic self-portraits in which he represents himself as both male and female, dominant and passive, black and white. He subscribes to Judith Butler's notion of gender as an impersonation wherein both masculinity and femininity are elaborately designed masquerades. According to Kobena Mercer, Harris's "strategic use of masquerade, which carnivalises the gendered surface of the body, renders Black masculinity into a strangely ambiguous version of femininity; that is, a category of identity characterised by its own highly constructed and composite artificiality."[13] In Harris's theatrical tableaux, gender is a completely fluid concept and male and female identities are easily interchanged as the artist traverses our culture's overdetermined codes. In Harris's photograph *Alexandra and Lyle* (p.20), two people embrace; one, with close-cropped hair wears a black leather jacket and directly meets our gaze, the other, in a black chiffon dress and full makeup looks askance. "He" is Alexandra and "she" is Lyle. Our attempt to locate or define masculinity has been quite thoroughly destabilized by the artist's provocative gender exchange.

Harris makes very little distinction between male and female. In fact, the categories of "butch" and "femme," as applied to both genders, have far greater validity for the artist, as the diverse range of his representations of self and others attest. In his recent Polaroid triptych *Brotherhood, Crossroads, and Etcetera* (pp.108–9) the artist depicts two

physically engaged nude black men as a butch and femme pair. The men are, in fact, the artist and his brother Thomas Allen Harris. In one image, the two kiss as Thomas presses a gun into Lyle's chest; in another, the embracing couple gaze at us as they point their guns in our direction. The pair pose before the vivid red, green, and black colors of Marcus Garvey's African national flag. This depiction of brotherhood undercuts the macho posturing of black militants of the sixties and seventies and illustrates society's continuing fascination with sex and violence, so often associated with young black males. Harris exposes the implicit homoeroticism underlying our culture's phallocentric focus on penises and guns in his invigorating and expansive gender masquerade.

The masculine, it seems, is not a monolithic and immutable gender but a complex conflation of personal, sexual, social, and historical conditions. Once assumed to be the normative, or authentic, gender role, defined in marked contrast to the masquerade of the feminine, masculinity is finally revealed to be, like femininity, an artificially constructed identity. From the mainstream masculinity policed by the superego, as seen in the work of Mary Kelly and Clegg & Guttmann, to the more transgressive identities forged by the id, as in Matthew Barney's and Lyle Ashton Harris's work, and allowing for multiple ego negotiations in between, masculinity proves itself to be a highly variable and often vulnerable construction. The personal and psychological demands of maleness, coupled with the political and social pressures to conform to its manifold codes, require the subject to be constantly vigilant, lest he suffer internal and external sanctions. In life as in the contemporary visual arts, the performance of the male role

13.
Kobena Mercer, "Dark & Lovely Notes on Black Gay Image-Making," *TEN.8* (Birmingham, Eng., spring 1991), 85.

presupposes the presence of a discriminating audience, and the performer knows that the success or failure of the masquerade is ultimately measured in the eyes of others.

I wish to express my sincere appreciation to David Dorsky and Andrew Perchuk for their valuable contributions to this exhibition and essay.

Pollock and Postwar Masculinity
Andrew Perchuk

He sat in front of it [the mural], completely uninspired for days, getting more and more depressed. . . .Then suddenly one day, after weeks of hesitation, he began wildly splashing on paint and finished the whole thing in three hours.

. . . .We had great trouble in installing this enormous mural, which was bigger than the wall it was destined for. Pollock tried to do it himself, but not succeeding, he became quite hysterical and went up to my flat and began drinking from all the bottles I had purposely hidden, knowing his great weakness. He not only telephoned me at the gallery every few minutes to come home at once and help place the painting, but he got so drunk that he undressed and walked quite naked into a party that Jean Connolly, who was living with me, was giving in the living room.[1]

As the guests looked on in dismay, he urinated in the fireplace.[2]

This anecdote, though quite possibly apocryphal, but nonetheless certain to be reproduced in the two competing Pollock bio pics currently under development, is a primary example of the mythology that almost immediately began to enshroud Pollock and Abstract Expressionism in the late 1940s and continues with remarkable persistence to the present day. The story is a succinct encapsulation of the essential elements of the Pollock myth: Pollock is unable to work for weeks, and then, in a burst of creative

inspiration, finishes this large painting in three hours; he becomes hysterical after initial failure; he takes to hitting the bottle heavily; in a drunken stupor he both exposes himself and pisses in public. Within the narrative, a number of the postwar period's masculine archetypes are readily apparent: the rebel, the tortured soul, the alcoholic or heavy drinker, the man suffering from "momism," or overreliance on women, the phallus worshiper (think of the plays of Tennessee Williams or William Inge), among others.

That the myth surrounding Pollock partook of, or possibly even helped to construct, masculine archetypes important to the contemporary culture has obvious interest for the biographer. But these masculine archetypes were further used to construct the masculinist narrative that has been central to the history of Abstract Expressionist painting and, through its influence, American postwar art in general. Some critics, particularly the long line of modernists, decry an emphasis on issues of masculinity as the intrusion of the extraneous and biographical into art history. And I would agree that if masculine display were solely a biographical element its emphasis would reduce Pollock's paintings to little more than visual illustrations of a discourse on sexual difference. However, in this essay,

1.
Peggy Guggenheim, *Out of this Century: Confessions of an Art Addict* (New York: Universe, 1979), 296.

2.
Deborah Solomon, *Jackson Pollock: A Biography* (New York: Simon & Schuster, 1987), 144.

3.
"A LIFE Roundtable on
Modern Art," *LIFE,*
Oct. 11, 1948, 56.

4.
"Jackson Pollock: Is He
the Greatest Living
Painter in the United
States?," *LIFE,* Aug. 8,
1949.

5.
T. J. Clark, "Jackson
Pollock's Abstraction,"
in *Reconstructing
Modernism: Art in
New York, Paris, and
Montreal, 1945–64,* ed.
Serge Guilbaut
(Cambridge: MIT Press,
1990), 229. Clark states
in his essay that Pollock's
painting "is a work
against metaphor, against
any one of his pictures
settling down inside a
single metaphorical frame
of reference." In my
essay, comments on
Pollock's work attacking
metaphor are references
to Clark's essay.

6.
Quoted in Michael Leja,
*Reframing Abstract
Expressionism:
Subjectivity and Painting
in the 1940s* (New
Haven: Yale University
Press, 1993), 277.

7.
Steven Naifeh and
Gregory White Smith,
*Jackson Pollock: An
American Saga*
(New York: Clarkson
N. Potter, 1989), 631.

I hope to demonstrate that, rather than being confined to Pollock's biography, certain processes of masculine display are at the core of the paintings themselves, are, in fact, constitutive of an entire masquerade of masculinity within the creation and reception of Pollock's paintings and were an irreducible component of these works acceptance by the culture during the social and political era in which they were produced and later canonized. To make this point, I will follow my own inclinations and the predilections of the period by focusing primarily on the major drip paintings of 1947–50.

Jackson Pollock's work struck a chord almost immediately in the American postwar psyche. In October 1948, only seven months after the exhibition that introduced the drip paintings, *LIFE* included a reproduction of Pollock's *Cathedral* in the magazine's "Round Table on Modern Art."[3] Less than a year later, the magazine posed the question to its five million readers, "Jackson Pollock— Is He the Greatest Living Painter in the United States?"[4] At the time, Pollock's major works were selling for $1,500, when they were selling at all, compared to $10,000 a canvas for a popular contemporary realist such as Walter Murch, who was certainly not receiving this type of media attention. In the next few years, Pollock's work was to take on a whole range of uses within the culture: as part of an advertisement for tract housing, as the backdrop for models in *Vogue,* as the symbol of America the citadel of individual freedom for the United States Information Agency (USIA), as the pinnacle of American culture for the Museum of Modern Art. The versatility and use-value of Pollock's paintings are attributable to many factors, among them the paintings' ability to satisfy, at least within the picture plane, some of the

tensions and anxieties that were creating a masculinity crisis in the immediate postwar period.

The connection between Pollock's postwar works, in particular the major drip paintings of 1947–50, and sexuality, usually configured in terms of masculine display, has been alluded to since their initial exhibition and reproduction. Recently, T. J. Clark, in his essay "Jackson Pollock's Abstraction," made the connection explicit: "For the drip paintings are clearly implicated in a whole informing metaphorics of masculinity: the very concepts that seem immediately to apply to them—space, scale, action, trace, energy, 'organic intensity,' 'being in the painting,' being 'One'—are all, among other things, operators of sexual difference."[5] Early critics of Pollock consistently described his work as being out of control; one commented that he "painted . . . in the throes of a nearly ungovernable passion," while another saw his work as "mere unorganized explosions of random energy."[6]

Though very often configured in terms of myth or the unconscious, or at times merely with pejorative intent, critical commentary on Pollock has consistently drawn connections between his paintings, sexuality, male display, and gender issues. Thomas Craven and Thomas Hart Benton accused Pollock in 1950 and 1951, respectively, of having made the drip paintings by ingesting paint and then pissing on the canvas (an allusion we will return to).[7] The work was so heavily engendered that when Francis Henry Taylor, director of the Worcester Art Museum, tried to dismiss the work of the Abstract Expressionists in general in *Time* magazine, in an article that focused largely on Pollock, he inverted the masculine theatrics of the work into a strangely negative female analogy: "They have merely substituted the rubber girdle for the whalebone corset."[8] Later on, Allan Kaprow said of Pollock that he saw in his example "a sort of ecstatic blindness" and that "this type of form allows us just as well an equally strong pleasure in participating in a delirium";[9] while Thomas Hess used the analogy that "With Mark Twain's river-boatman he [Pollock] could brag: 'Look at me through leather, boys,' or he'd blind you with power."[10] The emphasis on Pollock's physicality, his power, is an integral part of myriad investigations into the artist and his work. When *Art in America* asked "Who Was Jackson Pollock?" every one of the participants—his widow, Lee Krasner; one of his best friends, Tony Smith; his most important dealer, Betty Parsons; and his most significant contemporary collector, Alfonso Ossorio—considered it pertinent to describe his physical presence in heroic terms. "He was not a big man, but he gave the impression of being big. About five-foot-eleven—average—big-boned, heavy. His hands were fantastic, powerful hands . . . . All told, he was physically powerful." "Pollock had a strong face, a rugged physical presence." "I loved his looks. There was a vitality, an enormous physical presence. He was of medium height, but he looked taller. You could not forget his face. A very attractive man—oh very."[11] One gets the impression from these accounts that Pollock's physical attributes, his power and presence, are a necessary component for understanding his significance and his work.

Pollock's own descriptions of his working method and of his mental state during the process of creation serve to reinforce the centrality of his physical presence and sexuality to the paintings. "When I am in my painting, I'm not aware of what I'm doing. It is only after a sort of 'get acquainted' period that I

see what I have been about . . . . It is only when I lose contact with the painting that the result is a mess. Otherwise there is pure harmony, an easy give and take, and the painting comes out well."[12] Pollock here seems to be describing a familiar narrative of someone lost in the immediacy of sexual reverie: the loss of individualization, the impossibility of distance or perspective, an enveloping "oneness" with an object outside one's own body. Here one must remember the radicality of his process, best depicted in the Hans Namuth photographs of the artist at work. In one series reproduced in *LIFE* magazine, Pollock begins by walking into his canvas, his shoes trailing splattered paint; he crouches, dipping a dried-out brush into a large can of paint; as he flings, spatters, and pours paint onto the canvas, he is on his haunches, open-mouthed; the culmination of the series is an exhausted Pollock mopping his brow with a towel, the work session completed.[13] The inherent sexuality of this process is underscored by the metaphors used to describe it. For Thomas Hess, Pollock is a dancer: "The artist danced around his canvas, adding and obliterating, until the surface was transformed into an equivalent of the essence of the dance."[14] For Tony Smith, Pollock in the process of painting is a fertility god:

I never heard anyone mention it, but I think that his feeling for the land had something to do with his painting canvases on the floor. I don't recall if I had ever thought of this before seeing Hans Namuth's film. When he was shown painting on glass, seen from below and through the glass, it seemed that the glass was the earth, that he was distributing flowers over it, that it was spring.[15]

The heavily encoded masculine sexuality of Pollock's work has been obscured over the last forty years by two generations of modernist criticism. As Rosalind Krauss traces it in her recent

8.
"The Wild Ones," *Time*, Feb. 20, 1956, 75.

9.
Allan Kaprow, "The Legacy of Jackson Pollock," *Art News*, October 1958, 24–26; 53–55.

10.
Thomas Hess, "Pollock: The Art of a Myth," *Art News*, January 1964.

11.
"Who Was Jackson Pollock?" *Art in America*, May/June 1967, 48–59.

12.
Quoted in *The New American Painting* (New York: Museum of Modern Art, 1959), 64.

13.
"Baffling U.S. Art: What It Is About," *LIFE*, Nov. 9, 1959, 68–80.

14.
Hess, 64.

15.
"Who Was Jackson Pollock," 52.

16.
See Rosalind Krauss, *The Optical Unconscious* (Cambridge: MIT Press, 1993), 243–329. Krauss argues that modernist "opticality" constitutes a sublimation of Pollock's work, and her de-sublimation emphasizes the violence of Pollock's mark on the horizontal plane of the canvas. She extends this violence into the cultural through the analogy with the Freudian story of peeing on the fire, from *Civilization and Its Discontents*. My own analysis as it pertains to these subjects is deeply indebted to hers.

17.
Quoted in Steven Cohan, "Masquerading as the American Male in the Fifties. . .," in *Male Trouble*, ed. Constance Penley and Sharon Willis (Minneapolis: University of Minnesota Press, 1993), 211. My analysis of a sense of masculine inadequacy in postwar America is drawn largely from Cohan. See also "The Spy in the Gray Flannel Suit . . ." in the present volume.

18.
Quoted in Cohan, 212.

19.
Quoted in Cohan, 213.

20.
Barbara Ehrenreich, *The Hearts of Men: American Dreams and the Flight from Commitment* (Garden City, N.Y.: Anchor Press, 1983), 32.

book, the whole project of modernist criticism in relation to Pollock's work has been an attempt to sublimate it—to raise Pollock off his haunches and the work off the floor.[16] But the significance of the drip paintings' specific masquerade of masculinity lies within the crisis in masculine subjectivity being experienced at the time. In the early postwar period, American masculinity was felt to be under siege both at home and abroad, as Americans feared that what appeared to be unrivaled power and prosperity was either somehow hollow or could suddenly disappear. The two terms that recur continually in discussions of the era's masculinity are "conformity" and "inadequacy."

The frequency with which the latter term cropped up is best explained in light of the American public's reaction to the Kinsey reports on male and female sexuality, which were published in the late forties and early fifties. According to Kinsey, male sexual power peaks in the late teens and early twenties and then continuously decreases, while female sexuality doesn't peak until the late twenties or early thirties and then remains fairly constant. The significance of these findings was trumpeted throughout the popular press, and *Newsweek* even compared its impact to that of an atomic bomb.[17] The continuing emphasis on male sexual inadequacy was indicative of the contemporary crisis in which male identity was not only experienced without any degree of satisfaction but was being fundamentally redefined. The sociologist Helen Mayer Hacker commented that "Virility used to be conceived as a unilateral expression of male sexuality, but is regarded today in terms of the ability to evoke a full sexual response on the part of the female. . . . Sexual performance is more inextricably linked to feelings of masculine self-worth than even mother-

hood is to women."[18] *Look* magazine went so far as to publish a four-part series entitled "The Decline of the American Male," which warned that "Scientists who study human behavior fear that the American male is now dominated by the American female . . . .He is no longer the masculine, strong-minded man who pioneered the continent and built America's greatness. . . . Some authorities believe that his capacity is being lowered."[19] For these critics, America had become a female-dominated society after World War II, diminishing male potency and control.

This view was carried into the economic sphere, in which the newly dominant role of consumer was ascribed to women, and the traditionally dominant male role of producer had become subsidiary, and it is within the conformist consumer society of the postwar era that the other threat to American masculinity arose. In an extremely influential book published in 1950, *The Lonely Crowd*, David Reisman described the masculine type that was increasingly dominating postwar society: the other-directed person. In contrast to the inner-directed person, who had been the dominant type in industrial society up to that point, and whose personality was set by early formative experiences in the family, making him relatively immune to peer pressure, the other-directed person adopted his modes, tastes, and wishes based on conforming with others. He shifted his views with the crowd, paying "close attention to the signals from others." Barbara Ehrenreich, summarizing the impact of Reisman's description of the other-directed personality, remarked that "his book reinforced the average gray flannel rebel's gnawing perception that conformity, notwithstanding the psychologists' prescriptions, meant a kind of emasculation."[20] Ehrenreich goes on to detail the totality of this emasculation: The traits that Reisman found in the other-directed personality—the perpetual alertness to signals from others, the concern with feelings and affects rather than objective tasks—were precisely those that the patriarch of mid-century sociology, Talcott Parsons, had just assigned to the female sex. In Parson's scheme, the male (breadwinner) role was 'instrumental'—rational and task-oriented—and the female role was 'expressive'—emotional, attuned to the feelings of others. The other-directed man was a Parsonian woman.[21]

If, on the domestic front, the surface of prosperity was suffused with a gnawing sense of inadequacy, conformity, and ultimately emasculation for contemporary male subjectivity, America's international prestige was threatened by two conditions that characterized the Cold War mentality: alienation and fear. I. F. Stone referred to this period as haunted, because of the unmistakable social tensions behind the facade of homogeneity. Americans, believing themselves to be endangered by Communist aggression, internal sabotage, and the threat of nuclear war, feared that all the gains stemming from World War II might vanish. But as Arthur Schlesinger Jr., argued in *The Vital Center*, virtually the

cold warrior's handbook, the only alternative to the free man "devoured by alienation" was the totalitarian automaton, "ruthless, determined, extroverted, free from doubts or humility."[22] The frightening consequences of this dichotomy were manifested by the many who, anticipating the onslaught of the "red hordes," practiced civil defense in underground bomb shelters.[23]

The way in which the drip paintings were able to resolve aspects of the crisis in postwar masculinity, the specific work they were able to perform in the culture, can only be understood in relation to their origination and development. The drip paintings were born out of violence—violence against Pollock's previous imagery, against the notion of good painting, against the transparency of metaphor, and against the organic. Pollock's paintings of the early to mid-forties are, for the most part, unmistakably figurative. Often the figurative elements are constructed from an armature of black lines, as, for instance, in the paintings *Pasiphaë* and *The She Wolf*. But whether Pollock is at that moment experimenting with depictions of the unconscious or Surrealist-inspired automatic writing, the heads, parts of

21.
Ehrenreich, 34.

22.
Quoted in Serge Guilbaut, *How New York Stole the Idea of Modern Art: Abstract Expressionism, Freedom, and the Cold War* (Chicago: University of Chicago Press, 1983), 92.

23.
For a further discussion, see Elizabeth Bigham and Andrew Perchuk, "American Identity/American Art," in *Constructing American Identity* (New York: Whitney Museum of American Art, 1991), 7–16.

Jackson Pollock
The She Wolf, 1943
Oil, gouache and plaster on canvas
41 7/8 × 67 in.
Collection Museum of Modern Art, New York

Jackson Pollock
Reflection of the Big Dipper,
1947
Oil on canvas
43 3/4 × 36 3/16 in.
Collection Stedelijk
Museum, Amsterdam

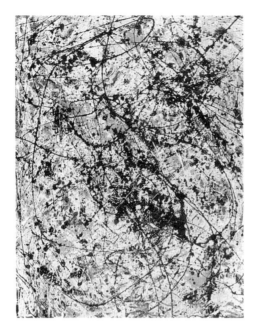

bodies, and creatures that characterized his work from the thirties and very early forties are still clearly visible. Even in works where the figuration is less immediately apparent, such as *The Key,* in which the figure/ground dilemma was largely overcome by a Hofmann-like segmentation of the picture plane and an abundance of calligraphic marks, the painting is bounded by figures on either side. The earliest drip paintings were produced through violence to these figures, by quite literally effacing them under a dense, tangled web of lines. In *Galaxy* and *Reflection of the Big Dipper,* the web obscures images that began as human figures. The debasement of the canvas, lying unstretched on the floor, extended beyond the drip technique. In *Full Fathom Five,* Pollock embedded detritus in the wet paint: a key, a comb, the caps from tubes of paint, a handful of tacks, cigarette butts, and burnt matches. *LIFE* magazine ironically mentioned that "Cigaret ashes and an occasional dead bee sometimes get in the picture inadvertently."[24] The violence to the picture surface reached its apex in a number of works from 1948–49, such as *Cut Out* and, most famously, *Out of the Web*

(Number 7), 1949, in which Pollock has gouged out large figurative sections of the painted surface, revealing the masonite backing below. While some critics continue to see figurative elements in the most famous drip paintings, Rosalind Krauss has shown that it is unnecessary for there to be actual figures in the underpainting for Pollock to be attacking the "figure."

In *Number 1, 1948* . . . one can barely make out an underdrawing that maps the surface with three more or less vertical poles, one at the center and the other two at either edge. It is this schema that is then buried by the avalanche of the poured skein. . . . Years of training in harness to Thomas Benton, analyzing Michelangelos and El Grecos by means of schematic plumb lines and implicit vectors, had left him a relation to figurative art that was visible through its most diagrammatic mapping. . . . In striking at the schema, the web cancels more than just this or that figure. It operates instead on the very idea of the organic, on the way composition can make the wholeness of the human form and the architectural coherence of the painting into analogues of one another, each repeating and magnifying the other's continuity.[25]

What is the significance of this annihilation of the figure, the organic, metaphor, especially as it relates to the culture of Pollock's time? In *Civilization and Its Discontents,* Freud remarks that among the first acts of civilization "the control of fire stands out as a quite extraordinary and unexampled achievement,"[26] and his speculative account as to how man harnessed the power of fire casts considerable light on the connection between the drip paintings and the crisis in postwar masculinity. Freud wrote:

It is as though primal man had the habit, when he came in contact with fire, of satisfying an infantile desire connected with it, by putting it out with a stream of his urine. The legends that we possess leave no doubt about the originally phallic view taken of the

24.
"Is He the Greatest . . . ," 45.

25.
Krauss, 263–64.

26.
Sigmund Freud, *Civilization and Its Discontents,* trans. James Strachey (New York: W. W. Norton, 1961), 40–41.

tongues of flame as they shoot upwards. Putting out the fire by micturating . . . was therefore a kind of sexual act with a male, an enjoyment of sexual potency in homosexual competition. The first person to renounce this desire and spare the fire was able to carry it off with him and subdue it to his own use. By damping down the fire of his own sexual excitation, he had tamed the natural force of fire. This great cultural conquest was thus the reward for his renunciation of instinct. Further, it is as though woman had been appointed guardian of the fire which was held captive on the domestic hearth, because her anatomy made it impossible for her to yield to the temptation of this desire.[27]

For Freud, then, culture begins when a man curbs or sublimates his natural instinct to piss on the fire, the same process, it will be remembered, by which Craven and Benton accused Pollock of producing the drip paintings. And it is precisely the resistance to modernist opticality—the raising of the drip paintings off the floor and onto the wall, where they become "painting," where the violence of Pollock's mark becomes "volatilizing abstractness" that "bounds and delimits nothing," where the fire is restored—that represents Krauss's desublimation of Pollock's work.[28]

What, then, has replaced the figure, optical verticality, metaphor, and the organic in the drip paintings? Urinating on the fire is a hint but seems to me the wrong marker of masculine display. For Rosenberg, as opposed to Greenberg, the canvas was reconfigured as an arena where the artist created not a picture but an event. The traditional pictorial qualities of form, color, and composition could be dispensed with, leaving the artist a space for self-revelation, a space consisting "of the same metaphysical substance as the artist's existence."[29] This line, continued by other critics, as we have seen, stresses the physical presence of the artist, the biography of the maker. Pollock is here an athlete, a gymnast, and the physical act of painting becomes as important as the painting itself. Pollock displays the fantastic strain to his body and acquires an authority over and above the work. Allan Kaprow said, "I am convinced that to grasp Pollock's impact properly, one must be something of an acrobat, constantly vacillating between an identification with the hands and body that flung the paint and stood 'in' the canvas, and allowing the markings to entangle and assault one into submitting to their permanent and objective character."[30] And certainly Pollock's insertion of his physical presence into the surface of the paintings, quite literally in the case of the handprints that bound the edges and corners of *Number 1, 1948* and *Lavender Mist,*

27.
Freud, 41n.

28.
"Volatizing abstractness" is a description Clement Greenberg applied to Pollock's work, while Michael Fried continued this line, stating that Pollock's line "bound and delimits nothing—except, in a sense, eyesight." Quoted in Krauss, 247.

29.
Harold Rosenberg, "The American Action Painters," *Art News,* December 1952, 23.

30.
Kaprow, 26.

Jackson Pollock
Out of the Web (Number 7),
1949
Oil and duco on masonite
47 7/8 × 96 in.
Collection Staatsgalerie,
Stuttgart

Jackson Pollock
Number 1, 1948, 1948
Oil on canvas
68 x 104 in.
Collection Museum of
Modern Art, New York

31.
"Jackson Pollock:
An Interview with
Lee Krasner," *Arts*,
April 1967, 38.

32.
Quoted in Leja, 277.

33.
Quoted in Jack Spector,
*The Aesthetics of Freud:
A Study in Psychoanalysis
and Art* (New York: Praeger,
1973), 100.

34.
See Krauss, 247.

is part of the overall masculine masquerade that Pollock wanted to project— and is intimately connected to the works' projection of authenticity. In answer to Hofmann's observation that he didn't paint from nature, Pollock responded, "I am nature."[31] Greenberg, the chief sublimator of Pollock's work, even hinted at this cultural utility in an early comment on the artist's work: "His emotion starts out pictorially; it does not have to be castrated and translated in order to be put into a picture."[32] But the claim that Pollock—through a superhuman effort— was able to impose his physical presence on the canvas in a way that no other artist had ever succeeded in doing is the stuff of myth, useful for the cultural work it was consciously or unconsciously created to perform: that is, to elevate Pollock above the masculinity crisis of the time. But the strain of this discourse, the energy expended to project Pollock as a classical hero who stands outside the laws that govern mere men, is indicative of the underlying uncertainty that arises from the unavoidable fact that Pollock and his body are also implicated in the inadequacy and emasculation of postwar

masculinity. So it seems to me that the specific display, the informing process, in the masquerade of the drip paintings is not, and cannot be, an insertion of the artist's own physical presence into the void left by the absence or destruction of metaphor and the organic. Rather, the paintings invert Freud's notion—first articulated in the *Three Essays* of 1905— that sexual curiosity can be diverted (sublimated) in the direction of art if its interest can be shifted away from the genitals onto the shape of the body as a whole.[33] For Freud it is man's erect posture, the movement from animal horizontality to the vertical, that allows him to replace smell with sight, opening up the possibility of diverting attention from the genitals to the whole body, transforming sexual excitement into the sublimated pleasure of beauty.[34] The drip paintings place art on the ground, and the picture surface is marked all over by signs of its own debasement. The flings, hurls, splatters, and drips, the puddles of coagulated paint themselves, constitute a trace of the processes that produced them; they do not reflect the presence of Pollock or his body but the presence of an overall sexuality spread to all corners of the horizontal, an index of the masculine display of ejaculation. This, not Pollock's physical and psychological straining, is the authentic display, which the culture probably unconsciously understood the paintings to represent.

I do not mean to suggest that Pollock had somehow magically gotten possession of the phallus, an obvious impossibility, or that he would have in any way accepted the cultural construction of the works' masquerade as an authentic phallic trace. Rather, possibly under Greenberg's influence, he wanted to stress control. "No chaos, damn it,"[35] he had responded to *Time* magazine's assertion of chaos and lack of control in his work. But where do we locate this control in the working method of the drip paintings? Another description of Pollock at work: "I prefer to tack the unstretched canvas to the hard wall or floor. I need resistance of a hard surface. On the floor I am more at ease. I feel nearer, more a part of the painting, since this way I can walk around it, work from the four sides, and literally be in the painting."[36] The last of the drip paintings were so large that Pollock could not lift them into the vertical for the famous 'get acquainted' periods. As Allan Kaprow commented, Pollock was not even able to see the entirety of the vast, resolutely horizontal canvases in one gaze[37] rather he seemed satisfied merely by leaving his mark.

It seems to me that the masquerade of the drip paintings offered two main gratifications for the immediate postwar culture. The first is the response of an unemasculated phallic display to the perceived emasculation implicit in the masculinity crisis of the period. There is a tremendous pleasure in the desublimated sexuality radiating across the surface of the picture plane, a reassertion of

virility as a thing in itself. Just as importantly, this sexuality seems to render the feminine unnecessary for its enjoyment. Rather, the phallic violence of the drip paintings seems specifically directed against the feminine. We return to the conclusion of the Freudian story about urinating on the fire: "Further, it is as though woman had been appointed guardian of the fire which was held captive on the domestic hearth, because her anatomy made it impossible for her to yield to the temptation of this desire." In this sense, when the drip paintings strike at the fire, the organic, culture, the object of that violence can be seen to be encodedly feminine. Betty Parsons has said of Pollock that "he associated the female with the negative principle.[38] But it is not necessary to locate the violence toward the feminine in the drip paintings within Pollock's biography, even though this is a rich source, considering his relationships with his mother, wife, and mistress. Significantly, the most common metaphors used by critics and curators to describe the vestigial representation of the drip paintings—web, labyrinth, spiral, vortex—are all markers for the feminine. And as discussed previously, there came to be an increasing identification between the conformist, consumer society of the time (with its emphasis on appearances, the ubiquitous keeping up with the Joneses, and the limitless number of taboos and prescriptions), and the feminine. Though Pollock eschewed the misogynist directness of de Kooning's attack on the markers of feminine masquerade—the Revlon smile, exaggerated makeup, and artificial breasts of the de Kooning woman—his debasement of the painting, what Krauss calls the bassesse of his method,[39] his going beneath the figure into formlessness, is violence directed at a feminized construction.

35.
Quoted in Solomon, 205.

36.
Quoted in *New American Painting*, 64.

37.
Kaprow, 26.

38.
"Who Was Jackson Pollock?" 55.

39.
Krauss, 284.

40.
Kaprow, 24.

41.
Quoted in Solomon, 178.

42.
New American Painting, 5.

43.
"Who Was Jackson
Pollock?" 15.

44.
Quoted in Leja, 269–70.

45.
New American Painting, 8.

46.
New American Painting,
10–11.

47.
Harold Rosenberg, "The
Search for Jackson Pollock,"
Art News, February 1961,
35.

The second of these gratifications is the perception of the authenticity that derives from the tremendous risk and strain needed to produce these images. Allan Kaprow has commented on Pollock's importance for a generation of artists: "In him the statement and the ritual were so grand, so authoritative and all-encompassing in its scale and daring, that whatever our private convictions, we could not fail to be affected by its spirit."[40] Risk and authenticity are so central to the myth that one could literally multiply the Kaprow account by a hundred, but to make the point I will confine myself to statements by two of Pollock's most important promoters: Betty Parsons and Alfred Barr. In Parson's view, "Some people are born with too big an engine inside them. If he hadn't painted, he would have gone mad."[41] For Barr, writing in the catalogue for *The New American Painting*, the exhibition that would introduce the Abstract Expressionists to the world, the artists share an all-consuming authenticity, "Many feel that their painting is a stubborn, difficult, even desperate effort to discover the 'self' or 'reality,' an effort to which the whole personality should be recklessly committed: I paint, therefore I am."[42] Pollock, at least as related by Krasner, shared in the belief in the primacy of authenticity: "I brought Hofmann to see Pollock. Hofmann, being a teacher, spent all the time talking about art. Finally, Pollock couldn't stand it any longer and said, 'Your theories don't interest me. Put up or shut up! Let's see your work.'"[43] The authenticity of the artist's struggle is proven by his ability to tear down, to go beneath the form into formlessness, to see nothingness in the paintings and stare directly into the void. Harold Rosenberg both described the nothingness that the Abstract Expressionists tried to represent and

informed the viewer that the same void resided inside himself. "The spectator has the nothing in himself, too. . . . There is no use looking for silos or madonnas. They have all melted into the void. But as I said, the void itself, you have that, just as surely as your grandfather had a sun-speckled lawn."[44] And as Schlesinger had said, the only alternative to alienation was totalitarian certainty. The work, as it made its way into the world, produced the desired effect. European critics' reaction to *The New American Painting* mirrored the alienated existentialism that had become the ideology of American foreign policy. In Italy, the work demonstrated that "the necessity of surviving as individuals without being crushed by the conformism of industrialized life, have added that charge of violence and of personal fury which each of these paintings conveys. It is like witnessing a shipwreck and their fight for survival."[45] While in Germany, the American artists were described in terms that might have made even the USIA blush:

They all use vast dimensions, not from megalomania, but because one cannot say these things in miniature. . . . Americans are world travelers and conquerors. They possess an enormous daring. One proves oneself in the doing, in the performance, in the act of creation. . . . these young Americans stand beyond heritage and psychology, nearly beyond good and evil.[46]

This process reached its conclusion when Harold Rosenberg, in his essay "The Search for Jackson Pollock," claimed Pollock as a modern-day Daniel Boone, venturing out into an unchartered and dangerous aesthetic wilderness.[47] In this formulation, alienation seemed no longer the curse of freedom, but an expression of heroic American individualism.

For the masculine masquerade of the drip paintings—characterized by the pleasure of phallic display, violence toward the feminine, and authenticity—to retain any cultural force, it could never reveal itself to be a masquerade. The artificiality conjured by the very idea of masquerade, the attempt to project a particular image, is almost the essence of femininity as it was conceived in this period. Over time, Pollock began to question the authenticity of his image, and the consciousness of his implication in producing a masquerade led to a crisis that resulted in the end of the drip paintings and, ultimately, his career. Pollock was introduced to the world by the *LIFE* magazine article "Is He the Greatest Painter?" In February 1949, Pollock spent the day with *LIFE* photographer Arnold Newman, for whom Pollock offered to demonstrate his technique. "He placed a fresh sheet of canvas on the floor of the barn, kneeled on top of it, and with slow studied movements dripped paint from a stick. He proceeded to pick up a can of sand, and crouching on his heels, added pinches of earth to his painting. Pollock, who had never painted for a photographer before and almost never allowed anyone to watch him work, was willing to paint for the five million readers of *LIFE*."[48] Dressed in a denim jacket, dungarees, and paint-splattered work boots, Pollock gave a performance as a Brandoesque rebel genius.

Pollock's willingness to participate in his own mythologizing had provoked Rothko to comment as early as 1947 that "Pollock is a self-contained and sustained advertising concern."[49] Harold Rosenberg called Pollock a "magpie,"[50] consistently acting out different parts. Pollock seems to have had doubts early on about the strain to produce his image, wavering between the poles of "I'm the only painter alive" and "I'm a fucking phony." When James Brooks and Bradley Walker Tomlin brought Pollock the *LIFE* magazine article, he

refused to look at it. And the careful crafting of an image to present to the world extended to the picture plane itself: the handprints that are present at the edges of *Number 1, 1948*, about which critics have made so much, announcing Pollock's physical presence, his being 'in' and being 'one' with the painting, were touched up to conceal the fact that Pollock was missing one of the fingertips on his right hand.[51]

The catalyst that brought to a head Pollock's self-consciousness of his masquerade was the film Hans Namuth made of the artist at work in the late summer and fall of 1950. After shooting a seven-minute black-and-white test reel of Pollock working in the studio, Namuth was able to raise two thousand dollars to film a professional color documentary. To accomplish this, high-powered movie lights needed to be focused on Pollock as he painted, and since his studio had no electricity, he had to paint outside. Namuth begins the movie with Pollock signing his name, and to coincide with the release date he signs "Pollock 51." The centerpiece of the movie is Namuth's attempt to accurately capture Pollock's working method. He convinced Pollock to attempt a painting on glass, which if secured on a platform a couple of feet in the air would allow Namuth to photograph the work session from a horizontal position. Namuth lay on his back beneath a four-by-six sheet of glass and recorded Pollock as he arranged pebbles and wire mesh on the surface and began to hurl paint. Pollock, crouching above the glass, could see the photographer through the transparent surface, and, one would like to believe poetically, possibly see his own reflection in the camera's lens. After the completion of the painting-on-glass scene, Pollock, who had been sober for more than two

48.
Solomon, 192–93.

49.
Quoted in Solomon, 176.

50.
Quoted in Krauss, 282.

51.
Solomon, 188.

Black-and-white still from the film *Jackson Pollock* (1950) by Hans Namuth showing the painting-on-glass scene.

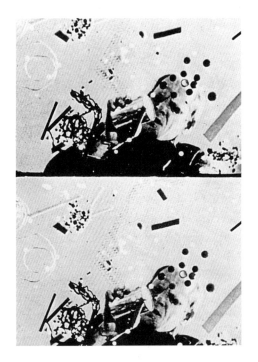

years, walked into the house and poured himself a large drink. At the dinner that followed, a drunken Pollock repeatedly shouted at Namuth, "I'm not a phony, you're a phony," before overturning the dinner table. He never got back on the wagon; the drip paintings, and his career, were effectively over.

In the process of shooting the movie, Pollock became self-conscious that the tremendous strain was not directed toward producing authenticity but a masquerade. He saw himself as a performer, and all the elements of his working method—the horizontality of the picture surface, the display that produced the drips, pours, and puddles, the presence that allowed him to be in the painting—became histrionics.

While the masquerade of the drip paintings ended, its gendered characteristics were canonized as the essential ingredients that confected "the triumph of American painting." That is, the processes of masculine display associated with the drip paintings and the notion of the authentic risk necessary to produce them became the definition of successful American art. This discourse became so legible that it could be self-consciously reproduced in an almost point-by-point manner thirty years later by Neo-Expressionist artists trying to create their own triumphant American painting. Though this is obviously the subject of a different inquiry, I would like to suggest that the heroization of masculine display within an entire masquerade of masculinity valorized certain artists and certain types of artistic production, creating a coherent but necessarily proscribed reading of postwar American art, with obvious consequences for those who could not or would not participate in it.

The Spy in the Gray Flannel Suit: Gender Performance and the Representation of Masculinity in *North by Northwest*
Steven Cohan

The poster for *North by Northwest* (1959, dir. Alfred Hitchcock) (figure 1) offers an arresting image of male vulnerability: Cary Grant suspended helplessly in space. Although he stretches out his arms as if ready to break the fall with his hands, Grant's bent legs and flung feet indicate an utter inability to support himself were he to reach the ground. Moreover, the expression on his face—his mouth agape, his eyes closed—testifies to, if not fear, then horror at his plight. The inclusion of Eva Marie Saint in the background behind Grant—where she stands, gun in hand, as the apparent cause of his danger—encourages us to read the poster as a reference to an actual moment in the film: when Eve Kendall (Saint) pretends to shoot Roger O. Thornhill (Grant)— who is posing as the nonexistent American spy George Kaplan—in order to convince her lover Phillip Vandamm (James Mason) that she has not wavered in her affection or loyalty. The choice of this scene for the poster was obviously a calculated one on the studio's part. Those who hadn't yet seen the film would presumably interpret Eve's shooting of Roger much as Vandamm himself does, deducing that Eva Marie Saint is a treacherous siren who puts Cary Grant's life in jeopardy. The theatrical trailer for the

Figure 1
The poster for *North by Northwest*

film uses voice-over narration to instruct uninitiated spectators to view the relation between Grant and Saint in just this fashion. It begins by addressing the star himself: "You can't fight it, Cary. Someone's out to get you. . . ." And it closes by reminding audiences what lies in store for them at their local cinemas: "It's one surprise after another. Adventurous Cary, romanced by the kind of blonde that gets into a man's blood, even if she has to shoot her way in." To illustrate, the trailer then shows the shooting scene.[1]

1.
All quotations from the trailer and the film are my transcriptions of the soundtrack to the MGM/UA laser disc, as verified by the published script: Ernest Lehman, *North by Northwest* (New York: Viking, 1972). For the continuity script recently published in the "Rutgers Films in Print" series, see James Naremore, ed., *North by Northwest* (New Brunswick, N.J.: Rutgers University Press, 1993).

Figure 2
The phony shooting scene

2.
Interestingly, this scene was a turning point for the film in more ways than one, since "the idea of Eve's shooting Thornhill with blanks" appears to have been the catalyst that started Ernest Lehman writing again in late 1957, after writer's block had stalled his completion of the last quarter of the screenplay. See Leonard J. Leff, "Hitchcock at Metro," *Western Humanities Review* 37 (1983), 105.

3.
George M. Wilson, *Narration in Light: Studies in Cinematic Point of View* (Baltimore: Johns Hopkins University Press, 1986), 65.

4.
Stanley Cavell, *North by Northwest, Critical Inquiry* 7 (1981), 775.

The publicity for *North by Northwest* prepares audiences to watch for a crucial scene in the film, the turning point, in fact, since it results in Roger Thornhill's recuperation as a full-fledged male hero who acts rather than reacts.[2] George Wilson maintains that "the false shooting scene constitutes the death of Roger Thornhill," but it would be more precise to say that this scene finally achieves the "demise" of George Kaplan, the fictional identity that has in effect been serving as an instructive masculine persona for Roger.[3] After the phony shooting, for the first time in the film Roger finally takes charge of the story: defying the command of the Professor (Leo G. Carroll), he changes clothes and escapes from the hospital, where "George Kaplan" has been taken for safekeeping, to go after Eve in his own name and on his own authority. Needless to say, while Eve's shooting of "Kaplan" may be nothing more than a put-up job, the heroic masculinity Roger displays in rescuing her afterward is meant to be read as the genuine article.

The poster, however, paints a somewhat different picture of this scene. Although Eva Marie Saint is still there threatening Cary Grant with a gun, the artwork does not actually reproduce that key moment as it occurs in the film, if for no other reason than because the perspective in the poster is—well, it's all wrong. In the film, Roger and Eve are first shown face to face in a medium shot. As she backs away, threatening him with the

gun, there are rapid cuts timed to each of her gunshots; the editing switches first to an extreme long shot, then to a medium shot looking over Roger's shoulder, so that, as Eve shoots again, he turns around to face the viewer, falling to the ground in the position that apparently inspired the poster's artwork (figure 2). When Roger performs his phony fall in the film, moreover, he hits the ground immediately after Eve fires the gun, landing with so much force that he gets a bruise on his side, which he shows to the Professor afterward in the hospital room. In contrast to the film, the poster, in its distortion of the unifying point of view normally associated with realist visual representation, reminds me more than anything else of a cubist's rendition of this scene. The difference in size between Grant and Saint, the spatially discontinuous perspectives from which their two figures are shown, their location in separate two-dimensional planes—these features all break up the trajectory of Saint's aim, giving the impression that the gunshot has launched Grant's body into space where, suspended in a moment of free fall by the Master of Suspense (so the ad seems to imply), the star hangs helplessly in midair, much to his consternation.

Perhaps the poster's image of Cary Grant suspended helplessly in space stands out because the climax of the film on Mount Rushmore—when Eve loses her footing and falls, only to be caught by Roger—plays on the similar danger that ends *Vertigo* (1958), the film Alfred Hitchcock made right before *North by Northwest*. As Stanley Cavell points out, *North by Northwest* averts the very catastrophic fate that concludes the earlier film, namely, "the woman's falling to her death."[4] Actually, the poster evokes the same fear of falling as the opening of *Vertigo*, when Scotty (James Stewart), in pursuit of a criminal, loses his footing and hangs helplessly from the roof of a building. Significantly, this moment of extreme male vulnerability in *Vertigo* is not mediated by a female figure, as it is in the endings of both that film and *North by Northwest*. The lack of female mediation explains (for Scotty, for Hitchcock, for male audiences) the opening's terrifying implication of symbolic castration.[5] Dialogue in *Vertigo* later gives contradictory accounts of Scotty's weakness on the roof, on the one hand explaining his fear of heights as the effect of his trauma, which remains to haunt him through the recurring symptom of vertigo, while on the other hand considering it an inherent debility that, predating his trauma, caused his dizziness and paralysis when he lost his footing on the roof. "What a time to find out I had it," Scotty reflects of his acrophobia. *North by Northwest* raises this same fear of falling, with the same implication of emasculation; but, like the last moments of *Vertigo*, it also alleviates that masculine anxiety through the mediating figure of a vulnerable woman. The climax puts Roger on (relatively) firm footing on the monument while Eve dangles helplessly in midair, prevented from plummeting to her death (as Judy [Kim Novak] does in *Vertigo*) only by the grip of Roger's hand—which invites Vandamm's sadistic henchman, Leonard (Martin Landau), to grind his heel on Roger's other hand. The poster, by contrast, pulls the ground out from under Roger's body, leaving him without any observable means of support whatsoever, much the same way that the opening of *Vertigo* strands Scotty on the rooftop to expose his complete and utter vulnerability.

Although an image of male helplessness may actually seem incongruent with the power normally projected by male American movie stars throughout the tenure of the studio system, it is highly

appropriate that MGM used it to advertise *North by Northwest*. The studio's publicity department even went so far as to reproduce the poster at the start of the theatrical trailer. In putting the danger back into the hero's phony fall, as it were, the poster exploits the very fear of male vulnerability—of a symbolic castration at the hands of an armed and dangerous female—that *North by Northwest* itself makes every effort to resolve (indeed, effectively to erase, since in the film itself she shoots with blanks) through its highly entertaining Cold War spy plot. As depicted by the poster, Cary Grant's "fall" is a rather haunting image of masculinity in crisis, and the film itself cannot completely exorcise this anxiety, even though its closure on Mount Rushmore gives every appearance of doing just that; the very premise of this type of thriller, after all, means that at the very least the actor playing the hero must be repeatedly placed in great physical danger.

Prompted by its advertising campaign, I want to examine *North by Northwest* as a representation of what the culture perceived during this period as a "masculinity crisis." To be sure, at the time of its release in July 1959, *North by Northwest* was extremely popular with critics and audiences alike because of its adventure and comedy, not for its social currency. Praised as the director's return to form after the box-office failures of *The Wrong Man* (1956) and *Vertigo*, *North by Northwest* still stands out today

5.
Tania Modleski suggests that, in both *Vertigo* and *North by Northwest*, a fear of heights is associated with femininity—more specifically, with "femininity" as a construction of symbolic male lack. See Tania Modleski, *The Women Who Knew Too Much: Hitchcock and Feminist Theory* (New York: Routledge, 1988) 90.

Figure 3
The climactic scene on Mount Rushmore.

6.
Robert E. Kapsis, *Hitchcock: The Making of a Reputation* (Chicago: University of Chicago Press, 1992), 56.

7.
Robert J. Corber, *In the Name of National Security: Hitchcock, Homophobia, and the Political Construction of Gender in Postwar America* (Durham, N.C.: Duke University Press, 1993), 191.

as "the quintessential Hitchcock film":6 thrilling and romantic adult escapist entertainment that appears to have little sense of history, no concern at all with real social problems, and, unlike *Rear Window* (1954) or *Vertigo*, an unproblematic portrait of masculinity as constituted in a patriarchal culture. As the climactic setting on Mount Rushmore makes clear, however, the film is by no means that ideologically innocent or emptied of history. Whatever other purposes Hitchcock and screenwriter Ernest Lehman may have had in mind when inventing Roger O. Thornhill, this character was a commercially shrewd intuition of what fifties America wanted to believe, for better *and* worse, about masculinity in its historical setting.

The historical specificity of *North by Northwest* has been mentioned by critics in the past but not analyzed in depth as a significant mediation of the culture's own preoccupation with a masculinity crisis. Generally, critics maintain that *North by Northwest* resecures the ideological status quo through its portrait of Roger's psychological development, which is initially triggered by the spy plot and then celebrated by the marriage that closes the romance plot. Even as recently as 1993, one of Hitchcock's acutest critics, Robert J. Corber, singled out *North by Northwest* as the postwar film of the director which most obligingly delivers, through its narrative account of Roger's Oedipalized masculinity, a straightforward, unproblematic, and homogeneous reproduction of the postwar consensus supporting Cold War liberalism. While I recognize that, in its closure, *North by Northwest* does actively work toward a resolution demonstrating how "gender and nationality functioned as mutually reinforcing categories of identity,"7 in my own historicized reading of the film I emphasize what Corber does not, which is that

North by Northwest yields from its crisis narrative a much more ideologically conflicted representation of the masculine masquerade. Gender and nationalism were indeed wedded in dominant representations of all kinds during the fifties, which is why I also begin my analysis of *North by Northwest* by looking at the way marriage appears to center the ideological imperatives that govern the film's narrative action most transparently. But as my analysis then goes on to make evident, the pressing need to see gender and nationalism reinforcing each other made masculinity a ready site of ideological crisis because neither ever rested on a singular or stable platform; the national interest shifted, depending on the perspective from which it was viewed, and so did expectations about what constituted proper gender identities and behavior.

I therefore call into question the stability with which *North by Northwest* represents masculinity through the period's dominant breadwinner and Cold War ideologies (which motivate the film's romance and spy plots, respectively), and I accomplish this primarily by historicizing Roger Thornhill's masquerade as George Kaplan with reference to the performative ethic that identifies Thornhill as a member of the new professional-managerial class, an advertising executive. Rereading the film's conservativism through this performance ethic, I argue that Roger's identity crisis, symptomatic of that new class's own anxieties about self-presentation, ends up destabilizing the expected relation between gender and representation; and I go on to examine, in conclusion, how Roger's masculinity, no less than Eve's femininity, is itself an ongoing and potentially discontinuous performative masquerade, particularly when set against the informing context of Cary Grant's male star image, with its own intertextual implications of theatricality and masquerading. Put simply, I take George Kaplan as the film's emblem of masculinity as a gender performance, and my purpose is to help historicize the masculine masquerade in popular American culture, while recognizing, too, the importance that the masquerade has had for contemporary feminism as a powerful theoretical accounting of gender.

Marriage Makes the Man

Starting with Robin Wood's 1965 auteurist appreciation of the art with which Hitchcock takes Roger Thornhill on his breathless journey toward his final union with Eve Kendall, the social and sexual conservatism of *North by Northwest* has been demonstrated repeatedly, usually through careful attention to the film's structure as a narrative of psychological growth: As he works his way through the three faces of this film's Eve (first she is his seducer, then his betrayer, ultimately his mate), Roger reconciles his dependency on his mother, mistrust of women, and fear of commitment.[8] *North by Northwest* is clearly as preoccupied with achieving the marriage of its hero as it is with spinning an amusing adventure plot of espionage and mistaken identities.[9] It is therefore tempting to agree with Leslie Brill's claim that the film is a mythic quest originating out of "Roger Thornhill's search for identity and a proper mate—two aspects, it usually turns out, of a single goal."[10] But the film's motivation, however banal, is much more timely than that, since it also follows the culture in believing that "marriage—and, within that, the breadwinner role—was the only normal state for the adult male."[11] The film thus puts the question of its hero's maturation explicitly in terms of his getting married; if he is to revitalize the patronizing, insincere, manipulative, and self-absorbed masculinity he displays in the first scene on

Madison Avenue, Roger must learn the difference between a "proposition" (what he calls Eve's intention when she confesses that she bribed the waiter to seat him at her table in the dining car) and a "proposal" (what he names his invitation, while they are still on the monument, to take the train back to New York City together).

But for much of the film, Roger's behavior actually parodies the breadwinner ideal. "I'm an advertising man, not a red herring!" he exclaims to the Professor when the latter requests that he accompany him to Rapid City to help put Vandamm's mind at ease about Eve. "I've got a job, a secretary, a mother, two ex-wives, and several bartenders waiting for me, and I don't intend to disappoint them all and get myself slightly killed." While phrased as if to emphasize the many economic dependents he has taken on in his private life, Roger's flippant declaration actually indicates his irresponsibility. Psychiatrist Abram Kardiner's diagnosis of "momism" summarized fifties thinking about masculinity in a manner that describes Roger to a tee:

The attachment to a strong, dominant mother can have various characterological outcomes. Thus we have the case of a man of thirty-five who is an only child and who complains that he has difficulties with women. There is no disturbance of orgastic potency or performance, only difficulties in adjusting to females. He has had many affairs without much tenderness. His difficulties arise from his wanting only to take from a woman and to give nothing. . . . [His mother] was his protector but a tyrannical one. He now seeks a life situation in which he can reproduce the situation with his mother, in order to be the exclusive object of his wife's attention and to be supported by her. Were it not for the ease with which women are currently available for "affairs," he would never consort with them at all.[12]

With Roger exhibiting this very pattern of behavior in his relations with

8.
Robin Wood includes his 1965 book on Hitchcock in *Hitchcock's Films Revisited* (New York: Columbia University Press, 1989); for his analysis of *North by Northwest* as a growth narrative, see pp. 131–41.

9.
Following the example of the screwball comedies he analyzes elsewhere in *Pursuits of Happiness: The Hollywood Comedy of Remarriage* (Cambridge: Harvard University Press, 1981), in his article on *North by Northwest*, Cavell places the film "in the genre of remarriage . . . which means to [him] that its subject is the legitimizing of marriage" (762–63).

10.
Leslie Brill, *The Hitchcock Romance: Love and Irony in Hitchcock's Films* (Princeton, N.J.: Princeton University Press, 1988), 8.

11.
Barbara Ehrenreich, *The Hearts of Men: American Dreams and the Flight from Commitment* (New York: Doubleday, 1983), 15.

12.
Abram Kardiner, "The Flight from Masculinity," in *The Problem of Homosexuality in Modern Society*, ed. Hendrik M. Ruitenbeek (New York: Dutton, 1963), 28.

13.
Quoted in Robert Coughlan, "Changing Roles in Modern Marriage," *Life*, Dec. 24, 1956, 114.

14.
J. Ronald Oakley, *God's Country: America in the Fifties* (New York: Dembner, 1986), 413.

15.
The three pieces and their original dates of publication are: J. Robert Moskin, "The American Male: Why Do Women Dominate Him?" *Look*, Feb. 4, 1958, 77–80; George B. Leonard Jr., "The American Male: Why Is He Afraid to Be Different?" *Look*, Feb. 18, 1958, 95–102; William Attwood, "The American Male: Why Does He Work So Hard?" *Look*, Mar. 4, 1958, 71–75. The three were then republished later that same year in book form, under the title *The Decline of the American Male*, by the editors of *Look* (New York: Random House, 1958).

16.
Moskin, 77.

women, including his flighty mother, his characterization is consequently encoded in such a way as to encourage audiences to identify him with "the increasing emotional immaturity of the American male," a syndrome of postwar life one expert traced back to the inability of many men to adapt to a military environment during World War II. "Most of them were emasculated males," this psychiatrist stated. "They wanted to depend on somebody else. Instead of giving and protecting, they wanted to be protected. They had never learned to accept responsibility—somewhere they had lost the male image."[13] Roger's immaturity thus evokes the ideology of Cold War global politics alongside that of the breadwinner ethic: The dread that the American male's emotional dependency (of the sort Roger indirectly reveals in his speech to the Professor), which led to his social as well as personal irresponsibility (Roger's failed marriages and drinking problem), in turn made him unduly dependent upon a woman (his mother) and, consequently, susceptible to pernicious influences (Communism).

The suspicion that attractive, middle-class American men like Roger had gone "weak," making themselves and their country vulnerable, was part of a "decline in national prestige and confidence" generally recognized during the latter part of the decade. During this "period of self-examination . . . the nation was criticized for its conformity, materialism, complacency, apathy, dull homogeneity, and confusion about its national purpose and goals."[14] Given the way the culture identified the national identity with masculinity, much of this self-examination focused on the strength or weakness of American men. Making masculinity a problem of immediate national concern helped give articulation to what was much harder to formulate, namely, irreconcilable ideolog-

ical demands being made on the representation of male strength and power: how to negotiate the "tough" masculinity demanded of the cold warrior abroad, which produced one ideological account of the nation's manhood, with the "soft" masculinity expected of the breadwinner at home, which produced a contrary one.

Because of the imbrication of gender in nationalism, the culture itself understood this ideological conflict as bewilderment about the proper masculine role, as evident in the debates about the state of American manhood that took place in the large circulation magazines during the mid-fifties. The crisis in the nation's masculinity reached such a pitch that *Look* eventually published a series of editorials analyzing what it named "The Decline of the American Male."[15] Appearing in 1958, the first article set the tone for this examination, commenting: "scientists worry that since the end of World War II, [the American male] has changed radically and dangerously; that he is no longer the masculine, strong-minded man who pioneered the continent and built America's greatness."[16] Each piece in the series concentrated on a different symptom of masculinity's decline: that men let themselves be dominated by women, that they worked too hard for their own physical and spiritual good, and that they conformed to the values of the crowd much too readily. With the allusion to Gibbon and falling empires in the wording of its title, *Look*'s series clearly meant to have ominous implications about ebbing U.S. strength in world politics.

For all the wear and tear on his nervous system, the American male has provided himself and his family with goods and services unmatched in any other country. . . . (The danger, of course, is that we will become too soft, too complacent and too home-oriented to meet the challenge of other dynamic nations like China and the Soviet Union.) . . . The answer—if there is to be one—is for the

American male to grow up emotionally so that he can learn to live with the pressures of this society and balance the demands of job, community and home without ruining his health and disposition.[17]

From the perspective of international politics, the breadwinner ethic of domestic ideology, which encouraged men to become "too soft, too complacent and too home-oriented," could all too easily be seen as a weakening of masculinity, which in turn was read as a symptom of the nation's own emasculation in the face of its Communist enemies.

We should therefore not forget the casual allusions in *North by Northwest* to the Cold War setting in which Roger Thornhill learns to grow up emotionally in order to rehabilitate himself as a responsible breadwinner through his marriage to Eve Kendall. As the Professor remarks after the phony shooting scene, the U.S. has already lost a few cold wars, and he is clearly worried about losing additional ground. Particularly when glossed through the Professor's concern about America's waning strength against Communists, audiences in 1959 would no doubt have seen the film's initial characterization of Roger as momma's boy, womanizer, and alcoholic, together with its ultimate recuperation of him as a responsible breadwinner through marriage, as a representation of the decline and renewal of the national character. When Roger bests the effete Vandamm by getting away with Eve *and* the figurine containing the stolen microfilm, our hero's triumph equates the revived health of his masculinity with that of his nation. As Corber points out, the film's spy and romance plots converge by the end of the film to align the successful realization of Roger's Oedipalized masculinity with the active performance of his patriotic duty; gender and nationalism then end up rationalizing each other, with the fate of the nation appearing to depend upon the

status of American manhood, and vice versa.[18] Evoking the Cold War mythology of endangered masculinity in its spy plot, *North by Northwest* responds by proposing a solution through its romance plot: the maturity implied by Roger's new willingness to accept responsibility for a woman. The phony-shooting scene, in fact, effects the turning point in Roger's relation to Eve precisely by placing the freedom she enjoys in the plot as an inscrutable federal agent under the controlling thumb of his own male play-acting: Then *his* performance can subordinate her activity to his, containing her sexuality within the terms of his own masquerade as George Kaplan.

He's an Advertising Man, Not a Red Herring

While it is important not to discount the way in which the Cold War and domestic ideologies of the period intertwine in *North by Northwest,* reading Roger's masculinity solely through this framework makes the film seem more somber and humorless than its text warrants. After all, *North by Northwest* is a funny as well as thrilling adventure, characterized by continuous tongue-in-cheek wit. As it wends its way toward that conservative closure on Mount Rushmore, when Roger proposes to Eve and saves the nation from its Communist enemies, *North by Northwest* wryly, often outrageously, places the familiar cultural idiom of fifties America in highly inappropriate contexts. The crop-dusting sequence, for instance, makes the banal Indiana cornfield turn sinister, just as the film's many jokes quote clichés at inopportune moments to give them an unexpected edge, as when the unflappable Mrs. Thornhill calls out to her forty-something son as he flees from Vandamm's men at the Plaza Hotel, "Roger, will you be home for dinner?"

17.
Attwood, 74–75.

18.
Corber, 191–92, 194–202.

19.
Erving Goffman, *The Presentation of Self in Everyday Life* (New York: Anchor, 1959), 238. The volume was first published in shorter form in 1956, as an academic monograph.

20.
Goffman, 62.

21.
Wilson also refers to the film's thematic defense of illusionism, but rather than historicizing it, as I am doing, he interprets this theme as an instance of Hitchcockian metacinema: a "wry apologia for the sort of illusionistic art —more specifically, for the sort of illusionistic cinema— that Hitchcock, paradigmatically, has always practiced" (64). But in this regard, the film is also every bit an Ernest Lehman text as it is an Alfred Hitchcock classic: With its adept and knowing positioning of Roger within the social milieu of the other-directed media professional, *North by Northwest* bears a strong similarity to Lehman's previous film, *Sweet Smell of Success* (1957), a *film noir* depiction of the night life of newspaper columnists and publicity mongers. I don't think it is an understatement to say that Lehman's contribution to the film's thematic preoccupation with illusions and performances is what helps to give *North by Northwest* the historical context I am emphasizing.

The gags reenact on a verbal or visual level what the film itself does to Roger by pulling the rug out from under his identity when Vandamm's men mistake him for Kaplan. This mistake occurs, not through any resemblance on Roger's part to the person of Kaplan, but because of Roger's accidental proximity to the name (at the same time they page "Kaplan," recall, Thornhill is actually signaling the bellboy to send a wire to his mother). Not only does Roger get mistaken for "George Kaplan," himself just a contrivance of superficial clues, metonymic signs of masculinity (a hairbrush, business suits, a name) left by the Professor's cohorts to convince Vandamm of this decoy's existence; but in the process of trying to prove his innocence, Roger learns just how easily the conventional signs of his own masculinity (that is, his relation to business affairs, social drinking, women, and the Oedipus complex— all sketched out in a conversation with his secretary that begins the narrative) can be quickly dissociated from his very ordinary identity. In the last analysis, Roger's identity is a persona, or mask, much like the identity made up for Kaplan. Only when he realizes this fact himself can Roger then begin to overcome his troublemakers by beating them at their own game: *performance.*

Clothes Make the Man

In an important book republished in paperback the same year as the film's release, the sociologist Erving Goffman claimed that performance actually constituted the ground of identity, "the presentation of self in everyday life." Goffman's analysis of various professional as well as personal forms of interaction as instances of "impression management" well describes the role-playing that occurs at many levels within the diegesis of *North by Northwest.*[19] When Roger claims that

"in the world of advertising there is no such thing as a lie . . . only the Expedient Exaggeration," the comment prepares the way for the film to link him to both Vandamm and the Professor. Goffman showed that this axiom was not simply limited to the advertising profession or espionage but, in fact, characterized the games and gambits of social relations generally:

[I]n everyday life it is usually possible for the performer to create intentionally almost any kind of false impression without putting himself in the indefensible position of having told a clear-cut lie. Communication techniques such as innuendo, strategic ambiguity, and crucial omissions allow the misinformer to profit from lies without, technically, telling any.[20]

In *North by Northwest* an important consequence of the phony shooting scene is that it marks the apparent end of identity play in the film by bringing the curtain down on the various performances actually occurring as part of the narrative action. Afterward, Vandamm learns who the double agent really is, Roger goes to rescue her in his own name, the Professor shows up with real bullets, and all the deceit and feigning necessary for Cold War espionage appear to be securely set off from domestic reality at the film's closing. But the film actually takes a more complicated stand toward the playacting of Cold War spy games. Consequently, while outwardly committed to resecuring the most orthodox representation of masculinity, as critics from Robin Wood to Robert Corber have argued, in its social setting *North by Northwest* also recognizes, with just as much conviction, the basis of meaningful representation in performance, with identity displaced from its moorings in the gender-nationalism equation and understood instead as a dynamic and unstable social production involving the continuous deployment of masks, role-playing, and theatricality.[21]

In light of the film's proposal that *all* identities may only be realized through performances of what Goffman calls a "sign activity,"[22] one has to ask: what makes one identity (Roger's, say) any more real than another (Kaplan's)? I suppose the answer is: whichever one wears better. Although Roger's faith in his identity is continually challenged, and although a first-time viewer's confidence in him as an innocent bystander may be shaken when Vandamm's men mistake him for George Kaplan, there is one constant, one yielding and intractable given throughout his many sincere professions of innocence and accidental performances of guilt. I am referring to the seemingly indestructible gray business suit Roger wears almost without exception until after the phony shooting, when his change of clothing signifies that he is finally taking charge of the narrative action.[23]

Until he retires his suit along with the persona of George Kaplan, Roger looks fastidiously neat at almost all times. His clothes appear clean and freshly pressed regardless of circumstance, both to suggest the hero's cartoonlike indestructibility and to reflect the presence in that role of Cary Grant, who was celebrated for both his fashion sense and his fastidiousness when it came to his tailored clothes. According to a press release at the time:

His shirts, also always tailor-made, have fly fronts concealing the buttons. He never folds his jacket pocket handkerchief in points, always folds it square and just tucks it in carelessly. His ties are never pointed, always have rounded edges. He prefers monotone ties, or sombre-colored ties with small, sparse print. He never wears bright ties, bright colors of any kind in any part of his apparel.

His favorite daytime or informal suit is dark gray, pin-striped, single-breasted, and he always wears cream-white shirts. He prefers a gray tie, a shade darker or lighter than his suit. With this he wears silk-and-wool mixture socks, sometimes plain, sometimes with a black clock. Extremely dark brown shoes, almost gunmetal brown, are his preference.[24]

As this description of Grant's signature wardrobe also implies, the well-tailored and seemingly imperishable gray suit worn by the hero of *North by Northwest* identifies his social class. "The hero is an advertising man (a significant choice of profession)," Lawrence Alloway noted at the time of the film's release in 1959, "and though he is hunted from New York to South Dakota his clothes stay neatly Brooks Brothers. That is to say, the dirt, sweat, and damage of pursuit are less important than the package in which the hero comes . . . the urbane Madison Avenue man."[25] In its review, *Daily Variety* similarly saw Roger as "a Madison Avenue man-about-Manhattan, sleekly handsome, carelessly twice-divorced, debonair as a cigarette ad."[26] *North by Northwest* celebrates this packaging of masculinity as one of its running gags about the star power of Cary Grant, not the least at those times when Roger's suit should by all rights appear the worse for wear: as when Eve packs it in her overnight case so that Roger can get off the train disguised as a redcap, or after the crop-dusting sequence, when he decides to get it sponged and pressed, giving her an opportunity to lead him to Vandamm. The copy in another one of the advertisements for the film made no bones about the comic indestructibility of Roger's gray flannel uniform, exclaiming: "The spies come at you from all directions . . . run from the cops, killers, secret agents, beautiful women . . . and see if you can do all this without wrinkling your suit!"[27]

Why is Roger's suit so important that it should not—and in fact *does* not—

22.
Goffman, 2.

23.
There is also a technical motivation for Roger to take off his gray suit at this point: His figure will soon need to stand out against the gray backdrop of the monument. This is the same reason why, after wearing black for the phony shooting, Eve changes to bright orange when she dresses to go off with Vandamm.

24.
20th Century–Fox press release, 1957; Cary Grant clipping file, Academy library. The release was used to publicize the production of *An Affair to Remember* (1958), but the characterization of Grant's fashion sense applies as well to *North by Northwest*.

25.
Lawrence Alloway, *The Long Front of Culture* (1959); quoted in Pacific Film Archive program notes for April 14, 1991; *North by Northwest* clipping file, Academy library.

26.
"Powe," rev. *North by Northwest*, *Daily Variety*, June 30, 1959, 3.

27.
Pressbook, *North by Northwest* clipping file, Academy library.

28.
In *Acting in the Cinema* (Berkeley: University of California Press, 1988), James Naremore comments on the way the gray color of Roger's clothing has caught the eye of many fans of the film, though his concern is to talk about the suit as it accentuates Grant's body in support of the star's performance style (214–16).

29.
Lehman, 2.

30.
Charles Higham and Roy Moseley, *Cary Grant: The Lonely Heart* (1989; reprint, New York: Avon, 1990), 274. According to the authors, moreover, Hitchcock sent Martin Landau to Grant's tailors because the director wanted Leonard to look better dressed than Roger—using the clothes competition, as it were, "symbolically, to show him [Leonard] as menacing and dominant." Seeing Landau's suits, Grant coveted them, the biographers continue, and used his contract to finagle them for his own personal wardrobe after the picture was completed (273–74).

31.
"The Shoulder Trade," *Time,* August 2, 1954, 62.

Figure 4
Roger flees from the cropduster in his indestructible gray suit.

escape notice?[28] It is revealing that the published screenplay pictures his suit a bit differently than viewers tend to remember it, describing Thornhill as "tall, lean, faultlessly dressed (and far too original to be wearing the gray-flannel uniform of his kind)."[29] Fair enough, particularly since the gray suit Cary Grant wears for most of the film varies in its chromatic tones according to the light and location, so that sometimes it seems more blue than gray, at other times more gray than blue. But while Roger's suit may not be your run-of-the-mill gray flannel uniform purchased off the racks at Brooks Brothers—it was actually tailored for Grant by Quintino of Wilshire Boulevard—it still means to register in the form of that class uniform; through most of the film (until after the phony shooting, in point of fact), the characters surrounding Roger are dressed in darker colors (charcoal, navy, black) to emphasize the gray color of his clothing.[30] Visually, this is to say, he even exemplifies that exquisite contradiction of fifties conformity described by Lehman's screenplay: In his designer suit, Roger Thornhill is instantly recognizable as the "original" representative of "his kind," the professional-managerial coalition that emerged within the middle class to dominate the entire culture during the postwar era.

Roger's affiliation with this particular segment of the middle class is his most salient, most stable, most incontestable characteristic. The one crucial measure-

ment of continuity for him (and for audiences in 1959) throughout the film, this identity remains clear enough to invest his character with a social if not moral authority, no matter what happens, no matter what he does. As *North by Northwest* keeps placing this man in the gray flannel suit before an audience's eyes, it has the effect of repositioning his masculinity in another, less transparent ideological context, one representing gender to America with just as much historical currency for the culture as the Cold War and domestic ideologies discussed earlier. Much of the significance of The Man in the Gray Flannel Suit as a pervasive cultural figure had to do with the way advertising, increasingly directed toward male shoppers as well as female ones, revised what had been presumed to be an absolute gender divide: masculine production versus feminine consumerism. So, for example, when *Time* noticed that "in the postwar decade the do-it-yourself craze has become a national phenomenon," the magazine was observing the increasing numbers of men who, like their wives, were becoming active consumers in their own right.[31] The launching of *Playboy* and *Sports Illustrated* magazines in 1953 also recognized the growing and potentially diverse male market. The Man in the Gray Flannel Suit was perceived as the agent of this disturbing—but also, everyone recognized, economically advantageous—absorption of masculinity into consumerism; what is more, he himself came to personify the corresponding conflation of substance and packaging.

The manipulator of media images, an advertising executive like Roger Thornhill exemplifies the postwar transformation of the disreputable and disheveled radio huckster into the respectable, well-dressed public relations man. As Eve tells Roger on the train between kisses: "You're an advertising man, that's all I know. . . . You've got taste in clothes. . . . Taste in food. . . . You're very clever with words. You can probably make them do anything for you. . . . Sell people things they don't need. . . . Make women who don't know you fall in love with you." Eve says all of this in a tone meant to be excited rather than disproving. Despite the instant criticism of Roger's masculinity implied through his association with Madison Avenue hucksterism, it is still the case that he generates considerable sympathy in audiences as well as Eve from the moment the film opens and puts his life in jeopardy. Cary Grant's relaxed and confident performance contributes to his character's attractiveness, but so does the film's insistence for all of Roger's immaturity and insincerity, not to mention his own resemblance to the spies as a fellow manipulator of masks and performance—upon his *ordinariness* as a harried businessman thrust into the dangerous and duplicitous world of foreign intrigue and CIA machinations. Truth to tell, the ordinary man or woman in the audience would not have had the economic power and social position that Roger arrogantly wields in the opening scene on Madison Avenue; but it is nevertheless the case, particularly once the film begins to correct his arrogance and dishonesty, that the audience is encouraged to identify with Roger as, in Robin Wood's phrase, "a modern city Everyman."[32]

Speaking more precisely, though, wouldn't it be more correct to describe Roger, not as every man, but as the exemplary fifties man? His profession immediately tells us that he belongs to the emerging power base of postwar America, in historian Jackson Lears's words, "a hegemonic historical bloc . . . formed by the groups often characterized as a "new class" of salaried managers,

administrators, academics, technicians, and journalists—people who manipulated symbols rather than made things, whose stock in trade consisted of their organizational, technical, conceptual, or verbal skills."[33] Analyzed during this period as "the other-directed character,"[34] "the organization man,"[35] and "the diploma *élite*,"[36] these college-trained professionals were, to use Vance Packard's description, "the big, active, successful people who pretty much run things," in contrast to "the supporting classes contain[ing] the passive non-big people who wear both white and blue collars: the small shopkeepers, workers, functionaries, technical aides." As Packard saw it in 1959, this new social and political allegiance between the "real upper class" (that is, old money) and the "semi-upper class" (that is, managerial and professional people) actually stratified the seemingly homogeneous middle class, with far-reaching consequences for the American class system because that invisible division then achieved "a more revolutionary blurring of the boundary line between white and blue-collared people."[37] As a result, the lower middle class was, without knowing it, living out the consequences of a reorganization of social power; nonetheless, low-level wage earners continued to identify with the interests of their employers and failed to recognize the actual incompatibility.

Technically speaking, the new grouping of educated media and managerial professionals lacked the coherence and unity of a "class" in the strictest sense of the term, but it nevertheless possessed real power and yielded palpable influence as, in Lears's words, "a historic hegemonic bloc, [which identified] its own problems and interests with those of society and indeed humanity at large." As Lears further points out, this was "a coalition of groups which differed in many ways but

32.
Wood, 134.

33.
Jackson Lears, "A Matter of Taste: Corporate Cultural Hegemony in a Mass-Consumption Society," in *Recasting America: Culture and Politics in the Age of Cold War*, ed. Lary May (Chicago: University of Chicago Press, 1989), 50. For a more generalized discussion by Lears of the concept of "cultural hegemony" and "historic bloc," their basis in Antonio Gramsci's writings, and their usefulness to American Studies, see his article "The Concept of Cultural Hegemony: Problems and Possibilities," *American Historical Review* 90 (1985), 567–93.

34.
David Reisman, in collaboration with Reuel Denney and Nathan Glazer, *The Lonely Crowd: A Study of the Changing American Character* (New Haven: Yale University Press, 1950), 35.

35.
William H. Whyte Jr., *The Organization Man* (New York: Simon & Schuster, 1956).

36.
Vance Packard, *The Status Seekers* (1959; reprint, Harmondsworth, Eng.: Pelican, 1961).

37.
Packard, 41, 36.

38.
Lears, "A Matter of Taste,"
50.

39.
Peter Biskind, *Seeing Is Believing: How Hollywood Taught Us to Stop Worrying and Love the Fifties* (New York: Pantheon, 1983), 15, 20.

40.
Barbara Ehrenreich, *Fear of Falling: The Inner Life of the Middle Class* (New York: Pantheon, 1989), 12, 14.

41.
"Freedom—New Style," *Time*, Sept. 27, 1954, 23.

which were bound together (up to a point) by common interests, common experiences, and a common worldview."[38] This bloc, moreover, found its overt political expression in what Peter Biskind describes as the "bipartisan coalition of moderates from both parties, who made up the rules of the game" and who governed, speaking culturally as well as politically, through "the power of consensus" (which Biskind condescendingly calls "the fifties' most important product").[39] Although this coalition of educated professionals and corporate managers began to break apart during the sixties, its consensus unraveling over issues of civil rights and the Vietnam War, some social historians now refer to it and its successive reformations in the seventies and eighties simply as "the professional middle class" in order to name that social group in American society which (1) is distinguished by an "economic and social status . . . based on education, rather than on ownership of capital or property," and (2) "uses consumption to establish its status, especially relative to the working class."[40] No single professional figure epitomized American deployment of capital solely in the interest of selling consumerism more vividly than The Man in the Gray Flannel Suit, the advertiser who worked on Madison Avenue and who himself blended seamlessly and effortlessly into the crowds of nameless, similarly dressed professional men filling up downtown streets in every U.S. city—the scene, in fact, with which *North by Northwest* opens.

Writing in 1954 to answer the question posed on its cover, "what is the American character?," *Time* looked at some of the consequences of the economy's shift in emphasis from production to consumerism. The magazine read the nation through the hegemonic lens of the men who made consuming their business,

and noted, "Increasingly, businesses group themselves in trade associations and businessmen look to their competitors rather than to their own accounting department, for the signals that mean success. Their attitude toward their own work is not that of producers, but of consumers. Morale is bucked up when a business decision meets the approval (and imitation) of the "antagonistic cooperators" of the adult peer group."[41] *Time* further observed that consumerism, the bedrock of the United States's postwar domestic economy, had begun to transform the "business mind" to the point of reorienting its epistemology totally around the exchange of what Goffman would soon analyze as "performance signs," the communication skills newly required for success in business. These demanded a heightened sensitivity to outer appearances which in turn induced the "business mind" to see social identity as a persona, or mask. Since advertising literally trades on the manufacturing of signs, an advertising executive like Roger Thornhill quite naturally personified this new type of man. *North by Northwest* dramatizes his quickness to pick up on "the signals that mean success" by showing how readily Roger himself takes to performance in response to (and imitation of) his own "antagonistic cooperators," namely, Vandamm and his men.

Time's comments on contemporary business life appeared in a cover story on David Reisman's *The Lonely Crowd* which had been published four years earlier. By 1954, that hugely influential book had already introduced into the popular idiom the standard way of characterizing the personality of the new middle-class, consumer-driven, professional businessman: the "modern" other-directed conformist, personified by the organization man as a *consumer*, as opposed to the "old-fashioned" inner-directed individualist, personified by the nineteenth-century captain of industry, who was, above all, a *producer*. Reisman himself explained the trend this way:

It would be premature, however, to say that it [other-direction] is already the dominant mode in America as a whole. But since the other-directed types are to be found among the young, in the larger cities, and among the upper income groups, we may assume that, unless present trends are reversed, the hegemony of other-direction types lies not far off.

If we wanted to cast our social character types into social class molds, we could say that inner-direction is the typical character of the "old" middle class—the banker, the tradesman, the small entrepreneur, the technically oriented engineer, etc.—while the other-direction is becoming the typical character of the "new" middle class—the bureaucrat, the salaried employee in business etc. Many of the economic factors associated with the recent growth of the new "new" middle class are well known. . . . There is a decline in the numbers and in the proportion of the working population engaged in production and extraction—agriculture, heavy industry, heavy transport—and an increase in the numbers and the proportion engaged in white-collar work and the service trades.[42]

What Reisman described as a trend "among the young, in the larger cities, and among the upper income groups" would, as a consequence of that group's hegemony, eventually cause U.S. society to turn away from Horatio Alger and embrace Roger O. Thornhill as its cultural role model instead.

From the moment that Vandamm accidentally sets the stage for Roger Thornhill to think of his identity as a performance, this spy in the gray flannel suit turns out to be the epitome of both the other-directed professional man *and* the ideologies sustaining the hegemony of Thornhill's class by confirming the value of his masculinity. In the first scene, the film gently satirizes Roger as a Madison Avenue type; in the second scene, it abruptly challenges his identity; and from that point on, it seeks to restore his affiliation with the professional-managerial class as a symbolic means of legitimizing that bloc's cultural hegemony in American society. In the process of saving both the woman he loves and the state's stolen secrets, Roger lives out the romance of the postwar armchair adventurer: He survives fantastically daring escapades, wins the prize (the blonde), and returns triumphant, to Madison Avenue. The narrative urgency for this romance to succeed comes from the need to validate Roger's masculinity, which was imperiled, it would seem, more by his job than by Vandamm. "The typical 'manly' or masculine vocations are rapidly disappearing," remarked the psychiatrist Henrik M. Ruitenbeek. "If masculine occupations are decreasingly important in a technological economy—and one largely oriented to finance and public relations rather than to production at that—the masculine role in the family has also changed."[43] A highly condensed and ideologically overdetermined event, Roger's marriage at the end of *North by Northwest* means to recuperate the endangered masculinity of the *professional* middle-class male.

Gender and Performance Anxiety

Because the film's closure is so ideologically overdetermined, particularly in equating Roger's revived manhood with the national interest, it is important to appreciate that *North by Northwest* also dramatizes the threat that the performance ideology of the professional-managerial class posed to the alignment of gender and nationalism as mirror images. The other-directed persona of this new class, to start with, severely undercuts the stability and singularity of "identity," projecting in its place a

42.
Reisman, 21.

43.
Hendrik M. Ruitenbeek, "Men Alone: The Male Homosexual and the Disintegrated Family," in *The Problem of Homosexuality in Modern Society*, ed. Ruitenbeek , 86.

Figure 5
His familiar face concealed
by dark glasses, Roger
meets Eve on the train.

44.
Orrin E. Klapp, *Heroes,
Villains, and Fools:
The Changing American
Character* (Englewood Cliffs,
N.J.: Prentice-Hall, 1962)
2, 96, 98.

45.
Klapp, 107.

heterogeneous field of social types, what the sociologist Orrin Klapp described as the "cafeteria style" of personality formation in U.S. society. Looking back on American social life of the fifties at the close of the decade, Klapp noted that, contrary to the American ideology of individualism, "in our society we do not have, as one might at first suppose, freedom from typing but a choice of type." Significantly, he characterized the diversity and confusion of self-presentation in American society by metaphorically equating the performance of an identity with the consumerist economy that underwrote it: "Americans find themselves in a kind of bargain basement with a bewildering variety [of roles] to choose from—the models may not all be equally becoming, but nothing prevents us from trying them on."[44]

Roger well epitomizes what Klapp, in a modification of Reisman's other-directed personality type, called "the audience-directed hero of today . . . He is at home anywhere, has 'stage presence,' and always manages to land on his feet."[45] Roger's skill in performance, which enables him to survive one dangerous predicament after another as he moves across the United States from the Northeast to the midwestern hinterlands, redefines his personality as the site of repeated identity displacements. These displacements occur over time and across a range of overlapping but not identical ideologies (those of the breadwinner

ethic, Cold War politics, and the new professional-managerial class), and each performance theatricalizes his personality according to different masculine personae (Madison Avenue executive, kidnap victim, alcoholic, momma's boy, murderer, fugitive, lover, redcap, and so on). The same is true of Eve. Each time she readjusts her mask to suit the particular scenario of the moment, she reveals her lack of a core identity, the stability of which would transcend the circumstances that instead require her to adapt one feminine persona or another for her own survival. This blonde is dangerous, not because she wields a gun, but because, with her identity produced through a series of masks, she shoots with blanks in more ways than one. She exemplifies how every social identity is, to borrow Goffman's phrase again, a "sign activity" requiring adeptness in theatricality, flexibility in handling her multiple personae, and attention to the demands of a constantly shifting audience. Like Roger's masculinity, her feminine identity is not *expressive,* in the sense of referring back to a coherent, continuous self beneath the layers of masquerade (the "real" Eve), because it is *performative,* continually being reconstituted in a theatricalized representation.

In showing how the social act of self-presentation destabilizes identity, *North by Northwest* calls into question the authenticity of *any* representational activity. To maintain its social dominance, the professional-managerial class relied on controlling representation, so it made the commodification of representations its primary business; but it also mistrusted representation in principle. From the spy scandals at the beginning of this period to the quiz show scandals at the end, apprehensions about the dangers of professional misuse of representation made both the advertiser and his profession persistent objects of criticism and satire within the new class itself. Functioning as scapegoats for the insincerity and conformity of the dominant corporate mentality, the advertising industry and its gray-suited practioners were accused of equating substance with its packaging—and then suspected of doing even worse: selling an empty package to an unsuspecting public.

The instability of all forms of representation in *North by Northwest* has particularly disruptive consequences for the seemingly stable position of masculinity in its various ideological settings. For if a social identity displaces the "real" person with a persona, then don't genders, sexual inflections of "identity," involve the same degree of imitation and fakery? In asking this question, I have in mind Judith Butler's theorization of gender as an ongoing performance, "the repeated stylization of the body, a set of repeated acts within a highly rigid regulatory frame that congeal over time to produce the appearance of substance, of a natural sort of being." She explains:

The distinction between expression and performativeness is crucial. If gender attributes and acts, the various ways in which a body shows or produces its cultural signification, are performative, then there is no preexisting identity by which an actor or attribute might be measured; there would be no true or false, real or distorted acts of gender, and the postulation of a true gender identity would be revealed as a regulatory fiction.[46]

From this perspective, "masculinity" does not refer to a male nature but instead imitates a dominant regulatory fiction authorizing the continued representation of certain types of gender performances for men (like the breadwinner), marginalizing others (like the momma's boy), and forbidding still others (like the homosexual). By the same token, Butler models her argument about gender not on the regulatory fictions of straight masculinity and femininity, but

on their subversion: gay and lesbian drag. "The replication of heterosexual constructs in nonheterosexual frames brings into relief the utterly constructed status of the so-called heterosexual original. Thus, gay is to straight *not* as copy is to original, but, rather, as copy is to copy."[47] Gender is a symbolic representation perceived in culture as a mimetic one; it always involves some element of masquerade. That is why, as self-conscious performance, drag, with its crossed and parodic references to binarized heterosexuality, functions so well as the normative framework in Butler's account.

To be sure, criticism of The Man in the Gray Flannel Suit's masculinity by popular and academic writers in the 1950s was directly aimed at his social behavior (in being passive before women, in conforming too wholeheartedly, in working too hard for his body's own good), not his sexual identity as a male. The masculinity crisis, heralded by *Look* as the "Decline of the American Male," was by no means talked about as an instability in or disruption of the symbolic category of gender itself. However, the identifying characteristic of the other-directed professional was nonetheless a gender attribute—he was, after all, a *man* in a gray flannel suit. Butler's theorization of gender as a performance helps to articulate what was not stated directly during the fifties but nonetheless continually suggested by this period's anxiety about a

46.
Judith Butler, *Gender Trouble: Feminism and the Subversion of Identity* (New York: Routledge, 1990), 33, 141. For a related discussion by Butler focusing on the issue of gender and imitation, see her article, "Imitation and Gender Insubordination," in *Inside/Out: Lesbian Theories, Gay Theories*, ed. Diana Fuss (New York: Routledge, 1991), 13–31.

47.
Butler, *Gender Trouble*, 31.

Figure 6
Roger is stopped by the woman in the hospital room before she gets a good look at him.

48.
Lawrence K. Frank, "How Much Do We Know About Men?" *Look*, May 17, 1955, 53. Emphasis is in the original.

49.
Butler, *Gender Trouble*, 25.

50.
Joan Riviere, "Womanliness as a Masquerade" (1929), reprinted in *Formations of Fantasy*, eds. Victor Burgin, James Donald, and Cora Kaplan (New York: Methuen, 1986), 38. The major articles that apply Riviere's ideas to film, and to which I allude in my comments here, are: Stephen Heath, "Joan Riviere and the Masquerade," in *Formations of Fantasy*, eds. Burgin et al. (45–61); Mary Ann Doane, "Film and the Masquerade: Theorizing the Female Spectator" (1982) and "Masquerade Reconsidered: Further Thoughts on the Female Spectators" (1988–89), both reprinted in her *Femmes Fatales: Feminism, Film Theory, Psychoanalysis* (New York: Routledge, 1991), 17–43; and John Fletcher, "Versions of Masquerade," *Screen* 29, no. 3 (summer 1988),43–69.

51.
See Chris Holmlund's critique of the limits that have been placed on the masquerade as a conceptualization of male sexuality, in "Masculinity as Multiple Masquerade: The 'Mature' Stallone and the Stallone Clone," in *Screening the Male: Exploring Masculinities in Hollywood Cinema*, eds. Steven Cohan and Ina Rae Hark (London: Routledge, 1993), 216–19.

52.
Butler, *Gender Trouble*, 25; see also 136, and "Imitation and Gender Insubordination," 24.

masculinity crisis. For instance, in one of its pieces on masculinity, *Look* magazine recognized that, since "masculinity" was the set of cultural expectations defining "what his society expects the male *to do and be*,"[48] then the ongoing engendering of men as "masculine" also meant that *being* a man was not necessarily the same as *doing* what a man's gotta do. ("Gender is always a doing," Butler states, "though not a doing by a subject who might be said to preexist the deed."[49]) If the gender attributes of masculinity were indeed performative, as *Look* implied, then they were also socially determined fictions, representations without an origin beyond the act of representation itself. The performance of gender required men and women alike to engage in masquerades of the sort that Roger and Eve undertake in *North by Northwest,* doing what the culture expected of men and women in order for them to appear to be properly "masculine" or "feminine."

By now there is a tradition in feminist film and cultural studies of analyzing femininity as a masquerade along the lines set out by Joan Riviere's famous case study of 1929, which associated femininity exclusively with the masquerade and posited that the feminine mask covered up a female's theft of the phallus. "Womanliness therefore could be assumed and worn as a mask," she explained, "both to hide the possession of masculinity and to avert the reprisals expected if she was found to possess it." Riviere's conclusion that there is no difference between "genuine womanliness and 'the masquerade'"—"whether radical or superficial, they are the same thing"— has dominated examinations of the feminine masquerade in cinema, particularly as it concerns female spectatorship and subjectivity.[50] The masquerade has recently been applied to masculinity as well, but because it has been invoked so often to explain the cultural construction of femininity, any overt theatricalization of the "masculine" through the masquerade is still believed to result in the implicit feminization of the male masquerader (as in Riviere's own examples of gay men putting on the mask of heterosexual virility).[51]

With my own analysis of the masculine masquerade in *North by Northwest,* I am more interested in picking up its theatrical rather than phallocentric implications, so I am using the term in accordance with Butler's theorization of gender as "performative—that is, constituting the identity it is purported to be," an effect achieved by treating the expressions of a gendered identity as if they were its causes as well as its results.[52] A gender masquerade of this sort does not conceal a deep dark secret (the theft of the phallus in Riviere's formulation) so much as it defines identity in terms of opposing— and also shifting—planes in order to establish the impression of dimensionality: an outside in relation to an inside, surface to depth, figure to ground, performance to authenticity. Far from raising questions of concealment and dissembling in order to imply a hidden and more real identity, what a gendered persona—the mask itself—signifies is the mark, or the playing out, of those differences.

This understanding of a gender masquerade is especially pertinent to cinema because of its institutional reliance upon stardom. The movie star—whose screen personality is, not accidentally, termed a *persona*—brings to the foreground of popular representation the epistemological problems that Butler describes in her deconstruction of sexual identities. On the one hand, a star bears a seemingly fixed and authentic relation to a referent in the real world, as epitomized by the photographic still, used extensively by the industry to promote films and their leading players.[53] But on the other hand, the star is also an "image" in more than a purely visual sense. The "star image" is an institutional product, a construction resulting from a complex, often overdetermined, sometimes underdetermined, interplay of biographical details, film roles, body codes, and media coverage, and extending, often in contradictory ways, across the duration of a performer's career.[54] Far from reproducing the original person, a star image on film is itself always a copy of a copy, a mask, or persona, meant to authenticate a social, racial, and gender type in the theatricalized settings of a movie and its promotion.

In their performance of gender types, Hollywood stars produce an effect akin to drag insofar as they, too, cross seemingly rigid binarized categories, such as the oppositions seeming/posing, natural/artificial, sincere/deceptive, which themselves carry a secondary gender inflection of masculine/feminine. According to Richard Dyer, "star images function crucially in relation to contradictions with and between ideologies, which they seek variously to 'manage' or resolve"—or even subvert by provoking a "clash of codes." While all stars embody "values that are under threat," as Dyer observes, some stars are extremely popular because their screen personae vividly stage or at least provoke ideological rupture.[55] That Cary Grant, voted the most popular male movie star of 1958, could so well represent heterosexual American masculinity speaks volumes about the ambiguous and unfixed status of masculinity in the culture at that time. Consequently, as *North by Northwest* unfolds and makes repeated and quite self-conscious allusions to the presence of its star player in the hero's part, the star image of "Cary Grant" supplies another

important layer of gender performance in the film text.

The Familiar Face of Cary Grant

Roger: I know, I look vaguely familiar.
Eve: Yes.
Roger: You feel you've seen me somewhere before.
Eve: Yes.
Roger: Funny how I have that effect on people. Something about my face.
Eve: It's a nice face.

Despite his legendary status in the fifties as Hollywood's quintessential leading man, Cary Grant was something of a paradoxical romantic hero for this period.[56] His biographers explicitly call his fifties screen image a "mask," by which they mean, with reference to his "sexual problems," "his false image, so carefully sustained, of unequivocal masculinity and strong emotional security."[57] While successfully personifying an image on and off screen of eternal youthfulness, Americanness, heterosexual attractiveness, bachelorhood, and sartorial elegance, Grant was actually middle-aged, British, bisexual, married (he was not yet divorced from Betsy Drake), and a secret cross-dresser (apparently wearing women's nylon panties underneath his expensively tailored suits[58]). The star's postwar screen persona, in short, refashioned his own age, class, nationality, sexual orientation, and marital status to represent something else entirely: the ever youthful American bachelor businessman, the role that Hitchcock and Lehman tailored expressly for him in *North by Northwest*.[59]

In the fifties, the apparent agelessness of Grant's face (which he seemed to have borrowed from the picture of Dorian Gray) contributed to the inescapable impression that the appeal of his star persona had more than a little to do with performance and masquerade. From the start of his career as Mae West's costar in the 1930s, Grant's value as a leading man

53.
Richard Dyer, "A Star is Born and the Construction of Authenticity" (1982); reprinted in *Stardom: Industry of Desire*, ed. Christine Gledhill (London: Routledge, 1991), 135.

54.
These comments draw upon Richard Dyer, *Stars* (London: British Film Institute, 1979).

55.
Dyer, *Stars*, 38, 32.

56.
My brief discussion of Grant in this essay follows the reading of his star persona in my article "Cary Grant in the Fifties: Indiscretions of the Bachelor's Masquerade," *Screen* 33 (winter 1992), 394–412. There I analyze the paradoxical implications of Grant's fifties star image in more detail, examining in particular how the masquerade functions in his romantic comedy *Indiscreet* (1958).

57.
Higham and Moseley, 248.

58.
"They were easy to drip dry when one was traveling," Grant reportedly told reporter Joe Hyams in explanation about five months before the release of *North by Northwest* (Higham and Moseley, 280).

59.
According to Donald Spoto, *North by Northwest* was written and planned with Cary Grant expressly in mind, and Hitchcock had to keep putting off James Stewart, who assumed he would do it as a matter of course after *Vertigo*. See Donald Spoto, *The Dark Side of Genius: The Life of Alfred Hitchcock* (Boston: Little, Brown, 1983), 402.

60.
Richard Schickel, *Cary Grant: A Celebration* (Boston: Little, Brown, 1983), 9.

61.
Jack Moffitt, rev. *North by Northwest*, Hollywood Reporter, June 30, 1959, 3.

had derived from his male beauty; in the postwar era he then became legendary for his eternal youthfulness—ever tanned, ever handsome, ever the same. As Richard Schickel puts it: "some time in his fifties, while he still looked as if he were in his forties—happily combining an elegant and easeful maturity with an undiminished capacity for playfulness—he simply ceased to age. Just plain stopped. As far as we in the audience could see."[60] Grant's irresistible good looks never coarsened with age but continued openly to attract the gaze of the female spectator, on screen as well as in the audience, often making her and not him the sexual aggressor, no matter what their difference in age. The seduction scenes in the two Hitchcock films of the fifties in which Grant starred—*To Catch a Thief* (1955), and *North by Northwest*—when the cool, sophisticated younger blonde becomes aroused enough by his good looks to break with convention, putting the moves on him, exemplify the extent to which "Cary Grant" signified desirable maleness and, hence, active sexual excitement in women. In his films, Grant didn't need to trick a woman into acting upon her desire for him; he simply had to let her look at him.

Grant's postwar films self-consciously acknowledge this important extratextual dimension of his star image through both verbal and visual references to his famous looks. Often giving Grant the kind of glamorous buildup usually reserved for female stars, the films of this period play up his desirability as a male through the closeups that introduce him and make his face comparable to the female lead's; the recognizability of his face, moreover, even became something of an in-joke in the late fifties, as when Roger and Eve discuss the familiarity of his face when they meet on the train in *North by Northwest*. The wit in their banter clearly arises from the interplay of extradiegetic references pressing against the diegetic immediacy of the scene. As well as establishing the fact that Eve has identified Roger from the photograph of him in the newspapers, and so has to reckon with the potential danger he might pose to her as a suspected murderer, the dialogue alludes to what the reassuring *and* exciting sight of Cary Grant's familiar face means in a romantic movie like this one. Eve's comment that Roger can make strange women fall in love with him likewise acknowledges Grant's status as the consummate screen lover, and the significance of this reference is then compounded when Eve, as if recognizing the commodification of the actor's famous face, goes on to equate his star power with his selling power. An even more self-conscious allusion to Grant's iconic status as the quintessential leading man occurs much later in the film, when Roger sneaks through a woman's hospital room, and she *twice* tells him to stop, the second time after she has gotten a better look at him with her glasses on, so that the repetition of "stop" now means "stay."

North by Northwest also takes note of Grant's famous face in the editing of his performance through closeups, which direct repeated attention to his apparently ageless face. The *Hollywood Reporter*'s characterization of Grant's performance simply takes for granted that his appearance on-screen functions as an image designed to be watched:

He delivers a marvelous series of closeups . . . he keeps you enthralled by doing nothing at all . . . [in the crop-dusting scene] he arouses more fear than a dozen movie Joan of Arcs being burned at the stake. The women will be attracted to him every minute, particularly in a hospital scene when he strides about clad only in a bath towel.[61]

Along with the camera's attention to his good looks, the highly mannered idiom of Grant's acting relies, in *North by*

Northwest as in his other films, upon an ensemble of predictable (which is not to say unpleasurable) theatrical effects as a performer.[62] As a consequence, Grant's celebrated diction, smile, double takes and pratfalls—all featured prominently in *North by Northwest,* as when Roger escapes from Vandamm in Glen Cove— like his famous clothes sense, openly play up the theatricality of his masculine persona over its authenticity, without in any way belittling the star's sexual appeal or his cinematic value as a leading man.

Because his screen image as the suave, consummate, and ageless lover arose from his construction of an attractive male identity out of artifice and theatricality, Cary Grant's star persona was ideally suited for the identity play that characterizes the narrative action in *North by Northwest.* (In fact, in one way or another, most of Grant's films of the postwar era have him undertaking some form of disguise, however flimsy the pretense, innocent the motivation, and transparent the mask.) When the film then has Grant engage in a masquerade as part of its plot, with Roger assuming the persona of Kaplan, it reproduces in the diegesis the very signs of the star's own performing, blurring the boundaries separating his character's acting from his own.

Furthermore, since "Cary Grant" is also a made-up name attached to a fabricated persona, Archie Leach's rise to stardom in Hollywood mirrors the invention of George Kaplan perhaps even more closely than the star's theatricalized image resembles the role-playing of Roger Thornhill.[63] "George Kaplan" and "Cary Grant" are both personae that signify all the more powerfully and credibly in being complete *and* successful fabrications. Their implicit comparability, moreover, helps us to see how the invention of the imaginary spy functions for *North*

by Northwest much as the invention of "Madeline Elster" does for *Vertigo.* To paraphrase Scotty's own realization in that film's final scene, the Madeline of Scotty's fantasy life turns out to be the seemingly first "fake" or "counterfeit," and her lack of authenticity exposes the basis of gender itself in ongoing acts of performance and masquerading. To be sure, when *Vertigo* pulls the veil away from Madeline's blondeness to expose her position in a chain of forged copies, it confirms what fifties culture already believed about femininity as a performance of womanliness that relied upon the manufacturing of gender attributes in an activity of masquerading which the Hollywood star system itself celebrated as female glamour and beauty. When *North by Northwest* lets Roger be mistaken for Kaplan, this chain of forged *male* copies results in a similar revelation, but, because it involves masculinity, it is far less expected: Roger Thornhill's masculinity—no less than George Kaplan's *or* Cary Grant's—is as much of a performative masquerade as a woman's femininity; it, too, is a gendered persona lacking an origin beyond representation and repeatedly needing to be reconstituted in one. The depiction of a masculinity crisis in the film's poster—with the image of Cary Grant falling in space, the ground pulled out from under him—epitomizes the unstable position of masculinity in such a chain of cultural representations of gender. Significantly enough, Grant's point of reference in the poster is itself another representation, a copy of a copy, of a scene in the film—the one, in fact, which happens to bring out Roger's full and willing complicity in performance: the phony-shooting scene.

Crisscrossed by so many levels of masquerades and identity play, *North by Northwest* calls into question whether masculinity can *ever* be assumed to be a

62.
For a more detailed analysis of the technique behind Grant's seemingly effortless performance style in *North by Northwest,* see Naremore, 211–35.

63.
Naremore also notes that both Kaplan and Roger are similar to Cary Grant the star as fabricated identities. See Naremore, 221–22.

coherent and singular, not to say authentic, condition in culture; this is ultimately the reason why the film then has to work all the harder to restore the period's dominant ideologies of gender in its closure. But by the same token, because that effort exposes the complex ideological machinery driving Roger on his road to maturity, marriage, and manhood, the ending of *North by Northwest* can also be viewed as one more gender performance. In its famous parting shot of the train speeding through the tunnel on its way back to Grand Central Station, the film winks all the more boldly at the domestic and Cold War ideologies motivating its closure, particularly the presumption of male entitlement which Roger's marriage to Eve is supposed to represent. In drawing this inference I do not mean to suggest that *North by Northwest* seriously challenges or revises the hegemonic status of Roger Thornhill's masculinity; this film is not utopian or revolutionary in its intent by any means. But I am claiming that, in its subtle historical understanding of the performance ideology motivating the personae of both its hero and its leading man, *North by Northwest* encourages our perception of the masquerading that forms the basis of gender identities, of masculinity as well as femininity, in our culture.

Constructed out of a series of performative masquerades, Roger's masculinity is not just a history—that is, a biography, as the film's Oedipal trajectory implies—since it also participates *in* history, the history of masculinity in the fifties. When American popular culture dwelled on its masculinity crisis during this period, whether the site was *North by Northwest* or *Look*'s "Decline of the American Male," it was registering the postwar realignment of American society around the professional-managerial historic bloc, but imagining the resulting social tremors

in terms of gender, not class. Clearly, the hegemony of the professional-managerial class had repercussions for the way fifties culture understood masculinity, particularly within the shifting locations of the dominant ideologies that *North by Northwest* cites; and just as clearly, the other-directed performative ethic of this new class implicitly challenged the status of masculinity as something natural, as the automatic effect of being male. That challenge occurred at the same time that the idea of masculinity itself, made comparable to nationalism and the interests of the national security state, became deeply complicit in the Cold War ideology that, most critics have argued, this film endorsed in one way or another. That challenge, moreover, as *North by Northwest* shows, resulted in the breakdown of the culture's consensus about masculinity, in effect requiring the renegotiation of what gender meant to Americans in the fifties.

"Lifelike": Imagining the Bodies of People with AIDS

Simon Watney

A youngster hardly twenty three hangs on,
sustained by a hateful necessary tube
taped up to his forehead, exciting his nose,

so ancient no one visits anymore.

—Michael Lynch,
"Late May—Toronto"

Scared families are flocking to leave a council skyscraper branded Britain's first "AIDS Ghetto." One great-gran said relatives are too frightened to visit because many of her neighbors—half are gay—are dying from the HIV virus. Other residents at Birmingham's Clydesdale Tower are so scared of touching the lift buttons they don protective gloves.

—Frank Curren,
"Our Hell Living in AIDS Ghetto"

Throughout the history of the HIV/AIDS pandemic, questions concerning the proximity of those known or thought to be uninfected to the bodies of people living with HIV or AIDS have played a central role in public discourse. The populist press has always reported on the AIDS crisis as if HIV were miasmatically contagious, and furthermore, as if the presence of people living with HIV or AIDS in the community is intrinsically surprising and therefore noteworthy. Characteristically, the *Daily Star* recently quoted "young mum Michelle Bishop,

26," who lives on the twenty-sixth floor of a Birmingham tower block with her six-year-old daughter, Danielle: "I've lived here five years and I'm desperate to leave. There are many people living here with AIDS and I'm living in fear and want to get out." [1]

Such reporting remains far from unusual in the U.K., where HIV has had a disproportionately limited impact compared to most other European countries—largely as the result of early community-based HIV education developed in the eighties by and for gay men, and the government's introduction of widespread needle exchanges since 1986. In a country with a total population of approximately fifty-eight million, there have been twenty-five thousand reported cases of HIV to date, and approximately ten thousand cases of AIDS. In this context, it is important to note that the mass media's representation of people with AIDS will always be linked to shifting national levels of seroprevalence—responding to the overall rate of new cases in the national population. Where HIV and AIDS remain comparatively rare, there is likely to be less pressure to modify representations that emerged at the earliest stages of the epidemic. Thus, proximity is indeed an

Michael Lynch's poem, "Late May—Toronto," appeared in *Tribe: An American Gay Journal* 1 (spring 1990): 44. Frank Curran's "Our Hell Living in AIDS Ghetto" appeared in the *Daily Star*, Aug. 29, 1994.

1.
As reported in the *Daily Star*, (London) Aug. 29, 1994, 44.

2.
For example, see Michael Callen, *Surviving AIDS,* (New York: HarperCollins, 1990).

3.
Tim Miles, "Reagan Fury over Benetton AIDS Ad," *Sunday Express,* June 26, 1994.

4.
Ibid.

important factor in our understanding of the representation of people with AIDS—especially in relation to perceptions of risk.

Yet such perceptions are organized in very different ways for different sections of the population. HIV/AIDS education developed for heterosexuals has generally tended to problematize the HIV status of one's sexual partner. The straight AIDS message regards its target audience as uninfected, and thus "at risk" from familiar, dangerous types of people—bisexuals, junkies, prostitutes, "the promiscuous," and so on. Materials produced by and for gay men, however, usually proceed from a pragmatic acknowledgment that many gay men are already infected—as many as fifty percent it is estimated in some U.S. cities. The gay AIDS message thus tends to emphasize the fact that risk may be *to* one's sexual partners, not simply *from* them. It is not difficult to follow the displaced anxieties that continue to inform much public and private AIDS commentary, anxieties about having intimate physical contact with somebody who has been "polluted" by equally direct prior contact to a member of the deadly dramatis personae of heterosexual HIV dread, bisexuals, junkies, and so on. Unpacked, the logic of the anxiety frequently seems to be the fear that one is having sex with someone who has had anal sex, or who has had sex with someone else who likes anal sex.

It is, frankly, pointless to complain at this stage of the epidemic that such fears and representations are largely groundless and irrational, for it is precisely their irrationality that sustains them. At the same time, however, we also live with a tenacious legacy of counter-representations, often mobilized by people with HIV/AIDS, working to correct the demonizing processes at work elsewhere. Since the early years of the

epidemic, people living with AIDS have been involved in a long-term contestation of representations deemed to be misleading, "stereotypical," and so on.[2] A complex politics of representation has played prominently in the history of HIV/AIDS, as rival sets of images mobilized rival explanations of the crisis. The image of someone with AIDS is, thus, inescapably caught up in a dense field of conflict, in which all too often the sadistic over-simplifications of racists, misogynists, and homophobes are countered by equally oversimplified idealizations. While it is undoubtedly just as important as before to refuse and refute casual, unthinking talk of "AIDS victims," for example, this stance becomes absurd to whatever extent it makes anyone living with AIDS feel he or she can't talk about the too commonly shared experience of being victimized, or if it further obscures the objective processes of systematic victimization.

Positive Bodies

When the Benetton clothing company recently produced an advertisement showing ex-president Ronald Reagan's face ostensibly covered with the Kaposi's sarcoma lesions commonly associated with AIDS, a colleague reportedly said that Mr. Reagan "feels sickened that his image is being used in such a disgusting fashion."[3] Photographer and art director Oliviero Toscani, who created the ad, defends his actions, saying: "I did this because Reagan disregarded alarms about the AIDS threat when he was President."[4] One is obliged to point out that Toscani has employed specific signs of physical deformation in order to demonize Reagan in precisely the same way that others have used those same signs to demonize people with AIDS in general. In either case, AIDS is held to be intrinsically disgusting—supposed "evidence" of depravity and immorality, or, as in the

Benetton ad, of government neglect and hypocrisy. Both the *Daily Star* and Benetton share the popular assumption that AIDS is indeed shameful.

Such routine transformations of the physical appearance of people with AIDS into cyphers or emblems of supposed moral worth hardly serves to clarify most people's perceptions of their own personal risk. Yet we should not simply complain that AIDS imagery targeted at heterosexuals presents HIV as a distant risk: In fact abundant epidemiological evidence demonstrates that, throughout the developed world, heterosexuals who have unprotected sexual intercourse are demonstrably far less likely to contract HIV than gay men. What is noteworthy is that the dominant imagery of AIDS has not yet adjusted to accommodate changing medical information. For example, epidemiological surveys now suggest that "a substantial proportion [of HIV positive individuals] will probably be free of AIDS 20 and 25 years after HIV-1 infection."[5] Such reliable reports provide grounds for cautious optimism for the many millions living with HIV throughout the developed world.[6] The extreme fatalism that characterizes most populist AIDS discourse *requires* that AIDS be painful, hideous, and uniformly fatal. Yet for the HIV positive "non-progressor," things are very different. Thus Jonathan Grimshaw has eloquently described "the paradox of having on the one hand something wonderful—more years of life than one had anticipated. And on the other hand the idea of life as a sentence, as a prisoner might be 'sentenced' for life."[7]

Behind all this lies the physiological question of HIV status, one's own and that of one's sexual partners—whether it is "known" or just "perceived." For most heterosexuals HIV is understandably felt as rather remote, because for most

heterosexuals it is indeed rather remote. Consequently, the fantasy that the epidemic can be stopped by magically identifying all so-called "AIDS carriers" remains potent. Indeed, the very notion of the "AIDS carrier" itself speaks volumes about the ways in which early commentators successfully framed the supposed "meaning" of the epidemic (for heterosexuals) in terms of the need to avoid whole classes of people. If you inhabited one of the groups heterosexuals were meant to avoid, things were, of course, rather different. For gay men, HIV status has become a presiding issue in all our social and amorous transactions—not because we seek to avoid HIV, but because it is literally unavoidable.

Throughout the entire history of the epidemic, doctors, epidemiologists, government officials, and many others have called on gay men to come forward for HIV testing. This is somehow imagined by analogy with the national blood-transfusion service as a "responsible" and even "manly" thing to do, a matter of common sense. But *whose* common sense, and *of what?* Any gay man having sex with another man whose HIV status he doesn't know faces the extremely high probability that he or his partner, or both, are already infected. In gay men over twenty-five, this has long been an everyday fact of life, something you learn to "get used to." In the United States, most gay men over thirty will have friends and acquaintances at all stages of HIV-related illness, and a decade of funerals behind them. In Britain, AIDS deaths appear only in the register of mortality statistics, and there has been no mass media recognition of the ways in which the epidemic is experienced in all its complexity from the perspective of those for whom death is increasingly a part of "everyday life"—"everyday life" as another, distant planet as far as journalists

5.
"Long-term Survival in HIV-1 Infection," *British Journal of Medicine*, July 30, 1994, 283–84.

6.
The survey quoted and others drawing similar conclusions were conducted in the developed world; consequently, inferences from these data may only be drawn with respect to the developed world and may or may not be applicable to the Third World.

7.
Jonathan Grimshaw, "'Life' for a Non-Progressor," plenary talk given at *Second International Conference on Biopsychosocial Aspects of HIV and AIDS*, Brighton, Eng., July 7–10, 1994.

8.
Diseased Pariah News 4
(1991): 1.

9.
Allen Barnett, "Philostorgy,
Now Obscure," in
The Body and its Dangers
(New York: St. Martin's
Press, 1990), 52.

are concerned. It remains important in Britain to depict AIDS in all its awful complexity, since its reality is not lived as directly and widely as in America. This is especially important in relation to younger gay men, who are unlikely knowingly to have any direct contact whatsoever with HIV or AIDS.

The "good news" about increased life-expectancy prospects for the already infected also signals a new challenge to gay health educators, since it seems likely that more people are likely to remain unknowingly infectious far longer than we had previously calculated. For some, the answer to such issues will be HIV testing. For others it will be an equally principled decision to continue living with uncertainty—the dominant mode of psychic reality for most gay British men in the nineties. We know the medical evidence, and it is not good. We live our life as best we can. Love affairs end. Ardor cools. Opportunity beckons. In such respects, gay men are hardly unique.

It would be difficult, if not impossible to do justice to the emotional complexity surrounding the entire question of HIV testing among gay men. For heterosexuals however, "AIDS testing" is invariably sensationalized and sentimentalized. As a gay man, it is difficult to think of a more spectacularly nauseating species of journalism than the oft repeated spectacle of the star (or more often starlet) describing his or her terrible anxieties before getting HIV-test results back. One gasps at the innuendoes: Forbidden love? Sexual pleasure? God forbid! And always, always, always, they are negative. When my friends test, here in London, one in four is statistically likely to be positive. This is how *we* think of "positive bodies."

"I Have AIDS"

Diseased Pariah News is published in San Francisco. It describes its mission as "a quarterly publication of, by, and for people with HIV disease. We are a forum for infected people to share their thoughts, feelings, art, writing, and brownie recipes in an atmosphere free of teddy bears, magic rocks, and seronegative guilt."[8] I ask myself which heterosexuals I know would begin to understand the notion of "seronegative guilt," let alone the different registers of meaning it evokes in gay men who think or believe themselves to be negative, or gay men who suspect they are possibly infected, or those who suspect they are probably infected, or those who know they are "positive." *Diseased Pariah News* has a regular hot porno gay PWA centerfold, and its most fabulous (and practical) regular column is "GET FAT, don't die!"

In a story by my late friend and colleague Allen Barnett, a gay man learns:

. . . that the body can recall things on its own. There were nights when he felt the recent dead getting into bed, climbing over him as if they had just come from the shower. He felt their bodies against his own, or beneath him, a sack of balls loose between their legs, wet hair on the nape of their necks. He could feel the way each of them used to push into the mattress on their way to sleep. It was even comforting to have them there, to be remembered by them before they got up to lie briefly, like this, in someone else's bed. There were dead men he could still arouse himself for. [9]

And, presumably, there were dead men for whom feelings of arousal were simply too painful to imagine, or to follow, or to follow through on.

There is furthermore a dimension of political and ethical solidarity closely involved in gay men's relations with one another's HIV statuses, since HIV is overwhelmingly the most important issue facing our various communities, though this is rarely acknowledged by the ostensible lesbian and gay political "leadership" organizations in Britain or the United States. They in turn seek admission to the cleaner airs of "official" national politics, and HIV has long been an embarrassment to Rainbow Coalitionists. Hence, we should also recognize the discursive impact of the research subject who speaks from "science" back into everyday life. In this manner Mark Harrington's presentation at the 1994 Tenth International Conference on AIDS in Yokohama exemplified a very different order of political intervention, welcoming delegates, and thanking the organizers for asking him to speak on the vexed topic of "When to Begin Antiretroviral Treatment?":

The topic is obviously a timely one, not only for the AIDS field in general, but also for myself in particular. Some of you were in Amsterdam two years ago and may have seen me present slides of my left auxiliary lymph node biopsies in April 1992, in situ hybridization of which demonstrated, in the words of one of my doctors, that my lymph node was "crammed with virus." At the time I had somewhat over 600 CD4 cells; they are now, two years later, somewhat over 400, and I remain asymptomatic.[10]

He then delivered a paper concluding that, from the perspective of people living with HIV; "all the advances in high-tech virology and immunology have yet to be applied or confirmed in well-designed studies which provide *clinical evidence of benefit.*[11]

A powerful poem by my late best friend, Charles Barber, graphically describes what it is like to be treated for such advanced symptoms of HIV disease as CMV retinitis. He is describing the type of catheter routinely inserted into the chests of people with AIDS whose regular veins can no longer take injections or IV drips:

The dream.
Finally well,
Over me lies his arm;
The hole in my chest a lip-smudge,
Stamped, sealed.
Grotesque,
Life-supporting,
Deforming and healing;
Not a cure; insistent I be
Life-like.[12]

At a time when the metaphor for people with HIV as "living timebombs" remains widely in use, we can only speculate about the extent popular "concern" about AIDS is about imaginary "fallout" rather than about the real, substantial issues of risk and death among gay men, injecting drug users, and their sexual partners.[13]

While comparisons between the signs of leprosy and plague in previous centuries and current representations of people with AIDS provide interesting parallels, all too often they are used to obscure or deflect attention away from what is unique to HIV/AIDS in the late twentieth century. This has less to do with lay perceptions possibly bearing traces of premodern notions of the body's "humors," than with institutionized homophobia and racism, with the complete inability of late-twentieth-century public political discourse to acknowledge the actual sexual choices and diversity of the populations politicians claim to represent. The answer to these and other current dilemmas does not lie in pretending that HIV is some kind of "equal opportunity" virus, as it is so often depicted. There is a truth that precedes representation, and it is faithfully mapped in the many epidemiological tables that measure changing patterns of public health and illness. How those tables are themselves translated into public discourse is thus a central question for AIDS activists who

10.
Mark Harrington, "When to Begin Antiretroviral Treatment?", paper given on Thursday, Aug. 11, 1994, at the *Tenth International Conference on AIDS*, at Yokohama.

11.
Ibid., emphasis in original.

12.
Charles Barber, "Thirteen Things About a Catheter," in Rachel Hadas, ed., *Unending Dialogue: Voices from an Aids Poetry Workshop* (Boston: Faber & Faber, 1990), 23.

13.
For example, Gill Swain, "AIDS TIMEBOMB: Where Life Really Is for Living," *Daily Mirror* (London), June 22, 1994.

wish to establish policies firmly based in the real epidemic rather than in the domains of collective cultural hallucinations.

This is why the question of how we imagine the bodies of people with AIDS matters. More than most, such bodies are inspected, evaluated, weighed, measured. More than most, they deserve the ordinary decencies of privacy. While the "truth claims" made from the position of speaking "as" a person with HIV or AIDS guarantees nothing about the accuracy or utility of what is said, nonetheless the claim has a fundamental validity. How we imagine the bodies of people with AIDS is always a reflection of how we all regard our own bodies, and that regard is charged with a dimension of sexual object-choice, which is as fundamental as any question of age or race or gender. Who's your next fuck?

Reconstructing Black Masculinity
bell hooks

Black-and-white snapshots of my childhood always show me in the company of my brother. Though he is less than a year older than me, we looked like twins, and for a time in life we did everything together. We were inseparable. As young children, we were brother and sister, comrades, in it together. As adolescents, he was forced to become a boy and I was forced to become a girl. In our southern black Baptist patriarchal home, being a boy meant learning to be tough, to mask one's feelings, to stand one's ground and fight; being a girl meant learning to obey, to be quiet, to clean, to recognize that you had no ground to stand on. I was tough, he was not. I was strong willed, he was easygoing. We were both a disappointment. Affectionate, full of good humor, loving, my brother was not at all interested in becoming a patriarchal boy. This lack of interest generated a fierce anger in our father.

We grew up staring at photos of our father, in a boxing ring, or playing basketball, or posing with his black infantry troop in World War II. He was a man in uniform, a man's man, able to hold his own. Despising his only son for not wanting to become the strong, silent type (my brother loved to talk, tell jokes, and make us happy), our father let him know early on that he was no son to him, that

real sons want to be like their fathers. Made to feel inadequate, less than male, in his childhood, a boy in a house filled with six sisters, he became forever haunted by the idea of patriarchal masculinity. All that he had questioned in his childhood was sought after in his early adult life in order to become a man's man—phallocentric, patriarchal, and masculine. In traditional black communities, when one tells a grown male to "be a man," one is urging him to aspire to a masculine identity rooted in the patriarchal ideal. Throughout black male history in the United States there have been black men who were not at all interested in the patriarchal ideal. In the black community of my childhood, there was no monolithic standard of black masculinity. Though the patriarchal ideal was the most esteemed version of manhood, it was not the only version. No one in our house talked about black men being no good, shiftless, trifling. Head of the household, our father was a "much man," a provider, lover, disciplinarian, reader, and thinker. He was introverted, quiet, and slow to anger, yet fierce when aroused. We respected him. We were in awe of him. We were afraid of his power, his physical prowess, his deep voice, and his rare, unpredictable but intense rage. We were never allowed to forget that, unlike other black men, our father was the fulfillment of the patriarchal masculine ideal.

Though I admired my father, I was more fascinated and charmed by black men who were not obsessed with being patriarchs: by Felix, a hobo who jumped trains, never worked a regular job, and was missing a thumb; by Kid, who lived out in the country and hunted the rabbits and coons that came to our table; by Daddy Gus, who spoke in hushed tones, sharing his sense of spiritual mysticism. These were the men who touched my heart. The list could go on. I remember them because they loved folks, especially women and children. They were caring and giving. They were black men who chose alternative life-styles, who questioned the status quo, who shunned a ready-made patriarchal identity and invented themselves. By knowing them, I have never been tempted to ignore the complexity of black male experience and identity. The generosity of spirit that characterized who they were and how they lived in the world lingers in my memory. I write this piece to honor them, knowing as I do now that it was no simple matter for them to choose against patriarchy, to choose themselves, their lives. And I write this piece for my brother in hopes that he will recover one day, come back to himself, know again the way to love, the peace of an unviolated free spirit. It was this peace that the quest for an unattainable, life-threatening patriarchal masculine ideal took from him.

When I left our segregated southern black community and went to a predominantly white college, the teachers and students I met knew nothing about the lives of black men. Learning about the matriarchy myth and white culture's notion that black men were emasculated, I was shocked. These theories did not speak to

the world I had most intimately known, did not address the complex gender roles that were so familiar to me. Much of the scholarly work on black masculinity that was presented in the classroom then was based on material gleaned from studies of urban black life. This work conveyed the message that black masculinity was homogeneous. It suggested that all black men were tormented by their inability to fulfill the phallocentric masculine ideal as it has been articulated in white-supremacist capitalist patriarchy. Erasing the realities of black men, who have diverse understandings of masculinity, scholarship on the black family (traditionally the framework for academic discussion of black masculinity) puts in place of this lived complexity a flat, one-dimensional representation.

The portrait of black masculinity that emerges in this work perpetually constructs black men as "failures" who are psychologically "fucked up," dangerous, violent, sex maniacs whose insanity is informed by their inability to fulfill their phallocentric masculine destiny in a racist context. Much of this literature is written by white people, and some of it by a few black men in academia. It does not interrogate the conventional construction of patriarchal masculinity or question the extent to which black men have historically internalized this norm. It never assumes the existence of black men whose creative agency has enabled them to subvert norms and develop ways of thinking about masculinity that challenge patriarchy. Yet, there has never been a time in the history of the United States when black folks, particularly black men, have not been enraged by the dominant culture's stereotypical, fantastical representations of black masculinity. Unfortunately, black people have not systematically challenged these narrow visions, insisting on a more accurate "reading" of black male reality. Acting in complicity with the status quo, many black people have passively absorbed narrow representations of black masculinity, perpetuated stereotypes, and myths, and offered one-dimensional accounts. Contemporary black men have been shaped by these representations.

No one has yet endeavored to chart the journey of black men from Africa to the so-called New World with the intent to reconstruct how they saw themselves. Surely the black men who came to the American continent before Columbus saw themselves differently from those who were brought on slave ships, or from those few who freely immigrated to a world where the majority of their brethren were enslaved. Given all that we know of the slave context, it is unlikely that enslaved black men spoke the same language, or that they bonded on the basis of shared "male" identity. Even if they had come from cultures where gender difference was clearly articulated in relation to specific roles, that was all disrupted in the New World context. Transplanted African men—even those who came from cultures where sex roles shaped the division of labor, where the status of men was different, and most often higher, than that of females—had the white colonizer's notions of manhood and masculinity imposed upon them. Black men did not respond to this imposition passively. Yet it is evident in black male slave narratives that black men engaged in racial uplift were often most likely to accept the norms of masculinity set by white culture.

Although the gendered politics of slavery denied black men the freedom to act as "men" within the definition set by white norms, this notion of manhood became the standard used to measure black male progress. Slave narratives document ways black men thought about

manhood. The narratives of Henry "Box" Brown, Josiah Henson, Frederick Douglass, and a host of other black men reveal that they saw "freedom" as that change in status that would enable them to fulfill the role of chivalric benevolent patriarch. Free, they would be men able to provide for and take care of their families. Describing how he wept as he watched a white overseer beat his mother, William Wells Brown lamented, "Experience has taught me that nothing can be more heart-rending than for one to see a dear and beloved mother or sister tortured, and to hear their cries and not be able to render them assistance. But such is the position which an American slave occupies." Frederick Douglass did not feel his manhood affirmed by intellectual progress. It was affirmed when he fought man to man with the slave overseer. This struggle was a turning point in Douglass's life: "It rekindled in my breast the smoldering embers of liberty. It brought up my Baltimore dreams and revived a sense of my own manhood. I was a changed being after that fight. I was nothing before—I was a man now." The image of black masculinity that emerges from slave narratives is one of hardworking men who longed to assume full patriarchal responsibility for families and kin.

Given this aspiration and the ongoing brute physical labor of black men that was the backbone of slave economy (there were more male slaves than black female slaves, particularly before breeding became a common practice), it is really amazing that stereotypes of black men as lazy and shiftless so quickly became common in the public imagination. In these nineteenth and early-twentieth-century representations, black men were cartoon-like creatures only interested in drinking and having a good time. Such stereotypes were an effective way for white racists to erase the significance of black male labor from public consciousness. Later on, these same stereotypes were evoked as reasons to deny black men jobs. They are still evoked today.

Male "idleness" did not have the same significance in African and Native American cultures that it had in the white mindset. Many nineteenth century Christians saw all forms of idle activity as evil, or at least a breeding ground for wrongdoing. For Native Americans and Africans, idle time was space for reverie and contemplation. When slavery ended, black men could once again experience that sense of space. There are no studies that explore the way Native American cultures altered notions of black masculinity, especially for those black men that lived as Indians or who married Indian wives. Since we know there were many tribes that conceived of masculine roles in ways that were quite different from those of whites, black men may well have found African ideas about gender roles affirmed in Native traditions.

There are also few confessional narratives by black men that chronicle how they felt as a group when freedom did not bring with it the opportunity for them to assume a "patriarchal" role. Black men who worked as farmers were often better able to assume this role than those who worked as servants or who moved to cities. Certainly, in the mass migration from the rural south to the urban north, black men lost status. In southern black communities there were many avenues for obtaining communal respect. A man was not respected solely because he could work, make money, and provide. The extent to which a given black man absorbed white society's notion of manhood likely determined the extent of his bitterness and despair when white supremacy continually blocked his access to the patriarchal ideal.

Nineteenth-century black leaders were concerned about gender roles. While they believed that men should assume leadership positions in the home and in public life, they were also concerned about black women's role in racial uplift. Whether they were merely paying lip-service to the cause of women's rights or were true believers, a number of exceptional black men advocated equal rights for black women. In his work, Martin Delaney continually stressed that both genders need to work in the interest of racial uplift. To him, gender equality was more a way to have greater involvement in racial uplift than a way for black women to be autonomous and independent. Black male leaders like Martin Delaney and Frederick Douglass were patriarchs, but as benevolent dictators they were willing to share power with women, especially if it meant they did not have to surrender any male privilege. In 1847, as co-editors of the *North Star,* Douglass and Delaney had a masthead that read: "Right is of no sex—truth is of no color. . . ." The 1848 meeting of the National Negro Convention included a proposal by Delaney stating: "Whereas we fully believe in the equality of the sexes, therefore, resolved that we hereby invite females hereafter to take part in our deliberation." In Delaney's 1852 treatise *The Condition, Elevation, Emigration, and Destiny of the Colored People of the United States, Politically Considered,* he argued that black women should have full access to education so that they could be better mothers, asserting that "The potency and respectability of a nation or people, depends entirely upon the position of their women; therefore, it is essential to our elevation that the female portion of our children be instructed in all the arts and sciences pertaining to the highest civilization." In Delaney's mind, equal rights for black women in certain public spheres, such as education, did not mean that he was advocating a change in domestic relations whereby black men and women would have co-equal status in the home.

Most nineteenth-century black men were not advocating equal rights for women. On the one hand, most black men recognized the powerful and necessary role black women had played as freedom fighters in the movement to abolish slavery and in other civil rights efforts; yet on the other hand, they continued to believe that women should be subordinate to men. They wanted black women to conform to the gender norms set by white society. They wanted to be recognized as "men," as patriarchs, by other men, including white men. Yet they could not assume this position if black women were not willing to conform to prevailing sexist gender norms. Many black women who had endured white-supremacist patriarchal domination during slavery did not want to be dominated by black men after manumission. Like black men, they had contradictory positions on gender. On the one hand, they did not want to be "dominated," but on the other hand, they wanted black men to be protectors and providers. After slavery ended, enormous tension and conflict emerged between black women and men as folks struggled to be self-determining. As they worked to create standards for community and family life, gender roles continued to be problematic.

Black men and women who wanted to conform to gender role norms found that this was nearly impossible in a white racist economy intent on continuing its exploitation of black labor. Much is made, by social critics who want to further the notion that black men are symbolically castrated, of the fact that black women often found work in service jobs while black men were unemployed. The

reality, however, was that in some black homes it was problematic when the woman worked and the man did not, or when she earned more than he, yet, in other homes, black men were quite content to construct alternative roles. Critics who look at black life from a sexist standpoint advance the assumption that black men were psychologically devastated because they did not have the opportunity to slave away in low-paying jobs for white racist employers when the truth may very well be that those black men who wanted to work but could not find jobs, as well as those who did not want to find jobs, may simply have felt relieved that they did not have to submit to economic exploitation. Concurrently, there were black women who wanted black men to assume patriarchal roles, and there were some who were content to be autonomous, independent. And long before the contemporary feminist movement sanctioned the idea that men could remain home and rear children while women worked, many black women and men had such arrangements and were happy with them.

Without implying that black women and men lived in gender utopia, I am suggesting that black sex roles, particularly the role of men, have been more complex and problematized in black life than is believed. This was especially the case when all black people lived in segregated neighborhoods. Racial integration has had a profound impact on black gender roles. It has helped to promote a climate wherein most black women and men accept sexist notions of gender. Unfortunately, many changes have occurred in the way black people think about gender, yet the shift from one standpoint to another has not been fully documented. For example: To what extent did the civil rights movement, with its definition of freedom as equal opportunity with whites, sanction white gender roles as the norm black people should imitate? Why has there been so little positive interest shown in alternative life-styles of black men. In every segregated black community in the United States there are adult black men—married, unmarried, gay, straight—who live in households where they do not assert patriarchal domination and yet live fulfilled lives, where they do not sit around worrying about castration. Again, it must be emphasized that the black men who are most worried about castration and emasculation are those who have completely absorbed white-supremacist patriarchal definitions of masculinity.

Advanced capitalism further changed the nature of gender roles for all men in the United States. The image of the patriarchal head of the household, ruler of this ministate called the "family," faded in the twentieth century. More men than ever before worked for someone else. The state began to interfere more in domestic matters. A man's time was not his own—it belonged to his employer—and the terms of his rule in the family were altered. In the old days, a man who had no money could still assert tyrannic rule over family and kin, by virtue of his patriarchal status, usually affirmed by Christian belief systems. Within a burgeoning capitalist economy, it was wage-earning power that determined the extent to which a man would rule over a household, and even that rule was limited by the power of the state. In *White Hero, Black Beast,* Paul Hoch describes the way in which advanced capitalism altered representations of masculinity:

The concept of masculinity is dependent at its very root on the concepts of sexual repression and private property. Ironically, it's sexual repression and economic scarcity that give masculinity its main significance as a symbol of economic status and sexual opportunity. The shrinkage of the concept of man into the narrowed and hierarchical conceptions of masculinity of the various work and consumption ethics also goes hand in hand with an increasing social division of labor, and an increasing shrinkage of the body's erogenous potentials culminating in a narrow genital sexuality. As we move from the simpler food-gathering societies to the agricultural society to the urbanized work and warfare society, we notice that it is a narrower and narrower range of activities that yield masculine status.

In feminist terms, this can be described as a shift from emphasis on patriarchal status (determined by one's capacity to assert power over others in a number of spheres, based on maleness) to a phallocentric model, where what the male does with his penis becomes a greater and certainly a more accessible way to assert masculine status. It is easy to see how the interests of a capitalist state, which was indeed depriving men of their rights, exploiting their labor in such a way that they only indirectly received the benefits, were furthered in the movement away from patriarchal power based on ruling others toward a masculine status that would depend solely on the penis.

With the emergence of a fierce phallocentrism, a man was no longer a man because he provided for his family; he was a man simply because he had a penis. Furthermore, his ability to use that penis in the arena of sexual conquest could bring him as much status as being a wage earner and provider. A sexually defined masculine ideal rooted in physical domination and sexual possession of women is accessible to any man. Hence, even unemployed black men could gain status, could be seen as the embodiment of masculinity, within a phallocentric framework. Barbara Ehrenreich's *The Hearts of Men* chronicles white male repudiation of the patriarchal masculine ideal that required a man to marry and provide for the material well-being of women and children, as white males increasingly embraced a phallocentric "playboy" ideal. At the end of the chapter "Early Rebels," Ehrenreich describes rites of passage in the 1950s which led white men away from traditional nonconformity into a rethinking of masculine status:

Not every would-be male rebel had the intellectual reserves to gray gracefully with the passage of the decade. They drank beyond excess, titrating gin with coffee in their lunch hours, gin with Alka-Seltzer on the weekends. They had stealthy affairs with secretaries, and tried to feel up their neighbors' wives at parties. They escaped into Mickey Spillane mysteries, where naked blondes were routinely perforated in a hail of bullets, or into westerns, where there were no women at all and no visible sources of white-collar employment. And some of them began to discover an alternative, or at least an entirely new style of male rebel who hinted, seductively, that there was an alternative. The new rebel was the playboy.

Even in the restricted social relations of slavery, black men had found a way to practice the fine art of phallocentric seduction. Long before white men stumbled upon the "playboy" alternative, black vernacular culture told stories about that nonworking man with time on his hands who might be seducing somebody else's woman. Blues songs often narrate the "playboy" role. Ehrenreich's book acknowledges that the varied expressions of masculinity in segregated black culture influenced white men. This suggests that the presence of black men in segregated black culture influenced white men.

The Beat hero, the male rebel who actually walks away from responsibility in any form, was not a product of middle-class angst. The possibility of walking out, without money or guilt, and without ambition other than to see and do everything, was not even imminent in the middle-class culture of the early fifties. . . . The new bohemianism of the Beats came from somewhere else entirely, from an underworld and an underclass invisible from the corporate "crystal palace" or suburban dream houses.

Alternative male life-styles that opposed the status quo were to be found in black culture. White men seeking alternatives to a patriarchal masculinity turned to black men, particularly black musicians. Norman Podhoretz's 1963 essay "My Negro Problem—And Ours" names white male fascination with blackness, and black masculinity:

Just as in childhood I envied Negroes for what seemed to me their superior masculinity, so I envy them today for what seems to be their superior physical grace and beauty. I have come to value physical grace very highly and I am now capable of aching with all my being when I watch a Negro couple on the dance floor, or a Negro playing baseball or basketball. They are on the kind of terms with their own bodies that I should like to be on with mine, and for that precious quality they seem blessed to me.

Black masculinity, as fantasized in the racist white imagination, is the quintessential embodiment of man as "outsider" and "rebel." They were the ultimate "traveling men" drifting from place to place, town to town, job to job.

Within segregated black communities, the "traveling" black man was admired even as he was seen as an indictment of the failure of black men to achieve the patriarchal masculine ideal. Extolling the virtues of traveling black men in her novels, Toni Morrison sees them as "truly masculine in the sense of going out so far where you're not supposed to go and running toward confrontations rather than away from them." This is a man who takes risks, what Morrison calls a "free man":

This is a man who is stretching, you know, he's stretching, he's going all the way within his own mind and within whatever his outline might be. Now that's the tremendous possibility for masculinity among black men. And you see it a lot. . . . . They may end up in sort of twentieth-century, contemporary terms being also unemployed. They may be in prison.

They may be doing all sorts of things. But they are adventuresome in that regard.

Within white-supremacist capitalist patriarchy, rebel black masculinity has been idolized and punished, romanticized yet vilified. Though the traveling man repudiates being a patriarchal provider, he does not necessarily repudiate male domination.

Collectively, black men have never critiqued the dominant culture's norms of masculine identity, even though they have reworked those norms to suit their social situation. Robert Staples, a black sociologist, argues that the black male is "in conflict with the normative definition of masculinity," yet this conflict has never assumed the form of complete rebellion. Assuming that black men are "crippled emotionally" when they cannot fully achieve the patriarchal ideal, Staples asserts: "This is a status which few, if any, black males have been able to achieve. Masculinity, as defined in this culture, has always implied a certain autonomy and mastery of one's environment." Though Staples suggests, "the black male has always had to confront the contradiction between the normative expectation attached to being male in this society and proscriptions on his behavior and achievement of goals," implicit in his analysis is the assumption that black men could only internalize this norm and be victimized by it. Like many black men, he assumes that patriarchy and male domination are not a socially constructed social order but a "natural" fact of life. He therefore cannot acknowledge that black men could have asserted meaningful agency by repudiating the norms white culture was imposing.

These norms could not be repudiated by black men who saw nothing problematic or wrong-minded about them. Staples, like most black male scholars writing about black masculinity, does not

attempt to deconstruct normative thinking; rather, he laments that black men have not had full access to patriarchal phallocentrism. Embracing the phallocentric ideal, he explains black male rape of women by seeing it as a reaction against their inability to be "real men" (i.e., assert legitimate domination over women). Explaining rape, Staples argues:

In the case of black men, it is asserted that they grow up feeling emasculated and powerless before reaching manhood. They often encounter women as authority figures and teachers or as the head of their household. These men consequently act out their feelings of powerlessness against black women in the form of sexual aggression. Hence, rape by black men should be viewed as both an aggressive and political act because it occurs in the context of racial discrimination which denies most black men a satisfying manhood.

Staples does not question why black women are the targets of black male aggression if it is white men and a white racist system that prevents them from assuming the "patriarchal" role. Given that many white men who fully achieve "normal" masculinity rape, his implied argument that black men would not rape if they could be patriarchs seems ludicrous. And his suggestion that they would not rape if they could achieve a "satisfying manhood" is pure fantasy. Given the context of this paragraph, it is safe to assume that the "satisfying manhood" he evokes carries with it the phallocentric right of men to dominate women, however benevolently. Ultimately, he is suggesting that if black men could legitimately dominate women more effectively they would not need to coerce them outside the law. Growing up in a black community where there were black men who critiqued normative masculinity, who repudiated patriarchy and its concomitant sexism, I fully appreciate our misfortune in knowing so little about their ideas of black masculinity. Without documentation of their presence, it has been easier for black men who embrace patriarchal masculinity, phallocentrism, and sexism to act as though they speak for all black men. Since their representations of black masculinity are in complete agreement with white culture's assessment, they do not threaten or challenge white domination—they reinscribe it.

Contemporary black power movement made synonymous black liberation and the effort to create a social structure wherein black men could assert themselves as patriarchs, controlling community, family, and kin. On the one hand, black men expressed contempt for white men, yet they also envied them their access to patriarchal power. Using a "phallocentric" stick to beat white men, Amiri Baraka asserted in the 1960s in his essay "american sexual reference: black male," that

Most American white men are trained to be fags. For this reason it is no wonder that their faces are weak and blank, left without the hurt that reality makes—anytime. That red flush, those silk blue faggot eyes. . . . They are the "masters" of the world, and their children are taught this as God's fingerprint, so they can devote most of their energies to the nonrealistic, having no use for the real. They devote their energies to the nonphysical, the nonrealistic, and become estranged from them. Even their wars move to the stage where whole populations can be destroyed by pushing a button. . . . Can you, for a second imagine the average middle class white man able to do somebody harm. Alone? Without the technology that at this moment still has him rule the world: Do you understand the softness of the white man, the weakness. . . .

This attack on white masculinity, and others like it, did not mean that black men were attacking normative masculinity, they were simply pointing out that white men had not fulfilled the ideal. It was a case of "will the real man please stand up." And when he stood up, he

was, in the eyes of black power movement, a black male.

This phallocentric idealization of masculinity is most powerfully expressed in the writings of George Jackson. Throughout *Soledad Brother*, he announces his uncritical acceptance of patriarchal norms, especially the use of violence as a means of social control. Critical of nonviolence as a stance that would unman black males, he insisted:

The symbol of the male here in North America has always been the gun, the knife, the club. Violence is extolled at every exchange: the TV, the motion pictures, the best-seller lists. The newspapers that sell best are those that carry the boldest, bloodiest headlines and most sports coverage. To die for king and country is to die a hero.

Jackson felt that black males would need to embrace this use of violence if they hoped to defeat white adversaries. And he is particularly critical of black women for not embracing these notions of masculinity:

I am reasonably certain that I draw from every black male in this country some comments to substantiate that his mother, the black female, attempted to aid his survival by discouraging his violence or by turning it inward. The blacks of slave society, U.S.A, have always been a matriarchal subsociety. The implication is clear, black mama is going to have to put a sword in that brother's hand and stop that "be a good boy" shit.

A frighteningly fierce misogyny informs Jackson's rage at black women, particularly his mother. Even though he was compelled by black women activists and comrades to reconsider his position on gender, particularly by Angela Davis, his later work, *Blood In My Eye*, continues to see black liberation as a "male thing," to see revolution as a task for men:

At the end of this massive collective struggle, we will uncover a new man, the unpredictable culmination of the revolutionary process. He will be better equipped to wage the real struggle, the permanent struggle after the revolution—the one for new relationships between men.

Although the attitudes expressed by Baraka and Jackson appear dated, they have retained their ideological currency among black men. Black female critiques of black male phallocentrism and sexism have had little impact on black male consciousness. Michele Wallace's *Black Macho and the Myth of the Super Woman* was the first major attempt by a black woman to speak from a feminist standpoint about black male sexism. Her analysis of black masculinity was based primarily on her experience in northern cities, yet she wrote as if she were speaking comprehensively about the collective black experience. Even so, her critique was daring and courageous. However, like other critics, she evoked a monolithic homogeneous representation of black masculinity. Discussing the way black male sexism took precedence over racial solidarity during Shirley Chisholm's presidential campaign, Wallace wrote:

The black political forces in existence at the time—in other words, the black male political forces—did not support her. In fact, they actively opposed her nomination. The black man in the street seemed either outraged that she dared to run or simply indifferent.

Ever since then it has really baffled me to hear black men say that black women have no time for feminism because being black comes first. For them, when it came to Shirley Chisholm, being black no longer came first at all. It turned out that what they really meant all along was that the black man came before the black woman.

In her autobiography, Chisholm documents the ways in which sexism stood in her way more than racism. Yet she also talks about the support she received from her father and her husband for her political work. Commenting on the way individuals tried to denigrate this support by hinting that there was something wrong with her husband, Chisholm writes:

"Thoughtless people have suggested that my husband would have to be a weak man who enjoys having me dominate him. They are wrong on both counts." Though fiercely critical of sexism in general and black male sexism in particular, Chisholm acknowledges the support she received from black men who were not advancing patriarchy. Any critique of "black macho," of black male sexism, that does not acknowledge the actions of black men who subvert and challenge the status quo cannot be an effective critical intervention. If feminist critics ignore the efforts of individual black men to oppose sexism, our critiques seem to be self-serving, appear to be antimale rather than antisexist. Absolutist portraits that imply that all black men are irredeemably sexist, inherently supportive of male domination, make it appear that there is no way to change this, no alternative, no other way to be. When attention is focused on those black men who oppose sexism, who are disloyal to patriarchy, even if they are exceptions, the possibility for change, for resistance, is affirmed. Representations of black gender relationships that perpetually pit black women and men against one another deny the complexity of our experiences and intensify mutually destructive internecine gender conflict.

More than ten years have passed since Michele Wallace encouraged black folks to take gender conflict as a force that was undermining our solidarity and creating tension. Without biting her tongue, Wallace emphatically stated:

I am saying, among other things, that for perhaps the last fifty years there has been a growing distrust, even hatred, between black men and black women. It has been nursed along not only by racism on the part of whites but also by an almost deliberate ignorance on the part of blacks about the sexual politics of their experience in this country.

The tensions Wallace describes between black women and men have not abated; if anything, they have worsened. In more recent years they have taken the public form of black women and men competing for the attention of a white audience. Whether in the realm of job hunting or book publishing, there is a prevailing sense within white-supremacist capitalist patriarchy that black men and women cannot both be in the dominant culture's limelight. While it obviously serves the interests of white supremacy for black women and men to be divided from one another, perpetually in conflict, there is no overall gain for black men and women. Sadly, black people collectively refuse to embrace nonpatriarchal gender roles that would undermine male domination in black communities.

Because the black power movement has, since the 1960s, worked overtime to let sisters know that they should assume a subordinate role to lay the groundwork for an emergent black patriarchy that would elevate the status of black males, the women's liberation movement has been seen as a threat. Consequently, black women were and are encouraged to think that any involvement with feminism was/is tantamount to betraying the race. Such thinking has not really altered over time. It has become more entrenched. Black people responded with rage and anger to Wallace's book, charging that she was a puppet of white feminists who were motivated by vengeful hatred of black men, but they never argued that her assessment of black male sexism was false. They critiqued her harshly because they sincerely believed that sexism was not a problem in black life and that black female support of black patriarchy and phallocentrism might heal the wounds inflicted by racist domination. As long as black people foolishly cling to the rather politically naive and dangerous assumption that it is in the interests of black liberation to support sexism and male domination, all our efforts to decolonize our minds and transform society will fail.

Perhaps black folks cling to the fantasy that phallocentrism and patriarchy will provide a way out of the havoc and wreckage wreaked by racist genocidal assault because it is an analysis of our current political situation that places a large measure of the blame on the black community, the black family, and, most specifically, black women. This way of thinking means that black people do not have to envision creative strategies for confronting and resisting white supremacy and internalized racism. Tragically, internecine gender conflict between black women and men strengthens white-supremacist capitalist patriarchy. Politically behind the times where gender is concerned, many black people lack the skills to function in a changed and changing world. They remain unable to grapple with a contemporary reality where male domination is consistently challenged and under siege. Primarily it is white male advocates of feminist politics who do the scholarly work that shows the crippling impact of contemporary patriarchy on men, particularly those groups of men who do not receive maximum benefit from this system. Writing about the way patriarchal masculinity undermines the ability of males to construct self and identity with their well-being in mind, creating a life-threatening masculinist sensibility, these white male feminists rarely discuss black men.

Most black men remain in a state of denial, refusing to acknowledge the pain in their lives that is caused by sexist thinking and patriarchal, phallocentric violence, which is not only expressed by male domination over women but also by internecine conflict among black men. We must question why it is that, as white culture has responded to changing gender roles and feminist movement, black people have turned to black culture and particularly to black men for articulations of misogyny, sexism, and phallocentrism. In popular culture, representations of black masculinity equate it with brute phallocentrism, woman-hating, a pugilistic, rapist sexuality, and flagrant disregard for individual rights. Unlike the young George Jackson, who, however wrong-minded, cultivated a patriarchal masculinist ethic in the interest of providing black males with a revolutionary political consciousness and a will to resist race and class domination, contemporary young black males espousing a masculinist ethic are not radicalized or insightful about the collective future of black people. Public figures such as Eddie Murphy, Arsenio Hall, Chuck D., Spike Lee, and a host of other black males blindly exploit the commodification of blackness and the concomitant exotification of phallocentric black masculinity.

When Eddie Murphy's film *Raw* (one of the most graphic spectacles of black male phallocentrism) was first shown in urban cities, young black men in the audience gave black power salutes. This film not only did not address the struggle of black people to resist racism, but Murphy's evocation of homosocial bonding with rich white men against "threatening" women who want to take their money even further conveyed his conservative politics. *Raw* celebrates a pugilistic eroticism, the logic of which tells young men that women do not want to hear declarations of love but want to be "fucked to death." Women are represented strictly in misogynist terms—they are evil; they are all prostitutes who see their sexuality solely as a commodity to be exchanged for hard cash, and after the man has delivered the goods they betray him. Is this the "satisfying masculinity" black men desire or does it expose a warped and limited vision of sexuality,

one that could not possibly offer fulfillment or sexual healing? As phallocentric spectacle, *Raw* announces that black men are controlled by their penises ("it's a dick thing") and asserts a sexual politic that is fundamentally anti-body.

If the black male cannot "trust" his body not to be the agent of his victimization, how can he trust a female body? Indeed, the female body, along with the female person, is constructed in *Raw* as threatening to the male who seeks autonomous selfhood, since it is her presence that awakens phallocentric response. Hence, her personhood must be erased; she must be like the phallus, a "thing." Commenting on the self-deception that takes place when men convince themselves and one another that women are not persons, Marilyn Frye, in her essay on patriarchal phallocentrism, "The Problem That Has No Name," asserts:

The rejection of females by phallists is both morally and conceptually profound. The refusal to perceive females as persons is conceptually profound because it excludes females from that community whose conceptions of things one allows to influence one's concept, it serves as a police lock on a closed mind. Furthermore, the refusal to treat women with the respect due to persons is in itself a violation of a moral principle that seems to many to be the founding principle of all morality. This violation of moral principle is sustained by an active manipulation of circumstances that is systematic and habitual and unacknowledged. The exclusion of women from the conceptual community simultaneously excludes them from the moral community.

Black male phallocentrism constructs a portrait of woman as immoral, simultaneously suggesting that she is irrational and incapable of reason. Therefore, there is no need for black men to listen to women or to assume that women have knowledge to share.

It is this representation of womanhood that is graphically evoked in Murphy's film *Harlem Nights*. A dramatization of black male patriarchal fantasies, this film reinvents the history of Harlem so that black men do not appear as cowards unable to confront racist white males but are reinscribed as tough, violent; they talk shit and take none. Again, the George Jackson revolutionary political paradigm is displaced in the realm of the cultural. In this fantasy, black men are as able and willing as white men to assert power "by any means necessary." They are shown as having the same desires as white men; they long for wealth, power to dominate others, freedom to kill with impunity, autonomy, and the right to sexually possess women. They embrace notions of hierarchical rule. The most powerful black man in the film, Quick (played by Murphy), always submits to the will of his father. In this world where homosocial black male bonding is glorified and celebrated, black women are sex objects. The only woman who is not a sex object is the postmenopausal mama/matriarch. She is dethroned so that Quick can assert his power, even though he later (again submitting to his father's will) asks her forgiveness. *Harlem Nights* is a sad fantasy, romanticizing a world of misogynist homosocial bonding where everyone is dysfunctional and no one is truly cared for, loved, or emotionally fulfilled.

Despite all his male bluster, Quick, the quintessential hero of black phallocentrism longs to be loved. Choosing to seek the affections of an able but unattainable black woman (the mistress of the most powerful white man), Quick attempts to share himself, to drop the masculine mask and be "real" (symbolized by his willingness to share his real name). Yet the black woman he chooses rejects him, only seeking his favors when she is ordered to by the white man who possesses her. It is a tragic vision of black heterosexuality. Both black woman and

black man are unable to respond fully to one another because they are so preoccupied with the white power structure, with the white man. The most valued black woman "belongs" to a white man who willingly exchanges her sexual favors in the interest of business. Desired by black and white men alike (it is their joint lust that renders her more valuable; black men desire her because white men desire her, and vice versa), her internalized racism and her longing for material wealth and power drive her to act in complicity with white men against black men. Before she can carry out her mission to kill him, Quick shoots her after they have had sexual intercourse. Not knowing that he has taken the bullets from her gun, she points it, telling him that her attack is not personal but "business." Yet when he kills her, he makes a point of saying that it is "personal." This is a very sad moment in the film, in that he destroys her because she rejects his authentic need for love and care.

Contrary to the phallocentric representation of black masculinity that has been on display throughout the film, the woman-hating black men are really shown to be in need of love from females. Orphaned, Quick, who is "much man" seeking love, demonstrates his willingness to be emotionally vulnerable, to share only to be rejected, humiliated. This drama of internecine conflict between black women and men follows the conventional sexist line that sees black women as betraying black men by acting in complicity with white patriarchy. This notion of black female complicity and betrayal is so fixed in the minds of many black men that they are unable to perceive any flaw in its logic. It certainly gives credence to Michele Wallace's assertion that black people do not have a clear understanding of black sexual politics. Black men who advance the notion that black women are complicit with white men make this assessment without ever invoking historical documentation. Indeed, annals of history that document the opposite assumption abound, showing that black women have typically acted in solidarity with black men. While it may be accurate to argue that sexist black women are complicit with white-supremacist capitalist patriarchy, so are sexist black men. Yet most black men deny their complicity.

Spike Lee's recent film *Mo' Better Blues* is another tragic vision of contemporary black heterosexuality. Like *Harlem Nights,* it focuses on a world of black male homosocial bonding, where black women are seen primarily as sex objects. Even when they have talent, as the black female jazz singer Clarke does, they must still exchange sexual favors for recognition. Like Quick, Bleek, the black hero, seeks recognition of his value in heterosexual love relations. Yet he is unable to see the "value" of the two black women who care for him. Indeed, scenes in which he makes love to Clarke but alternately sees her as Indigo—and vice versa—suggest the Dixie-cup sexist mentality (that is, all women are alike). And even after his entire world has fallen apart, he never engages in a self-critique that might lead him to understand that phallocentrism (he constantly explains himself by saying "it's a dick thing") has blocked his capacity to develop a mature adult identity, has rendered him unable to confront pain and move past denial. Spike Lee's use of Murphy's phrase establishes a continuum of homosocial bonding between black men that transcends the cinematic fiction.

Ironically, the film suggests that Bleek's nihilism and despair can only be overcome by his rejection of playboy, "dick thing" masculinity and rejection of the traditional patriarchal role he has unthinkingly accepted. His life crisis is resolved by the reinscription of a patriarchal paradigm. Since Clarke is no longer available, he seeks comfort with Indigo, pleads with her to "save his life." Spike Lee, like Murphy to some extent, exposes the essential, self-serving narcissism and denial of community that is at the heart of phallocentrism. He does not, however, envision a radical alternative. The film suggests that Bleek has no choice and can only reproduce the same family narrative from which he has emerged, effectively affirming the appropriateness of a nuclear family paradigm where women as mothers restrict black masculinity and black male creativity, and fathers hint at the possibility of freedom. Domesticity represents a place where one's life is "safe" even though one's creativity is contained. The nightclub represents a world outside the home, a world where creativity flourishes and with it an uninhibited eroticism—but that is a world of risk. It is threatening.

The "love supreme" (Coltrane's music and image is a motif throughout the film) that exists between Indigo and Bleek appears shallow and superficial. No longer sex object to be "boned" whenever Bleek desires, her body becomes the vessel for the reproduction of himself via siring a son. Self-effacing, Indigo identifies Bleek's phallocentrism by telling him he is a "dog," but ultimately she rescues the "dog." His willingness to marry her makes up for dishonesty, abuse, and betrayal. The redemptive love Bleek seeks cannot really be found in the model Lee offers, and as a consequence, this film is yet another masculine fantasy denying black male agency and the capacity of black men to assume responsibility for their personal growth and salvation. To achieve that agency and personal responsibility, black men must give up phallocentrism and envision new ways of thinking about black masculinity.

Even though individual black women adamantly critique black male sexism, most black men continue to act as though sexism is not a problem in black life and refuse to see it as the force motivating oppressive exploitation of women and children by black men. If any culprit is identified, it is racism. As in Staples's suggestion that the explanation for why black men rape is best understood in the context of racism, any explanation that evokes a critique of black male phallocentrism is avoided. Black men and women who espouse cultural nationalism continue to see the struggle for black liberation largely as a struggle to recover black manhood. In her essay "Africa On My Mind: Gender, Counter Discourse and African-American Nationalism," E. Frances White shows that overall black-nationalist perspectives on gender are rarely rooted purely in the Afrocentric logic they seek to advance, but rather reveal their ties to white paradigms:

In making appeals to conservative notions of appropriate gender behavior, African-American nationalists reveal their ideological ties to other nationalist movements, including European and Euro-American bourgeois nationalists over the past 200 years. These parallels exist despite the different class and power base of these movements.

Most black nationalists, men and women, refuse to acknowledge the obvious ways in which patriarchal phallocentric masculinity is a destructive force in black life, the ways in which it undermines solidarity between black women and men, or the ways in which it is life-threatening to black men. Even though individual black nationalists, like Haki Madhubuti, speak against sexism, progressive Afrocentric thinking does not have the impact that the old guard message has. Perhaps it provides sexist black men with a sense of power and agency

(however illusory) to see black women, and particularly feminist black women, as the enemy who prevents them from fully participating in this society. For such fiction gives them an enemy who can be confronted, attacked, annihilated— an enemy who can be conquered, dominated.

Confronting white-supremacist capitalist patriarchy would not provide sexist black men with an immediate sense of agency or victory. Blaming black women, however, makes it possible for black men to negotiate with white people in all areas of their lives without vigilantly interrogating those interactions. A good example of this displacement is evident in Brent Staples's essay "The White Girl Problem." Defending his "politically incorrect taste in women" (that is, his preference for white female partners) from attacks by black women, Staples never interrogates his desire. He does not seek to understand the extent to which white-supremacist capitalist patriarchy determines his desire. He does not want desire to be politicized. And, of course, his article does not address white female racism or discuss the fact that a white person does not have to be antiracist to desire a black partner. Many interracial relationships have their roots in racist constructions of the other. By focusing in a stereotypical way on black women's anger, Staples can avoid these issues and depoliticize the politics of black and white female interactions. His essay would have been a needed critical intervention had he endeavored to explore the way individuals maintain racial solidarity even as they bond with folks outside their particular group.

Solidarity between black women and men continues to be undermined by sexism and misogyny. As black women increasingly oppose and challenge male domination, internecine tensions abound.

Publicly, many of the gender conflicts between black women and men have been exposed in recent years with the increasingly successful commodification of black women's writing. Indeed, gender conflict between sexist black male writers and black female writers who are seen as feminists has been particularly brutal. The black critic Stanley Crouch has been one of the leading voices mocking and ridiculing black women. His recently published collection of essays, *Notes of Hanging Judge,* includes articles that are particularly scathing in their attacks on black women.

His critique of Wallace's *Black Macho* is mockingly titled "Aunt Jemima Don't Like Uncle Ben" (notice that the emphasis is on black women not liking black men; hence the caption already places accountability for tensions on black women). The title deflects attention away from the concrete critique of sexism in *Black Macho* by making it a question of personal taste. Everyone seems eager to forget that it is possible for black women to love black men and yet unequivocally challenge and oppose sexism, male domination, and phallocentrism. Crouch never speaks to the issues of black male sexism in his piece and works instead to make Wallace appear an "unreliable" narrator. His useful critical comments are thus undermined by the apparent refusal to take seriously the broad political issues Wallace raises. His refusal to acknowledge sexism, expressed as "black macho," is a serious problem. It destroys the possibility of genuine solidarity between black women and men, makes it appear that he is really angry at Wallace and other black women because he is fundamentally antifeminist and unwilling to challenge male domination. Crouch's stance epitomizes the attitude of contemporary black male writers, who are either uncertain about their political response to feminism

or are adamantly antifeminist. Much black male antifeminism is linked to a refusal to acknowledge that the phallocentric power black men wield over black women is "real" power, the assumption being that only the power white men have that black men do not have is real.

If, as Frederick Douglass maintained, "power concedes nothing without a demand," the black women and men who advocate feminism must be ever vigilant, critiquing and resisting all forms of sexism. Some black men may refuse to acknowledge that sexism provides them with forms of male privilege and power, however relative. They do not want to surrender that power in a world where they may feel otherwise quite powerless. The contemporary emergence of a conservative black nationalism that exploits a focus on race to deny the importance of struggling simultaneously against sexism and racism is both an overt attack on feminism and a force that actively seeks to reinscribe sexist thinking among black people who have been questioning gender. Any commodification of blackness that makes phallocentric black masculinity marketable makes the realm of cultural politics a propagandistic site where black people are rewarded materially for reactionary thinking about gender. Should we not be suspicious of the way in which white culture's fascination with black masculinity manifests itself? The very images of phallocentric black masculinity that are glorified and celebrated in rap music, videos, and movies are the representations that are evoked when white supremacists seek to gain public acceptance and support for the genocidal assault on black men, particularly youth.

Progressive Afrocentric ideology makes this critique and interrogates sexism. In his latest book, *Black Men: Obsolete, Single, Dangerous,* Haki Madhubuti courageously deplores all forms of sexism, particularly black male violence against women. Like the proclamations of a number of black male political figures of the past, Madhubuti's support of gender equality and his critique of sexism is not linked to an overall questioning of gender roles and a repudiation of all forms of patriarchal domination, however benevolent. Still, he has taken the important step of questioning sexism and calling on black people to explore the ways in which sexism hurts and wounds us. Madhubuti acknowledges black male misogyny:

The "fear" of women that exists among many Black men runs deep and often goes unspoken. This fear is cultural. Most men are introduced to members of the opposite sex in a superficial manner, and seldom do we seek a more in depth or informed understanding of them. Women have it rough all over the world. Men must become informed listeners.

Woman-hating will only cease to be a norm in black life when black men collectively dare to oppose sexism. Unfortunately, when all black people should be engaged in a feminist movement that addresses the sexual politics of our communities, many of us are tragically investing in old gender norms. At a time when many black people should be reading Madhubuti's *Black Men; Sister Outsider; The Black Women's Health Book; Feminist Theory: From Margin to Center* and a host of other books that seek to explore black sexual politics with compassion and care, folks are eagerly consuming a conservative tract, *The Blackman's Guide to Understanding the Blackwoman,* by Shahrazad Ali. This work actively promotes black male misogyny, coercive domination of females by males, and, as a consequence, feeds the internecine conflict between black women and men. Though many black people have embraced this work, there is no indication that it is having a positive impact on black communities, and there is every

indication that it is being used to justify male dominance, homophobic assaults on black gay people, and rejection of black styles that emphasize our diasporic connection to Africa and the Caribbean. Ali's book romanticizes black patriarchy, demanding that black women "submit" to black male domination in lieu of changes in society that would make it possible for black men to be more fulfilled.

Calling for a strengthening of black male phallocentric power (to be imposed by force if need be), Ali's book in no way acknowledges sexism. When writing about black men, her book reads like an infantile caricature of the Tarzan fantasy. Urging black men to assert their rightful position as patriarchs, she tells them: "Rise Blackman, and take your rightful place as ruler of the universe and everything in it. Including the black woman." Like *Harlem Nights,* this is the stuff of pure fantasy. That black people, particularly the underclass, are turning to escapist fantasies that can in no way adequately address the collective need of African Americans for renewed black liberation struggle is symptomatic of the crisis we are facing. Desperately clinging to ways of thinking and being that are detrimental to our collective well-being obstructs progressive efforts for change.

More black men have broken their silence to critique Ali's work than have ever offered public support of feminist writing by black women. Yet it does not help educate black people about the ways feminist analysis could be useful in our lives for black male critics to act as though the success of this book represents a failure on the part of feminism. Ali's sexist, homophobic, self-denigrating tirades strike a familiar chord because so many black people who have not decolonized their minds think as she does. While the black critic Nelson George critiques Ali's work, stating that it shows "how little Afrocentrism respects the advances of African-American women," he suggests that it is an indication of how "unsuccessful black feminists have been in forging alliance with this ideologically potent community." Statements like this one advance the notion that feminist education is the sole task of black women. It also rather neatly places George outside either one of these potent communities. Why does he not seize the critical moment to bring to public awareness the feminist visions of Afrocentric black women? All too often, black men who are indirectly supportive of feminist movement act as though black women have a personal stake in eradicating sexism that men do not have. Black men too benefit from feminist thinking and feminist movement.

Any examination of the contemporary plight of black men reveals the way phallocentrism is at the root of much black-on-black violence, undermines family relations, informs the lack of preventive health care, and even plays a role in promoting drug addiction. Many of the destructive habits of black men are enacted in the name of "manhood." Asserting their ability to be "tough," to be "cool," black men take grave risks with their lives and the lives of others. Acknowledging this in his essay "Cool Pose: The Proud Signature of Black Survival," Richard Majors argues that "cool" has positive dimensions even though it "is also an aggressive assertion of masculinity." Yet, he never overtly critiques sexism. Black men may be reluctant to critique phallocentrism and sexism, precisely because so much black male "style" has its roots in these positions; they may fear that eradicating patriarchy would leave them without the positive expressive styles that have been life-sustaining. Majors is clear, however, that a "cool pose" linked to

aggressive phallocentrism is detrimental to both black men and the people they care about:

Perhaps black men have become so conditioned to keeping up their guard against oppression from the dominant white society that this particular attitude and behavior represents for them their best safeguard against further mental or physical abuse. However, this same behavior makes it very difficult for these males to let their guard down and show affection.

Elsewhere, he suggests "that the same elements of cool that allow for survival in the larger society may hurt black people by contributing to one of the more complex problems facing black people today—black-on-black crime." Clearly, black men need to employ a feminist analysis that will address the issue of how to construct a life-sustaining black masculinity that does not have its roots in patriarchal phallocentrism.

Addressing the way obsessive concern with the phallus causes black men stress, in *No Name in the Street,* James Baldwin explains:

Every black man walking in this country pays a tremendous price for walking: for men are not women, and a man's balance depends on the weight he carries between his legs. All men, however they may face or fail to face it, however they may handle, or be handled by it, know something about each other, which is simply that a man without balls is not a man.

What might black men do for themselves and for black people if they were not socialized by white-supremacist capitalist patriarchy to focus their attention on their penises? Should we not suspect the contemporary commodification of blackness, orchestrated by whites, which once again tells black men not only to focus on their penis but to make this focus their all-consuming passion? Such confused men have little time or insight for resistance struggle. Should we not suspect representations of black men like those that appear in the movie *Heart Condition,* where the black male describes himself as "hung like a horse" as though the size of his penis defines who he is? And what does it say about the future of black liberation struggles if the phrase "it's a dick thing" is transposed and becomes "it's a black thing?" If the "black thing" that is, black liberation struggle, is really only a "dick thing" in disguise, a phallocentric play for black male power, then black people are in serious trouble.

Challenging black male phallocentrism would also make a space for critical discussion of homosexuality in black communities. Since so much of the quest for phallocentric manhood as it is expressed in black-nationalist circles rests on a demand for compulsory heterosexuality, it has always promoted the persecution and hatred of homosexuals. This is yet another stance that has undermined black solidarity. If black men no longer embraced phallocentric masculinity, they would be empowered to explore their fear and hatred of other men, learning new ways to relate. How many black men will have to die before black folks are willing to look at the link between the contemporary plight of black men and their continued allegiance to patriarchy and phallocentrism?

Most black men will acknowledge that black men are in crisis and are suffering. Yet they remain reluctant to engage those progressive movements that might serve as meaningful critical interventions, that might allow them to speak their pain. On the terms set by white-supremacist patriarchy, black men can name their pain only by talking about themselves in crude ways that reinscribe them in the context of primitivism. Why should black men have to talk about themselves as an "endangered species" in order to gain public recognition of their plight? And why are the voices of colo-

nized black men, many of whom are in the spotlight, drowning out progressive voices? Why do we not listen to Joseph Beam, one such courageous voice? He had no difficulty sharing the insight that "communism, socialism, feminism and homosexuality pose far less of a threat to America than racism, sexism, heterosexism, classism, and ageism." Never losing sight of the need for black men to name their realities, to speak their pain and their resistance, Beam concluded his essay "No Cheek To Turn" with these prophetic words:

I speak to you as a black gay pro-feminist man moving in a world where nobody wants to know my name, or hear my voice. In prison, I'm just a number; in the army, I'm just a rank; on the job and in the hospital, I'm just a statistic; on the street, I'm just a suspect. My head reels. If I didn't have access to print, I, too, would write on walls. I want my life's passage to be acknowledged for at least the length of time it takes pain to fade from brick. With that said I serve my notice: I have no cheek to turn.

Changing our society's representations of black men must be a collective task. Black people committed to renewed black liberation struggle, to the decolonization of black minds, are fully aware that we must oppose male domination and work to eradicate sexism. There are black women and men who are working together to strengthen our solidarity. Black men such as Richard Majors, Calvin Hemton, Cornel West, Greg Tate, Essex Hemphill, and others address the issue of sexism and advocate feminism. If black men and women take seriously Malcolm's charge that we must work for our liberation "by any means necessary," then we must be willing to explore the way feminism as a critique of sexism, as a movement to end sexism and sexist oppression, could aid our struggle to be self-determining. Collectively we can break the life-threatening chokehold that patriarchal masculinity imposes on black

men and create life-sustaining visions
of a reconstructed black masculinity,
which could provide black men with
ways to save their lives and the lives of
their brothers and sisters in struggle.

Reprinted in slightly revised form with the
permission of South End Press, from
Black Looks: Race and Representation.
© 1992 by Gloria Watkins.

A Feast of Scraps
Glenn Ligon

Porn is notorious for how quickly you can wear it out. You buy another magazine and put the old one in a cardboard box in the closet or under the bed, like family snapshots you were too lazy to place in an album. You may go back to the magazine occasionally, searching for a half-remembered face, a particular cock, or a story that kept you aroused, but eventually you put them in brown paper bags (you never just tie them up with string) and leave them at the curb to be picked up with the trash.

My friend Wayne said that when we think we know something, when we deem a thing no longer useful and throw it on the trashheap, that's the moment to examine it closely. I take his advice and go to Gay Treasures, a bookstore in Greenwich Village, to look at used porn magazines and photographs. Gay Treasures is full of things that we have thrown out, boxes and boxes of images that chronicle our histories and desires. A feast of scraps.

I ask the clerk to pull out the box labeled "Black Men." It is stuffed with black-and-white photos and Polaroids in clear plastic wrappers. The most intriguing images are six-packs of fading color photos from the late seventies, each pack showing the same model in a variety of poses. Pornographic images of black men usually fall into a narrow range of types: black men as closer to nature, sexually aggressive, enormously endowed. Black men *as* phallus. Fanon and others have argued that these stereotypes allay the fears of whites while serving their needs and desires.

Many of the images I'm looking at replay these stereotypes, yet as I try to put them aside I find I can't. A look, a face, a body, keeps bringing me back to them. The images are somehow familiar, like portraits of long-dead relatives you never met but in whose faces you can trace the contours of your own. I look closely and I begin to remember.

The seventies was the decade when I discovered I was sexually attracted to men. I had albums full of family pictures from that period, pictures of my male cousins and me as adolescents. These pictures record our unkempt afros, flowery polyester shirts, and pressed blue jeans, but they do not record my desire for my cousins. The photos of black men in Gay Treasures are the photos left out of my family albums, and when I look at them I see my cousins' faces and bodies and I remember my desire.

To say that stereotypical images of black men are constructed for white pleasure does not mean that the images have nothing to say to black people and that we must throw them out. To do so is not only to deny the ambivalence with which we look at the images but to deny the lives of the men depicted. We can still use the images, inhabit and change them, read against their intended meanings, critique ourselves with them, place our stories alongside them, use them to talk about our histories and desires. I set myself this task.

I had a dream. I was in a box labeled "Black Men." It was dark, and the images of men were pressed up against me and each other; we were all in a jumble. I couldn't tell where my body ended and another's began. We were indistinguishable. Then I realized that we were not in a box at all. We were in a tea room.

I would like to thank Suzan-Lori Parks, Megan Ratner, and Richard Meyer for their help with this project.

Necessity is a <u>mother</u>

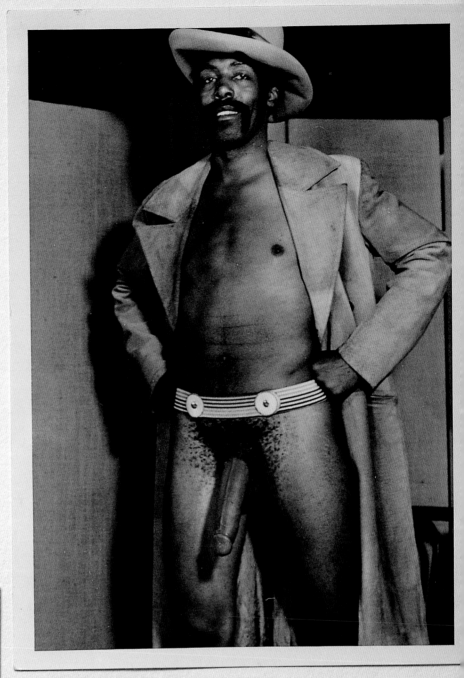

Daddy

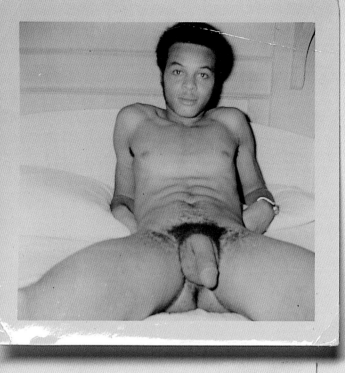

Brother

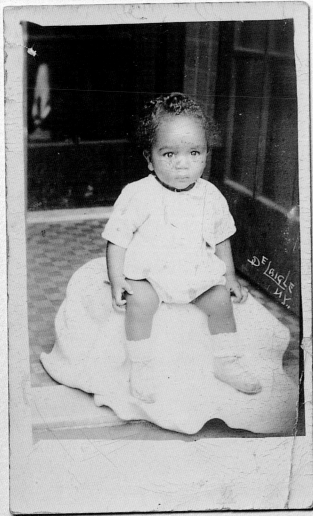

Thank

Miss

Jackson

11-9-71

You

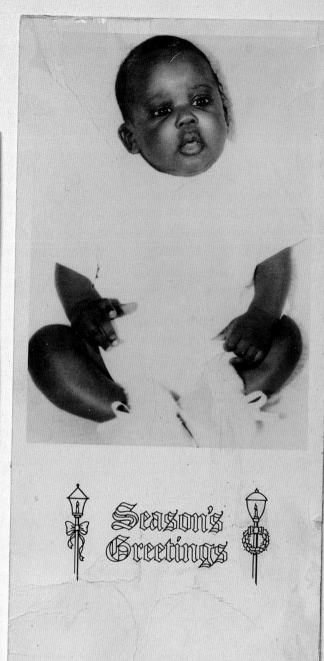

Season's
Greetings

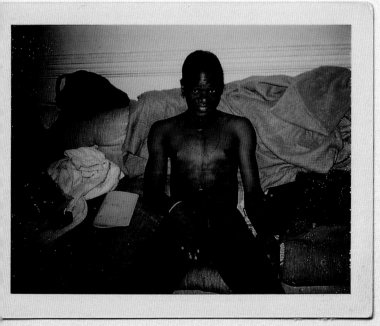

The baby's father

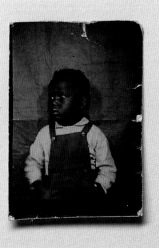

They told me I had to
change up

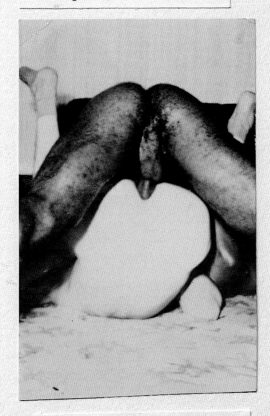

I just wanted somebody
who was down

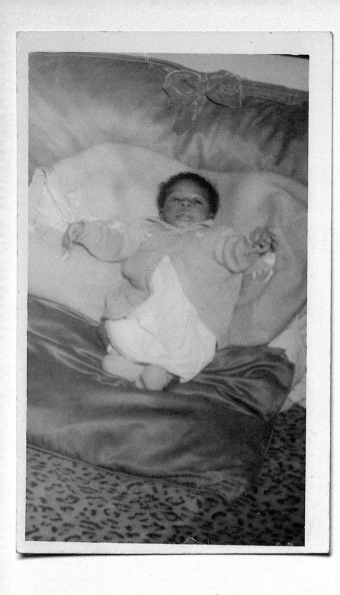

Yankee Doodle Lodge MT. SNOW, VT. 81

It's a process

It's not natural

Matthew Barney

Tina Barney

Clegg & Guttmann

Selected Works from the Exhibition

Graham Durward

Lyle Ashton Harris

Dale Kistemaker

Mary Kelly

Donald Moffett

Keith Piper

Charles Ray

Michael Yue Tong

Matthew Barney

Drawing Restraint 7, 1993
Mixed media
Room dimensions: 120 × 180 × 264 in.
Whitney Museum of American Art,
New York; Purchase, with funds
from the Painting and Sculpture
Committee 93.33

This page:
Spin Track

Facing page
from top to bottom:
Spin Track
Curl Track
Draw Track

Tina Barney
John's Den, 1985
Chromogenic color print (Ektacolor)
30 × 40 in.
Courtesy: Janet Borden, Inc.

The Boys, 1990
Chromogenic color print (Ektacolor)
48 × 60 in.
Museum of Fine Arts, Boston
Contemporary Curator's Fund,
including funds provided by
Barbara and Thomas Lee

Clegg & Guttmann

The Financiers, 1987

Cibachrome photograph

75 × 96 in.

Collection of Marc and Livia Straus

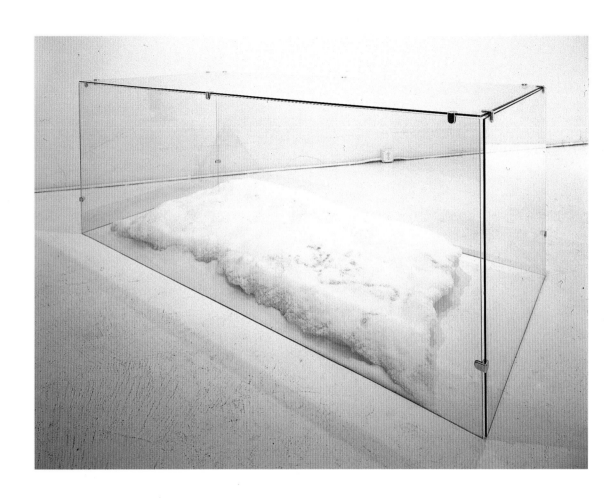

Graham Durward

Snow Drift, 1992
Glass and artificial snow
32 × 85 × 41 in.
Courtesy of the artist and
Sandra Gering Gallery

Lyle Ashton Harris
(in collaboration with Thomas Allen Harris)
Brotherhood, Crossroads and Etcetera #1, 1994
Unique Polaroid
24 × 20 in.
Courtesy of the artist and
Jack Tilton Gallery, New York

Brotherhood, Crossroads
and Etcetera #2, 1994
Unique Polaroid
24 × 20 in.
Collection of Blake Byrne

Brotherhood, Crossroads
and Etcetera #3, 1994
Unique Polaroid
24 × 20 in.
Collection of Thomas Allen Harris

Dale Kistemaker

His Bedroom, 1993

Mixed-media installation

Dimensions variable

Courtesy of the artist

First
she made sure the
thigh pads were in the
right position, then she went into a
lunk. Where was the lever and why was she
sweating even before she'd started? She despised it. Despised the
woman-thing, the soft thing that severed her will before a hard thing,
hard to do, hard to touch, hard to understand like the machine in front
of her. If only she could cut it off, cut off her sequacity and kill it.
Maybe she could find the adductor adjustment device and set it to
the appropriate range. She placed one leg at a time on the movement
arms of the apparatus, making sure to keep her inner thighs firmly
against the resistance pads and her shoulders square. After that,
she fastened her seat belt and prepared to inflict severe damage
on her flabby game. Her body tensed, muscles hardened, resolve
hardening. Search and destroy the flaccid hyle. Knees pried
apart in compliance with an ancient rule, she forced them
together slowly, deliberately refusing her allotted place and
held her new position hard and fast. Yes, fast and hardheaded,
she'd think in tough metaphors and eject tight sentences in
stringent tones, change her hair, her clothes and her name,
of course – from Mary Lou to Louie, or perhaps M.L. After
all, it was a free country, a free world, a free market and
she was free to free herself of her doecious destiny.
Returning to the stretch position she began again.
Deploy her assets. Project power. Pull with her
thighs and not her lower legs. Fit in. Weigh in
at the right weight and defeat her rivals.
She breathed out heavily. Hardhearted?
Not at all, she told herself. It was
a hard life. What she had was
hard-earned and, if anyone
objected, well, that was,
she spat on the floor,
hard luck,

Mary Kelly
Gloria Patri, 1992
(Details)

Gloria Patri, 1992
12 disks, 6 trophies and 5 shields
Screenprinted or etched polished aluminum
Dimensions variable
Courtesy of the artist

Donald Moffett

Sutured Snowman, 1992

Acrylic, felt, nylon and screws

52 × 34 × 38 in.

Courtesy of the artist

Choke, 1991
Polyurethane, acrylic and vinyl
15 × 15 × 8 in.
Courtesy of Ealan J. Wingate

Glory, 1991
Polyurethane, acrylic and vinyl
15 × 15 × 8 in.
Courtesy of Ealan J. Wingate

Keith Piper

Another Step into the Arena,
1992 (details)
Video installation with four monitors,
video projection, slides, boxing ring
and Amigo-generated computer animation
Dimensions variable
Courtesy of the artist

Charles Ray

Self-Portrait, 1990

Mixed media

75 × 26 × 20 in.

Collection Newport Harbor

Art Museum;

Museum purchase

Michael Yue Tong

Red Sky at Morning, 1992
Steel, black-and-white
photographs and velvet
30 × 84 × 30 in.
Courtesy of the artist

Matthew Barney

Drawing Restraint 7, 1993
Mixed media
Room dimensions 120 × 180 × 264 in.
Whitney Museum of American Art,
New York; Purchase, with funds from
the Painting and Sculpture Committee
93.33

Tina Barney

John's Den, 1985
Chromogenic color print (Ektacolor)
30 × 40 in.
Courtesy: Janet Borden, Inc.

Card Game, 1986
Chromogenic color print (Ektacolor)
48 × 60 in.
Courtesy: Janet Borden, Inc.

The Boys, 1990
Chromogenic color print (Ektacolor)
48 × 60 in.
Museum of Fine Arts, Boston
Contemporary Curator's Fund,
including funds provided by
Barbara and Thomas Lee

Clegg & Guttmann

The Financiers, 1987
Cibachrome photograph
75 × 96 in.
Collection of Marc and Livia Straus

The Assembly of Deans, 1989
Cibachrome photograph
60 × 216 in.
New School for Social Research

Graham Durward

Snow Drift, 1992
Glass and artificial snow
32 × 85 × 41 in.
Courtesy of the artist and
Sandra Gering Gallery

Black Emanation, 1993
Ink and conte crayon on velvet
96 × 144 in.
Courtesy of the artist and
Sandra Gering Gallery

Lyle Ashton Harris

Man and Woman I, 1987–88
Gelatin silver print
30 × 20 in.
Collection of Susan and Michael Hort

Man and Woman II, 1987–88
Gelatin silver print
30 × 20 in.
Courtesy of the artist and
Jack Tilton Gallery, New York

Untitled I, 1987–88
Gelatin silver print
20 × 30 in.
Courtesy of the artist and
Jack Tilton Gallery, New York

Untitled III, 1987–88
Gelatin silver print
30 × 20 in.
Courtesy of the artist and
Jack Tilton Gallery, New York

Alexandra and Lyle, 1994
Unique Polaroid
24 × 20 in.
Collection of Alexandra Epps

The Nigerians, 1994
Unique Polaroid
24 × 20 in.
Courtesy of the artist and
Jack Tilton Gallery, New York

Lyle Ashton Harris
(in collaboration with Thomas Allen Harris)

Brotherhood, Crossroads and Etcetera #1,
1994
Unique Polaroid
24 × 20 in.
Courtesy of the artist and
Jack Tilton Gallery, New York

Brotherhood, Crossroads and Etcetera #2,
1994
Unique Polaroid
24 × 20 in.
Collection of Blake Byrne

Brotherhood, Crossroads and Etcetera #3, 1994
Unique Polaroid
24 × 20 in.
Collection of Thomas Allen Harris

Dale Kistemaker

His Bedroom, 1993
Mixed-media installation
Dimensions variable
Courtesy of the artist

Mary Kelly

Gloria Patri, 1992
12 disks, 6 trophies and 5 shields
Screenprinted or etched
polished aluminum
Dimensions variable
Courtesy of the artist

Donald Moffett

Gays in the Military #1–5, 1990
Engraving and custom transfer type
on paper
11 × 13 1/2 in. each
Collection of Scott Watson

Choke, 1991
Polyurethane, acrylic and vinyl
15 × 15 × 8 in.
Collection of Ealan J. Wingate

Glory, 1991
Polyurethane, acrylic and vinyl
15 × 15 × 8 in.
Collection of Ealan J. Wingate

Mon Amour, 1992
Polyurethane, acrylic and vinyl
15 × 15 × 8 in.
Collection of Ealan J. Wingate

Sunshine, 1992
Polyurethane, acrylic and vinyl
8 in. diameter
Courtesy of the artist

Sutured Snowman, 1992
Acrylic, felt, nylon and screws
52 × 34 × 38 in.
Courtesy of the artist

Keith Piper

Another Step into the Arena, 1992
Video installation with four monitors,
video projection, slides, boxing ring and
Amigo generated computer animation
Dimensions variable
Courtesy of the artist

Charles Ray

Self-Portrait, 1990
Mixed media
75 × 26 × 20 in.
Collection Newport Harbor Art Museum;
Museum purchase

Michael Yue Tong

Red Sky at Morning, 1992
Steel, black-and-white photographs
and velvet
30 × 84 × 30 in.
Courtesy of the artist

Father Altar, 1993
Steel, lightbox, transparency,
satin and audiotape
168 × 60 × 72 in.
Courtesy of the artist

Mother Altar, 1993
Steel, lightbox, transparency,
satin and audiotape
168 × 60 × 72 in.
Courtesy of the artist

Matthew Barney

Born 1964 in San Francisco.
Lives and works in New York.

Education

BA, Yale University,
New Haven, Connecticut,
1989

Selected Solo Exhibitions

1994
Cremaster 4, Artangel Trust,
London

1991
Matthew Barney: New Work,
San Francisco Museum of
Modern Art

Barbara Gladstone Gallery,
New York

Stuart Regen Gallery,
Los Angeles

1989
Field Dressing, Payne Whitney
Athletic Complex,
Yale University, New Haven

1988
Scab Action, video exhibition
for the New York City
Rainforest Alliance,
Open Center, New York

Selected Group Exhibitions

1994
Drawing on Sculpture,
Cohen Gallery, New York

*Of the Human Condition:
Hope and Despair at the End
of the Century,*
The Spiral Building, Tokyo

The Ossuary, Luhring
Augustine, New York

*Acting Out—The Body
in Video: Then and Now,*
Royal College of Art, London

Sammlung Volkmann, Berlin

1993
Aperto 1993, 45th Venice
Biennale

1993 Biennial Exhibition,
Whitney Museum of American
Art, New York

*Don't Ask, Don't Tell, Don't
Pursue,* Fairfield University,
Fairfield, Connecticut

Barbara Gladstone Gallery,
New York

*Action/Performance And the
Photograph,* Turner-Krull
Galleries, Los Angeles

*Exhibition to Benefit the
Mapplethorpe Laboratory for
AIDS Research,* Barbara
Gladstone Gallery, New York

Works on Paper, Paula Cooper
Gallery, New York

1992
Documenta IX, Kassel, Germany

Périls et Colères, CAPC Musée
Bordeaux, France

Post Human, Musée d'Art
Contemporain Pully, Lausanne,
France. Traveled to Castello di
Rivoli, Torino, Italy; Deste
Foundation for Contemporary
Art, Athens; Deichtorhallen
Hamburg; Israel Museum,
Jerusalem.

*Matthew Barney, Sam Reveles,
and Nancy Rubins,*
Stein Gladstone Gallery,
New York

Speilhölle, U-Bahn Station,
Frankfurt

1991
Barbara Gladstone Gallery,
New York

Stuart Regen Gallery,
Los Angeles

ACT-UP Benefit Art Sale, Paula
Cooper Gallery, New York

1990
*Viral Infection: The Body and
its Discontents,* Hallwalls
Contemporary Arts Center,
Buffalo

Drawings, Althea Viafora
Gallery, New York

Video Library, Andrea Rosen
Gallery, New York

Selected Bibliography

1993
Cembalest, Robin, Mary Haus
and Meyer Raphael Rubenstein.
"Fast Forward, 19 Artists
Whose Works Are Gaining
Recognition." *Artnews,*
November 1993, 122–133.

Rees, Michael. "Yale Sculpture:
A Recent Breed of Critically
Trained Artists from the Noted
School of Art." *Flash Art,*
May/June, 65–67.

1992
Bonami, Francesco and
Benjamin Weil. "Matthew
Barney: The Artist as a Young
Athlete." *Flash Art,*
January/February, 100–103.

D'Amato, Brian. "The Last
Medium: The Virtues of Virtual
Reality." *Flash Art,*
January/February, 96–98.

Decter, Joshua. *Arts Magazine,*
January, 80–81.

Dworkin, Norine. *Artnews,*
February, 123–124.

Johnson, Ken. *Art in America,*
January, 115–116.

Riley, Robert. *Flash Art,*
November/December, 139.

Saltz, Jerry. *Flash Art,*
November/December, 136.

1991
Relyea, Lane. "Openings:
Matthew Barney." *Artforum,*
September, 124.

Riley, Robert and John
Caldwell. *Matthew Barney:
New Work.* San Francisco
Museum of Modern Art.

Saltz, Jerry. "Wilder Shores
of Art: Matthew Barney's
Field Dressing (orifill)."
Arts Magazine, May, 29–31.

Selwyn, Marc. *Flash Art,*
October, 133.

Tina Barney

Born 1945 in New York City. Lives and works in Watch Hill, Rhode Island.

Education

The Sun Valley Center for Arts and Humanities, 1976–79

Selected Solo Exhibition

1993
Janet Borden, Inc., New York

1992
Janet Borden, Inc., New York

1991
International Museum of Photography at George Eastman House, Rochester, New York

1990
The Museum of Modern Art, New York

Janet Borden, Inc., New York

Cleveland Center for Contemporary Art

1989
The Denver Art Museum

Janet Borden, Inc., New York

Weber College, Ogden, Utah

1988
Tatistcheff Gallery, Los Angeles

John Good Gallery, New York

1987
Milwaukee Art Center

1985
Tatistcheff & Co., New York

1984
Westover School, Middlebury, Connecticut

Selected Group Exhibitions

1993
In and Out of Place: Contemporary Art and the American Social Landscape, Museum of Fine Arts, Boston

Commodity Image, International Center of Photography, New York. Traveled to Institute of Contemporary Art, Boston.

Fictions of Self, Weatherspoon Art Gallery, University of North Carolina, Greensboro Traveled to Herter Art Gallery, University of Massachusetts, Amherst

In Camera, Museum of New Mexico, Santa Fe

1992
Multiple Exposure, Wesleyan University, Middletown, Connecticut

The Invention of Childhood, Kohler Art Center, Sheboygan, Wisconsin

1991
This Sporting Life, High Museum of Art, Atlanta. Traveled to Blaffer Gallery, University of Houston; De Saisset Museum, Santa Clara University, California; Delaware Art Museum, Wilmington; Albright-Knox Art Gallery, Buffalo, New York.

Forbidden Games, Jack Tilton Gallery, New York

Imaging the Family, Brown University, Providence, Rhode Island

Blood Relatives, Milwaukee Art Museum

1990
Identities: Portraiture in Contemporary Photography, Philadelphia Art Alliance

1989
The Photography of Invention, National Museum of American Art, Smithsonian Institution, Washington, D.C. Traveled to Museum of Contemporary Art, Chicago; Walker Art Center, Minneapolis.

Staged Documents, San Francisco Camerawork

1988
Cultural Participation, installation by Group Material, Dia Art Foundation, New York

Fictitious Truth: Photographs, Real Art Ways, Hartford, Connecticut

1987
1987 Biennial Exhibition, Whitney Museum of American Art, New York

American Dreams, Ministry of Culture, Madrid, Spain

1986
Relations, Tatistcheff & Co., New York

1985
· *Humanistic Visions,* San Jose State University

1984
Children Through Time & Light, Light Gallery, New York

1983
Big Pictures, The Museum of Modern Art, New York

Selected Bibliography

1992
Rimanelli, David. "People Like Us." *Artforum,* October, 70–73.

1991
Sullivan, Constance and Susan Weiley, eds. *Friends and Relations: Photographs by Tina Barney.* Washington and London: Smithsonian Institution Press.

1990
Grundberg, Andy. "Tina's World: In Search of the Honest Moment." *New York Times,* April 1, 39–41.

Sullivan, Constance, ed. *Women Photographers.* New York: Harry N. Abrams.

1988
Squiers, Carol. "Tina Barney." *American Photographer,* December, 42–47.

1987
American Dreams: 30 Abril– 6 Septiembre, 1987. Madrid: Ministerio de Cultura.

Mother & Daughters: That Special Quality: An Exploration in Photographs. New York: Aperture Foundation. Distributed by Farrar, Straus and Giroux.

Clegg & Guttmann

Michael Clegg

Born 1957 in Dublin.
Lives and works in New York.

Education

Chelsea School of Art,
London
School of the Visual Arts,
New York

Martin Guttmann

Born 1957 in Jerusalem.
Lives and works in New York.

Education

BA, The Hebrew University
of Jerusalem

MA, M. Phil., Ph. D.,
Columbia University, New York

Selected Solo Exhibitions

1994
*The Transformation of Data
into Portraiture,*
Kunstraum der Universität,
Lüneberg, Germany

*The Open Public Library,
Mainz,* Landesmuseum,
Mainz, Germany

Vérité, Galerie Christian Nagel,
Cologne

1993
*The Open Public Library,
Hamburg,* Kunstverein in
Hamburg

1992
*From the Index of Commisioned
and Non-Commisioned
Photographic Portraits: Gazes
in a Direction Perpendicular to
the Picture Plane, Placed in
a Sequence According to Their
Intensity, and Accompanied by
Varying Postures and Hand
Arrangements,* The Institute of
Contemporary Art, S. 1
Museum, Long Island City,
New York

*The Outdoor Exhibition Space:
Munich—San Francisco,*
Kunstraum Daxer, Munich

1991
Printing and Framing,
Galerie Christian Nagel,
Cologne

*A Model for an Open Tool
Shelter, Toronto,* The Power
Plant, Toronto

The Open Public Library, Graz,
Grazer Kunstverein, Austria

1990
Galleri Nordanstad-Skarstedt,
Stockholm

*The Free Public Library, New
York,* Jay Gorney Modern Art,
New York

Akira Akeda, Tokyo

*A Model for a Free-Standing
Outdoor Library,* Kabinett für
Aktuelle Kunst,
Bremerhaven, Germany

1989
Landscapes, Forum Stadtpark,
Graz, Germany

Corporate Landscapes,
Kunstverein Bremerhaven,
Germany

Galerie Peter Pakesch, Vienna

*Portraits de Groupes de
1980 à 1989,* CAPC Musée
d'Art Contemporain,
Bordeaux, France

1988
Portraits, Landscapes, Still Lifes,
Margo Leavin Gallery,
Los Angeles

Collected Portraits,
Würtembergischer Kunstverein,
Stuttgart

Galerie Hussenot, Paris

1987
Jay Gorney Modern Art,
New York

Achim Kubinski,
Stuttgart, Germany

The Israel Museum, Jerusalem

1986
*Clegg & Guttmann, Joseph
Kosuth,* Jay Gorney Modern
Art, New York

Rotterdam Art Foundation,
The Netherlands

1985
*Single, Double and Group
Portraits,* Galerie Löhrl,
Mönchengladbach, Germany

1983
Allegories of the Stock Exchange,
Olsen Gallery, New York

1981
Group Portraits of Executives,
Annina Nosei Gallery,
New York

Selected Group Exhibitions

1994
*'Back Stage'—Graffitti in the
Open Public Library, Hamburg,*
Kunsthalle Lauzanne,
Switzerland

1993
Kontextualizmus, Neue Galerie
am Landesmuseum Joanneum,
Graz, Germany

Project Unité, Firminy, France

*From the Inside Out: Eight
Contemporary Artists,*
The Jewish Museum, New York

1992
Post Human, Musée d'Art
Contemporain Pully, Lausanne,
France. Traveled to Castello di
Rivoli, Torino, Italy; Deste
Foundation for Contemporary
Art, Athens; Deichtorhallen
Hamburg; Israel Museum,
Jerusalem.

*Clegg & Guttmann, David
Robbins, Heimo Zobenrig,*
Jay Gorney Modern Art,
New York

*Multiple Exposure: The
Group Portrait in Photography,*
Center for the Arts,
Wesleyan University,
Middletown, Connecticut

*Knowledge: Aspects of
Conceptual Art,* University Art
Museum, University of
California, Santa Barbara.
Traveled to Santa Monica
Museum of Art, California;
North Carolina Museum of
Art, Raleigh.

1991
Metropolis, Walter Gropius Bau,
Berlin

1990
Art et Publicite, Musée National d'Art Moderne, Centre Georges Pompidou, Paris

Team Spirit, organized by Independent Curators Incorporated, New York. Traveled to Neuberger Museum, State University of New York at Purchase and Cleveland Center for Contemporary Art, among other sites.

Artificial Nature, Deste Foundation for Contemporary Art, Athens

1989
Image World: Art and Media Culture, Whitney Museum of American Art, New York

Wittgenstein: The Play of the Unsayable, Wiener Sezession, Vienna. Traveled to Palais des Beaux-Arts, Brussels.

Tenir l'Image à Distance, Musée d'Art Contemporain de Montréal

The Photography of Invention, National Museum of American Art, Smithsonian Institution, Washington, D.C. Traveled to Museum of Contemporary Art, Chicago; Walker Art Center, Minneapolis.

1988
This is Not a Photograph, The Ringling Museum of Art, Sarasota, Florida

Two to Tango: Collaboration in Recent American Photography, International Center of Photography, New York

The Castle, an installation by Group Material, Documenta VIII, Kassel, Germany

1987
1987 Biennial Exhibition, Whitney Museum of American Art, New York

Fake, The New Museum of Contemporary Art, New York

1986
Prospect '86, Kunstverein, Frankfurt

The Real Big Picture, Queens Museum, New York

Selected Bibliography

1991
Clegg, Michael and Martin Guttmann. "Cumulus from America." *Parkett,* spring, 163–164.

Wei, Lily. "On Nationality: 13 Artists." *Art in America,* September, 124–131.

1990
Mahoney, Robert. "Clegg and Guttmann's 'The Free Public Library'." *Arts Magazine,* summer, 92–93.

Nesbitt, Lois E. "Clegg & Guttmann: Jay Gorney Modern Art." *Artforum,* summer, 164.

Tallman, Susan. "Get the Picture?" *Arts Magazine,* summer 1990, 15–16.

1989
Clegg & Guttmann: Portraits de Groupes de 1980 a 1989. Bordeaux: CAPC Musée d'art Contemporain.

Staniszewski, Mary Ann. "Dressed for Success." *Afterimage,* September, 24–25

Graham Durward

Born 1956 in Aberdeen, Scotland.
Lives and works in New York.

Education

Whitney Museum Independent Study Program, New York, 1985–86

Edinburgh College of Art, Postgraduate, 1977–78

Edinburgh College of Art, 1973–77

Selected Solo Exhibitions

1994
Patrick Callery, New York

1993
Shedhalle, Zurich

1992
Sandra Gering Gallery, New York

1991
Randy Alexander Gallery, New York

1985
369 Gallery, Edinburgh

1984
Freidus-Ordover Gallery, New York

1982
369 Gallery, Edinburgh

Selected Group Exhibitions

1994
The Use of Pleasure, Terrain, San Francisco

1993
Bodily, Penine Hart Gallery, New York

1992
Mr. B's Curiosity Shop, Threadwaxing Space, New York

Pop Body, Sally Hawkins Gallery, New York

1991
Brooklyn, Jack Tilton Gallery, New York

Stendhal Syndrome, Andrea Rosen Gallery, New York

Reconnaissance, Simon Watson's Living Room, New York

Fragments, Parts, Wholes— The Body and Culture, White Columns, New York

1985
Critical Strategies, The British Art Show, Southampton, England. Traveled to Bristol, England; Newcastle, England; Edinburgh.

1984
Four Scottish Artists, Dart Gallery, Chicago

1983
Scottish Art Now, Fruitmarket, Edinburgh

Selected Bibliography

1993
Heartney, Eleanor. *Artnews,* March, 116.

Perchuk, Andrew. *Artforum,* April, 99–100.

Taylor, Simon. *Art in America,* March, 115.

1991
Decter, Joshua. *Arts Magazine,* May, 105.

Liu, Catherine. *Artforum,* April, 120–21.

1990
Liu, Catherine. "Manipulation & Photography." *Artforum,* April, 171.

Morgan, Robert C. "Fragments, Parts & Wholes—The Body in Culture." *Tema Celeste,* June.

Lyle Ashton Harris

Born 1965 in the Bronx, New York.
Lives and works in New York and Los Angeles.

Education

Whitney Museum Independent Study Program, New York, 1992

National Graduate Photography Seminar, Tisch School of the Arts, New York, 1991

MFA, California Institute of the Arts, Valencia, 1990

BA, Wesleyan University, Middletown, Connecticut, 1988

Selected Solo Exhibitions

1994
The Good Life, Jack Tilton Gallery, New York

Schmidt Contemporary Art, St. Louis

1993
Face, Broadway Window, The New Museum of Contemporary Art, New York

Simon Watson's Living Room, New York

Selected Group Exhibitions

1994
Black Male: Representations of Masculinity in Contemporary Art, Whitney Museum of American Art, New York

Telling . . . Stories, Randolph Street Gallery, Chicago

1993
42nd Street Art Project: Victory Parade, Times Square, New York

Dress Codes, Institute of Contemporary Art, Boston

Ciphers of Identity, Fine Arts Gallery, University of Maryland, Baltimore County. Traveled to Ronald Feldman Gallery, New York.

In Out of the Cold, Center for the Arts at Yerba Buena Gardens, San Francisco

1992
Fever, Exit Art, New York

In This World, Contemporary Art, Vancouver

Presenting Rearwards, Rosamund Felsen Gallery, Los Angeles

Reclaiming Sensuality, California Museum of Photography, Riverside

Body Politic, Santa Monica Museum of Art

1991
Disputed Identities, San Francisco Camerawork

AutoPortraits, Camerawork, London

Acquired Visions: Seeing Ourselves Through AIDS, Studio Museum in Harlem, New York

Someone or Somebody, Meyers/Bloom Gallery, Los Angeles

Situation, New Langton Arts, San Francisco

Selected Bibliography

1994
Aletti, Vince. "It's a Family Affair: Photographer Lyle Ashton Harris Scores a Strategic Hit." *The Village Voice,* Sept. 27, 39–40.

Atkins, Robert. "From Preppie to Orange Hair in an Amsterdam Minute." *The New York Times,* September 25, 39.

Avgikos, Jan. "Ciphers of Identity." *Artforum,* March, 91.

Cotter, Holland. "Art After Stonewall: 12 Artists Interviewed." *Art in America,* June, 63–64.

————. " 'Ciphers of Identity,' and 'Absence, Activism and the Body Politic'." *The New York Times,* June 24.

1993
White, Artress Bethany. "About Face: Lyle Ashton Harris." *A Gathering of the Tribes,* fall/winter, editor's page and 54–59.

Temin, Christine. "ICA's Provocative 'Dress Codes'." *Boston Globe,* March 10, 49, 53.

1992
Kotz, Liz. "The Body You Want." *Artforum,* November, editor's page and 82.

Ramsey, Ellen L. "Disputed Identities US/UK." *Parachute,* Jan./Feb./Mar., 59–60.

Hess, Elizabeth. "Give Me Fever." *The Village Voice,* December 29, 95.

Dent, Gina, ed. "Miss America." *Black Popular Culture: A Project by Michele Wallace,* Seattle: Bay Press, 326.

Rosenberg, Ann. "Sexual Images, Both Gay and Light-hearted." *Vancouver Sun,* May 2, 11.

1991
George, Eddie. "Black Body and Public Enemy." *Ten.8,* spring, 68–71.

Mercer, Kobena. "Dark and Lovely: Notes on Black Gay Image–Making." *Ten.8,* spring, 78–85.

Harris, Lyle Ashton. "Revenge of a Snow Queen." *Out/Look,* summer, cover and 7–13.

Walker, Christian. "The Miscegenated Gaze." *San Francisco Camerawork,* fall, 12–14.

1990
Hayes, William. "Out with the Boys." *Mother Jones,* July/August, 47–49.

Mary Kelly

Born 1941 in Fort Dodge, Iowa.
Lives and works in New York.

Education

Postgraduate Diploma, St. Martin's School of Art, London, 1970

MA, Pius XII Institute, Florence, Italy, 1965

BA, College of Saint Teresa, Winona, Minnesota, 1963

Selected Solo Exhibitions

1994
Uppsala Konstmuseum, Sweden

Helsingfors Stads, Konstmuseum, Finland

1993
Institute of Contemporary Arts, London

Contemporary Art, Vancouver

Postmasters Gallery, New York

1992
Ezra and Cecile Zilkha Gallery, Wesleyan University, Middletown, Connecticut

Herbert F. Johnson Museum of Art, Cornell University, Ithaca, New York

1990
Interim, The New Museum of Contemporary Art, New York. Traveled to Vancouver Art Gallery; The Power Plant, Toronto.

1989
Postmasters Gallery, New York

1988
LACE, Los Angeles

Powerhouse, Montreal

1986
Kettles Yard, Cambridge University, England

Riverside Studios, London

1985
Fruitmarket, Edinburgh, Scotland

1982
George Paton Gallery, Melbourne

University Art Museum, Brisbane, Australia

1981
Anna Leonowens Gallery, Nova Scotia College of Art & Design, Halifax

1979
University Gallery, Leeds, England

1976
Institute of Contemporary Arts, London

Selected Group Exhibitions

1993
Abjection in American Art, Whitney Museum of American Art, New York

Ciphers of Identity, Fine Arts Gallery, University of Maryland, Baltimore County. Traveled to Ronald Feldman Gallery, New York.

1992
Mistaken Identities, University Art Museum, Santa Barbara. Traveled to Museum Folkwang, Essen, Germany; Forum Stadtpark, Graz, Austria; Neues Museum, Weserburgh Bremen im Forum Langenstrasses, Bremen, Germany; Louisiana Museum of Modern Art, Humblebaek, Denmark.

Effected Desire, Carnegie Museum of Art, Pittsburgh

1991
1991 Biennial Exhibition, Whitney Museum of American Art, New York

1990
The Decade Show, Museum of Contemporary Hispanic Art, The New Museum of Contemporary Art, Studio Museum in Harlem, New York

Word as Image—American Art 1960-1990, Milwaukee Art Museum. Traveled to Oklahoma City Art Museum; Contemporary Arts Museum, Houston.

1989
Fashioning Feminine Identities, University Gallery, Essex, England

1987
State of the Art, Institute of Contemporary Arts, London. Traveled to The Laing Art Gallery, Newcastle.

The British Edge, Institute of Contemporary Art, Boston

Propositions: Works from the Permanent Collection, Art Gallery of Ontario, Toronto

1985
Difference: On Representation and Sexuality, The New Museum of Contemporary Art, New York. Traveled to The Renaissance Society at the University of Chicago; Institute of Contemporary Arts, London.

1984

The Critical Eye/I, Yale Center for British Art, New Haven

The British Art Show, City of Birmingham Museum and Art Gallery. Traveled to Ikon Gallery, Birmingham; Royal Scottish Academy, Edinburgh; Mappin Art Gallery, Sheffield; Southampton Art Gallery.

1983

The Revolutionary Power of Woman's Laughter, Protetch-McNeil, New York. Traveled to Art Culture Resource Center, Toronto; Washington College Art Gallery, Chestertown, Maryland.

1982

The 4th Biennale of Sydney, Gallery of New South Wales

1980

Issue, Institute of Contemporary Arts, London

1979

Feministische Kunste, Haags Gemeentemuseum, The Hague. Traveled to de Oosteerpoort, Groningen; Nooedbrabants Museum, Den Bosch; de Vleeshal, Middleburgh; Le Vest, Alkmar; de Beyerd, Buda; Nijmeegs Museum, Nijmegen.

Verbiage, Kettles Yard, Cambridge University, England.

1978

Art for Society, Whitechapel Art Gallery, London and Ulster Museum, Belfast

The Hayward Annual, The Hayward Gallery, London

Selected Bibliography

1994

Ayerza, Josefina. "Mary Kelly." *Flash Art,* January/February, 68–69.

1993

Berger, Maurice. "Displacements." *Ciphers of Identity.* Baltimore County: Fine Arts Gallery, University of Maryland.

1992

Mulvey, Laura. "Impending Time: Mary Kelly's 'Corpus'." *Lapis* (Milan).

Ottmann, Klaus. "Mary Kelly." *Journal of Contemporary Art,* fall, 15–22.

Solomon-Godeau, Abigail. *Mistaken Identities.* Santa Barbara: University Art Museum.

1991

Apter, Emily S. "Fetishism, Visual Seduction and Mary Kelly's Interim." *October,* fall, 97–108.

1990

Chadwick, Whitney. *Women, Art and Society.* New York: Thames and Hudson.

Foster, Hal, Marcia Tucker, Griselda Pollock and Norman Bryson. *Mary Kelly: Interim.* New York: The New Museum of Contemporary Art.

1989

Fisher, Jennifer. "Interview with Mary Kelly." *Parachute,* July–September, 32–35.

Mulvey, Laura. "Impending Time." *Visual and Other Pleasures.* Bloomington: University of Indiana Press.

1987

The British Edge. Boston: Institute of Contemporary Art.

Watney, Simon. "Mary Kelly." *Artscribe,* March/April, 71–72.

1986

Fraser, Andrea. "Post-Partum Document." *Afterimage,* March, 6–8.

"Mary Kelly and Laura Mulvey in Conversation." *Afterimage,* March, 6–8.

1985

Isaak, Joanna. "Difference: On Representation and Sexuality." *Afterimage,* April, 6–8.

Paoletti, John T. "Mary Kelly's Interim." *Arts Magazine,* October, 88–91.

1984

Osbourne, Caroline. "The Post-Partum Document." *Critical Texts.* New York: Columbia University.

Owens, Craig. "The Discourse of the Others: Feminists and Post-Modernism." *The Anti-Aesthetic.* Washington: Bay Press.

Paoletti, John T. "Mary Kelly." *The Critical Eye/I.* New Haven: Yale Center for British Art.

Publications by the Artist

1993

"Scatological Ejaculations, or, 'Letting Loose and Hitting 'em with All We've Got'" *Art Journal,* fall, 6–15.

"Gloria Patri: Two Narratives." *Assemblage 20,* April, 50–51.

1990

Interim. New York: The New Museum of Contemporary Art.

1987

"On Sexual Politics of Art." *Framing Feminism,* Edited by Rozsika Parker and Griselda Pollock. London: Pandora Press.

1984

"Reviewing Modernist Criticism." in *Art After Modernism,* New York: The New Museum of Contemporary Art, Boston: D. R. Godine.

1983

Post-Partum Document. London: Routledge & Kegan Paul.

Dale Kistemaker

Born 1948 in Cleveland, Ohio.
Lives and works in
San Francisco.

Education

MA, San Francisco State
University, 1975

BA, Ohio State University,
Columbus, 1972

Case Western Reserve
University, Cleveland, 1966–69

Selected Solo Exhibitions

1994
His Bedroom, The Friends
of Photography, Ansel Adams
Center, San Francisco

The Village, Robert Koch
Gallery, San Francisco

*Real Men, Dead Heroes,
His Bedroom,* and *The Village,*
California Museum of
Photography, Riverside,
California

1991
Real Men, Dead Heroes,
Southern Exposure Gallery,
San Francisco

1984
Oaxaca to Ohio, Art Matrix
Gallery, Long Beach, California

Selected Group Exhibitions

1991
Nuclear Matters, San Francisco
Camerawork

1990
Lines of Force, National Poetry
Association, Fort Mason
Center, San Francisco

Visual Voices Performance Series,
Southern Exposure Gallery,
San Francisco

1989
The Road Show, The John
Michael Kohler Arts Center,
Sheboygan, Wisconsin

1988
Boys and Their Toys, Robert
Koch Gallery, San Francisco

1985
*Extending the Perimeters of
20th Century Photography,*
The San Francisco Museum of
Modern Art

Curatorial Projects with Published Catalogues

1985–1986
*Jesse Alexander, Motor Racing
Photographs,* a 16 page
catalogue with curator's
introduction. Traveled to
Santa Barbara Museum of Art,
Santa Barbara; Akron Art
Museum; San Francisco
Camerawork.

1984–1986
*Passion and Precision:
The Photographer and Grand
Prix Racing 1894–1984,* a
119 page catalogue with essay.
Traveled to the Hall of
Champions, San Diego; Detroit
Institute of Art; Long Beach
Museum of Art, California.

Selected Bibliography

1992
Solnit, Rebecca. "San Francisco
Fax: Unveiling Masculinity and
Dale Kistemaker." *Art Issues,*
January/February, 29–30.

1991
Bonetti, David. "Alternative
Transformations." *San Francisco
Examiner,* August 9, D2.

Rapko, John. "Means of
Social Construction." *Artweek,*
September 5, 14–15.

1990
Cohn, Terri. "Interior
Destinations." *Artweek,*
August 20, 15–16.

Stein, Ruthe. "Gallery Puts Art
in Real-Life Settings."
San Francisco Chronicle,
Aug. 15, B3–B4.

Donald Moffett

Born 1955 in
San Antonio, Texas.
Lives and works in
New York City.

Education

BA, Trinity University,
San Antonio, Texas, 1977

Selected Solo Exhibitions

1991
I Know What Boys Like, Texas
Gallery, Houston

Wet Dreams, Simon Watson's
Living Room, New York

Wet Holes, Wessel O'Connor
Gallery, New York

1990
Oh-Oh-Harder-Oh-Oh, Wessel
O'Connor Gallery, New York

1989
*Homo Art: I Love It When You
Call Me Names,* Wessel
O'Connor Gallery, New York

Selected Group Exhibitions

1993
1993 Biennial Exhibition,
Whitney Museum of American
Art, New York

Building a Collection, Part I,
Museum of Fine Arts, Boston

Prospect, 1993, Frankfurter
Kunstverein, Frankfurt

Fawbush, New York

1992
Sculpture, Paula Cooper Gallery,
New York

*Dissent, Difference and the Body
Politic,* Portland Fine Arts
Museum, Portland, Oregon

Object Choice, Hallwalls
Contemporary Arts Center,
Buffalo

Gegendarstellung, Kunstverein in
Hamburg

Structural Damage,
BlumHelman Warehouse,
New York

From Media to Metaphor: Art About AIDS. Organized by Independent Curators Incorporated, New York. Traveled to Center on Contemporary Art, Seattle; Musée d'Art Contemporain, Montréal; Grey Art Gallery and Study Center, New York University among other sites.

Between the Sheets, PPOW, New York

1991
The Interrupted Life, The New Museum of Contemporary Art, New York

Outrageous Desire, Rutgers University, New Brunswick, New Jersey

(Dis)member, Simon Watson's Living Room, New York

When Objects Dream and Talk in Their Sleep, Jack Tilton Gallery, New York

Situation, New Langton Arts, San Francisco

Nayland Blake, Ross Bleckner, Donald Moffett, Simon Watson's Living Room, New York

Someone or Somebody, Meyers/Bloom, Los Angeles

The Art of Advocacy, Aldrich Museum of Contemporary Art, Ridgefield, Connecticut

Group Material's AIDS Timeline, Whitney Museum of American Art, New York

1990
Critical Realism, Perspektief Centre for Photography, Rotterdam

Against the Tide: The Homoerotic Image in the Era of Censorship and AIDS, Nexus Gallery, Atlanta

Spent, The New Museum at Marine Midland Bank, New York

Constructive Anger, Barbara Krakow Gallery, Boston

Eros/Thanatos—Death and Desire, Tom Cugliani Gallery, New York

The Indomitable Spirit, The International Center of Photography, New York

Strange Ways Here We Come: Felix Gonzalez-Torres and Donald Moffett, Fine Arts Gallery, University of British Columbia, Vancouver

1989
Art About AIDS, Freedman Gallery, Albright College, Reading, Pennsylvania

To Probe and To Push: Artists of Provocation, Wessel O'Connor Gallery, New York

Erotophobia: A Forum on Sexuality, Simon Watson's Living Room, New York

1988
Group Material: AIDS and Democracy, Dia Art Foundation, New York

Vollbild, The Full-Blown Picture, NGBK, Berlin, and Bern, Switzerland

Show of Provocation by ACT-UP, White Columns, New York

Selected Bibliography

1994
Cotter, Holland. "Art After Stonewall: 12 Artists Interviewed." *Art in America,* June, 62.

Watney, Simon. "Aphrodite of the Future." *Artforum,* April, 75–76, 119.

1993
Watney, Simon. "Memorialising AIDS: The Work of Ross Bleckner." *Parkett,* no. 38, 47-55.

1992
Glueck, Grace. *New York Observer,* Sept. 21, 1, 18.

1991
Mahoney, Robert. *Arts Magazine,* April, 104–105.

Nesbitt, Lois. *Artforum,* May, 139–140.

Schjeldahl, Peter. "Death Warmed Over." *The Village Voice,* Oct. 15, 113.

1990
Chua, Lawrence. "To Probe and to Push." *FlashArt,* January/February, 133–134.

Crimp, Douglas and Adam Rolston. *AIDSDEMOGRAPHICS.* Seattle: Bay Press.

"Democracy: A Project for Group Material." *Discussions in Contemporary Culture,* no. 5. Edited by Brian Wallis, Dia Art Foundation, Seattle: Bay Press.

Sokolowski, Thomas. "Iconophobics Anonymous." *Artforum,* summer, 114–119.

Smith, Roberta. *New York Times,* Feb. 16, C30.

1989
Cooper, Dennis. *Artforum,* September, 145.

Dechter, Joshua. *Arts Magazine,* September, 103.

Keith Piper

Born 1960 in Birmingham, England.
Lives and works in London.

Education

MA, Royal College of Art, London, 1986

BA, Trent Polytechnic, Nottingham, England, 1983

Selected Solo Exhibitions

1994
Tall Ships, Greenwich Park, London

Final Frontiers, The Royal Observatory, Greenwich Park, London

The Exploded City, Centre 181 Gallery, London

1993
Exotic Signs, Gallery Theesalon, Arnhem, The Netherlands

1992
Front, Het Kijkhuis, The Hague, The Netherlands

Tradewinds, Merseyside Maritime Museum, Liverpool

1991
A Ship Called Jesus, Camden Arts Centre, London. Traveled to Ikon Gallery, Birmingham.

Step Into the Arena, Rochdale Art Gallery, Rochdale, England.

Portrait of a Shopping Centre as a Cathedral, Dalston Cross Shopping Center, London

1990
The Devil Finds Work, Transmission Gallery, Glasgow

1989
Father I Have Done Questionable Things, Bedford Hill Gallery, London

1988
Chanting Heads, Various sites across the United Kingdom

1987
Another Empire State, Battersea Arts Centre, London

Adventures Close to Home, Pentonville Gallery, London

1984
Past Imperfect, Future Tense, The Black Art Gallery, London

Selected Group Exhibitions

1994
Down Town, Stichting Nederlands Instituut voor Fotografie, Rotterdam

Remote Control, Royal College of Art, London

1993
The Body in Ruin, V2, `s-Hertogenbosch, The Netherlands

Iterations: The New Image, International Center of Photography, New York

In the Ring, Newhouse Center for Contemporary Art, Snug Harbor Cultural Center, Staten Island, New York

British Artists of the 90's, VideoFest 93, Kunst-Werke, Berlin

Interrogating Identity, Duke University Museum of Art, Durham, North Carolina. Traveled to Walker Art Center, Minneapolis; Museum of Fine Arts, Boston; Grey Art Gallery and Study Center, New York University.

1992
Trophies of Empire, Arnolfini, Bristol, England

Photovideo, Impressions Gallery, York, England. Traveled to the Photographers Gallery, London.

1991
Tercera Bienal de la Habana '91, Havana, Cuba

Shocks to the System, Royal Festival Hall, London

1990
Black Markets, Cornerhouse, Manchester

1989
Tercera Bienal de la Habana '89, Havana, Cuba

1988
Essential Black Art, Laing Art Gallery, Newcastle. Traveled to Chisenhale Gallery, London.

1987
Depicting History: For Today, Mappin Art Gallery, Sheffield

Art History, The Hayward Gallery, London

State of the Nation, Herbert Art Gallery, Coventry

Piper & Rodney, Prema, Gloucestershire

1986
From Two Worlds, Fruitmarket, Edinburgh

Double Vision, Cartwright Hall, Bradford. Traveled to the Whitechapel Art Gallery, London.

Unrecorded Truths, The Elbow Room, London

New Contemporaries, Institute of Contemporary Arts, London

Monti Wa Maruma, Brixton Art Gallery, London

1985
No More White Lies, Chapter Arts Center, Cardiff, Wales

Black Skin, Blue Coat, Blue Coat Gallery, London

1984
Black Art Now, The Black Art Gallery, London

The Pan-Afrikan Connection, The Herbert Art Gallery, Coventry. Traveled to Africa Centre, London; Midlands Art Centre, Birmingham; The Midland Group, Nottingham; 38 King Street Gallery, Bristol; The Ikon Gallery, Birmingham.

1981
Black Art an' Done, Wolverhampton Art Gallery, Wolverhampton, England

Selected Bibliography

1993
Jones, Kellie. "In the Ring." Staten Island, N. Y.: Newhouse Center for Contemporary Art, Snug Harbor Cultural Center.

1992
Mercer, Kobena. "Engendered Species (Black Masculinity as Seen by Danny Tisdale and Keith Piper)." *Artforum,* summer, 74–77.

1991
Piper, Keith. *Step Into the Arena.* Rochdale, Eng.: Rochdale Art Gallery.

——————. *A Ship Called Jesus.* Birmingham: Ikon Gallery.

1989
Fisher, Jean. *Artforum,* May, 169–170.

1988
"Chanting Heads." *Arts Review,* Aug. 12 and 26, 554.

Charles Ray

Born 1953 in Chicago.
Lives and works in Los Angeles.

Education

MFA, Mason Gross School of
the Arts, Rutgers University,
New Brunswick, New Jersey,
1978

BFA, University of Iowa,
Iowa City, 1974

Selected Solo Exhibitions

1994
Charles Ray, Rooseum—Center
for Contemporary Art, Malmö,
Sweden; Institute of
Contemporary Arts, London;
Kunsthalle Bern; Kunsthalle
Zurich

1993
Feature, New York

Galerie Metropol, Vienna

1992
Feature, New York

Donald Young Gallery, Seattle

1991
Feature, New York

Galerie Metropol, Vienna

Galerie Claire Burrus, Paris

1990
Feature, New York

Burnett Miller Gallery,
Los Angeles

Newport Harbor Art Museum,
Newport Beach, California

Matrix Gallery, University Art
Museum, Berkeley, California

Galerie Claire Burrus, Paris

1989
Feature, New York

The Mattress Factory,
Pittsburgh

Burnett Miller Gallery,
Los Angeles

1988
Feature, Chicago

Burnett Miller Gallery,
Los Angeles

1987
Feature, Chicago

Burnett Miller Gallery,
Los Angeles

1985
Mercer Union, Toronto

New Langston Arts,
San Francisco

1983
64 Market Street, Venice,
California

Selected Group Exhibitions

1993
1993 Biennial Exhibition,
Whitney Museum of
American Art, New York

*Seeing the Forest through the
Trees,* Contemporary Arts
Museum, Houston

Images, Selections from the
Lannan Foundation Collection,
Los Angeles

1992
*Dirty Data: Sammlung
Schürmann,* Ludwig Forum für
Internationale Kunst, Cologne

Post Human, Musée d'Art
Contemporain Pully, Lausanne,
France. Traveled to Castello
di Rivoli, Torino, Italy;
Deste Foundation for
Contemporary Art, Athens;
Deichtorhallen, Hamburg;
Israel Museum, Jerusalem.

Documenta IX, Kassel, Germany

*Helter Skelter: L.A. Art in the
1990's,* Museum of
Contemporary Art, Los Angeles

1991
The Savage Garden, Fundación
Caja de Pensiones, Madrid

*Cadences: Icon and Abstraction
in Context,* The New Museum
of Contemporary Art,
New York

Mechanika, The Contemporary
Arts Center, Cincinnati

1990
Recent Drawings, Whitney
Museum of American Art,
New York

Blood Remembering, Newhouse Center for Contemporary Art, Snug Harbor Cultural Center, Staten Island, New York

1989
1989 Biennial Exhibition, Whitney Museum of American Art, New York

1988
Selections from the Permanent Collection, Newport Harbor Art Museum, Newport Beach, California

Recent Art from Los Angeles, Cleveland Center for Contemporary Art

1987
Industrial Icons, University Art Gallery, San Diego State University

Nature, Feature, Chicago

Selected Bibliography

1994
Ferguson, Bruce. Charles Ray. Malmö: Rooseum—Center for Contemporary Art.

1993
Heartney, Eleanor. "Identity Politics at the Whitney." *Art in America,* May, 43–47.

Smith, Roberta. "At the Whitney, A Biennial With a Social Conscience." *New York Times,* March 5, C1, C27.

1992
Pagel, David. "Charles Ray." *Forum International,* May, 79–82.

Relyea, Lane. "Charles Ray: In the NO." *Artforum,* September, 62–66.

Schimmel, Paul, Norman M. Klein and Lane Relyea. *Helter Skelter: L.A. Art in the 1990's.* Los Angeles: The Museum of Contemporary Art.

1991
Riley, Jan. *Mechanika.* Cincinnati: The Contemporary Arts Center.

Sangster, Gary. "Thinking Through Abstract Objects." in *Cadences: Icons and Abstraction in Context.* New York: The New Museum of Contemporary Art.

1990
Barnes, Lucinda and Dennis Cooper. *Charles Ray.* Newport Beach, Calif.: Newport Harbor Art Museum.

Brougher, Nora Halpern, "Charles Ray." *Flash Art,* November/December, 152.

Geer, Susan. "Marked by Art: Charles Ray at Newport Harbor Art Museum." *Artweek,* Sept. 6, 1, 20.

Pincus, Robert. "Charles Ray Brings Art Out of the Ordinary." *San Diego Union,* July 29, E2–3.

Rinder, Lawrence. "The Sculpture of Charles Ray." *University Art Museum Calendar* (University of California, Berkeley), November/December, 4.

1989
Myers, Terry R. "Charles Ray." *Flash Art,* October, 134.

1988
Palmer, Laurie. "Charles Ray." *Artforum,* April, 153.

Saunders, Wade. "Los Angeles." *Bomb,* winter, 75–78.

1987
Clothier, Peter. "Charles Ray: Edgy, Provocative Presences." *Artnews,* December, 97–98.

Knight, Christopher. "Beneath Art's Serene, Slick Surfaces, Danger Lurks." *Los Angeles Herald Examiner,* Mar. 22, E4.

1986
Tucker, Marcia. *Choices: Making an Art of Everyday Life.* New York: The New Museum of Contemporary Art, 37–38.

1985
Hugo, Joan. "Between Object and Persona: The Sculpture Events of Charles Ray." *High Performance,* 30, 26–29.

Michael Yue Tong

Born 1967 in Shanghai, China. Lives and works in Brooklyn, New York.

Education

MFA, University of Massachusetts, Amherst, 1993

BFA, State University of New York, College at Purchase, 1990

Selected Solo Exhibitions

1993
Dream of the Red Chamber, Hampden Gallery, University of Massachusetts, Amherst

1992
Red Sky at Morning, Hampden Gallery, University of Massachusetts, Amherst

Selected Group Exhibitons

1994
Fever, Wexner Center for the Arts, Ohio State University, Columbus

Untitled 1994, Institute of Progressive Art, Boston

Let the Artist Live, Exit Art, New York

1993
National Showcase Exhibition, Alternative Museum, New York

1992
Fever, Exit Art, New York

Workshop for Environmental Art, International Sculpture Exhibition, l'École National d'Art, Cergy Pontoise, France

Masculinity:
A Selective Bibliography of
Print Materials in English
Michael Leininger

Bibliographer's Note

The bibliographical terrain of masculinity lends itself to conflict, indignation, and anxiety. This should come as no surprise, since the explosion of theoretical research that erupted with the last great wave of feminism has affected thinking in a wide variety, if not all academic disciplines, representing an assault on previous assumptions about gender roles and male preeminence. Also not surprisingly, much of the literature encountered during the early years of feminist writing dealt primarily with women, albeit in their relation to oppressive patriarchies. Following quickly on the heels of this research, often growing out of it, came a wealth of gay and lesbian theory, as well as new ways of perceiving racial and ethnic groups. Women and minority groups, recognizing their positions as "others" within a web of patriarchal, racial, and class systems, began the process of constructing themselves as subjects, a process which came to be labeled "identity politics." Masculinity became the "usual suspect" which needed "rounding up" and, ultimately, deconstructing. The result, manifest in the publication dates of the citations which follow, is a level of interest in masculinity which is just

now accelerating, more than twenty years after the feminist wave began.

This bibliography is principally concerned with the representation of masculinity in the arts. Beyond that, it attempts to provide a reliable overview of literature from the humanities and the social sciences. Clinical literature is avoided, as well as dissertations, of which there are hundreds. Theoretical preference is given to works that constitute what might be called the "postmodern" view of masculinity, informed by a mixture of feminist, poststructuralist, Marxist, and psychoanalytic methods of analysis. What is left out is the literature from what might be termed "the other side"; that is, the writings of masculinists, conservative Christians, proponents of the men's movement, and so on.

The vastness of the subject and the necessity to choose, omit, and classify created many dilemmas. At least ten thousand citations were examined for an eventual selection of some five hundred. Why then have I cited so much gay material? Why do Robert Mapplethorpe and Pee-Wee Herman receive so much space at the expense of other underrepresented figures? Gender is most cogently evaluated at its sites of trans gression. It is because sexual minorities challenge and confound societal commonplaces about gender that the cultural production of these groups, as well as the criticism they generate, becomes central to any discussion of gender.

Finally, there was the problem of selecting categories. All citations that fit into the "Arts" category are put there. "Bisexuality," "cross-dressing," and other intermediate gender categories are assigned to the general category "Gender Studies." Several categories, such as "sports" and "war," which have extensive literatures of their own, were merged with "Gender Studies." Two categories that caused much anguish in their overlap were "Gay" and "Race." I chose the path I felt represented maximum "otherness" within the context of gender. Therefore, works concerning African American gays are found under "Gay" rather than "Race." I realize this decision is not universally approved. Indeed, the more I worked with this subject, the act of categorizing became increasingly suspect. If the study of gender is to unmask the fiction of fixed gender identities and open us to the widest possible range of human subjectivity, the old categories, which limit us by their boundaries, will need to be scrapped.

Art

Adler, Kathleen, and Marcia Pointon, eds. *The Body Imaged: The Human Form and Visual Culture Since the Renaissance.* Cambridge: Cambridge University Press, 1993.

Barthes, Roland. *The Responsibility of Forms: Critical Essays on Music, Art, and Representation.* New York: Hill & Wang, 1985.

Berger, Maurice, coordinator. "Man Trouble: A Project for 'Artforum'." Six articles. *Artforum* 32 (Apr. 1994): 74–83, 119, 122.

Bersani, Leo. *The Freudian Body: Psychoanalysis and Art.* New York: Columbia University Press, 1986.

Beurdeley, Cecile, ed. *L'Amour Bleu.* New York: Rizzoli, 1978.

Boime, Albert. *The Art of Exclusion: Representing Blacks in the Nineteenth Century.* Washington, D. C.: Smithsonian Institution Press, 1990.

Bowles, Norma, and Ernie Lafky. "Ironies in the Politics of Representation." *High Performance* 16 (spring 1993): 52–55.

Brett, Guy. *Through Our Own Eyes: Popular Art and Modern History.* London: Gay Men's Press, 1986.

Bryson, Norman. *Vision and Painting: The Logic of the Gaze.* New Haven: Yale University Press, 1983.

Bryson, Norman, and Penelope Wise, eds. *Visual Culture: Images and Interpretations.* Hanover, N.H.: University Press of New England for Wesleyan University Press, 1994.

Burgin, Victor. "Tea With Madeleine." In *Blasted Allegories: An Anthology of Writings by Contemporary Artists*, edited by Brian Wallis. New York: New Museum of Contemporary Art; Cambridge: MIT Press, 1987.

Burnham, Linda Frye. "Making Family: Gay Performance is Reaching Out to Make Family with Us, to Heal, to Help." *High Performance* 9, no. 4 (1986): 48–53.

Cameron, Daniel J., guest curator. *Extended Sensibilities: Homosexual Presence in the Contemporary Art of Charley Brown et al.* New York: The New Museum, 1982.

Cherry, Deborah, and Griselda Pollock. "Patriarchal Power and the Pre-Raphaelites." *Art History* 7 (Dec. 1984): 480–95.

Cooper, Dennis, and Richard Hawkins, eds. *Against Nature: A Group Show of Work by Homosexual Men, Jan. 6.–Feb. 12, 1988.* Los Angeles: Los Angeles Contemporary Exhibitions, 1988.

Cooper, Emmanuel. *Homosexuality and Art in the Last One Hundred Years in the West.* London: Routledge & Kegan Paul, 1986.

Cottingham, Laura. "Negotiating Masculinity and Representation." *Contemporanea* (Dec. 1990): 46–51.

Crimp, Douglas. *AIDS DemoGraphics.* Seattle: Bay Press, 1990.

Davis, Whitney. "Erotic Revision in Thomas Eakins's Narratives of Male Nudity." *Art History* 17 (Sept. 1994): 301–341.

Davis, Whitney, ed. *Gay and Lesbian Studies in Art History.* New York: Harrington Park Press, 1994.

Deutsche, Rosalyn. "Expertease: Rosalyn Deutsche on Men in Space." *Artforum* 28 (Feb. 1990): 21–23.

Dynes, Wayne R., and Stephen Donaldson, eds. *Homosexuality and Homosexuals in the Arts.* New York: Garland, 1992.

Failing, Patricia. "Invisible Men: Blacks and Bias in Western Art." *Art News* 89 (summer 1990): 152–55.

Fernandes, Joyce. "Exposing a Phallocentric Discourse: Images of Women in the Art of David Salle." *New Art Examiner* 14 (Nov. 1986): 32–34.

Floss, Michael, and Anastasia D. Shartin. "Notions of Masculinity." *Artweek* 23 (May 21, 1992): 21.

The Arts and Literature

Foster, Hal. *Compulsive Beauty*. Cambridge: MIT Press, 1993.

Frueh, Joanna, Cassandra L. Langer, and Arlene Raven, eds. *New Feminist Criticism: Art, Identity, Action*. New York: Icon Editions, 1994.

Goldin, Nan. *Witnesses: Against Our Vanishing, Nov. 16, 1989–Jan. 6, 1990*. New York: Artists' Space, 1989.

Goldman, Saundra, ed. *Gender, Fact or Fiction?* Austin: Texas Fine Arts Association, 1992.

Hall, Charles. "The Male Nude: The Woman's View." *Arts Review* (London) 43 (Apr. 1991): 189.

Hardison, Sam and George Stambolian. "The Art and Politics of the Male Image: A Conversation Between Sam Hardison and George Stambolian." *Christopher Street* 4 (Mar. 1980): 14–22.

Hargrove, June Ellen. "Shaping the National Image: The Cult of Statues to Great Men in the Third Republic." *Studies in the History of Art* 29 (1991): 48–63.

Harper, Glenn, ed. "Special Issue on Contemporary Black Artists." *Art Paper* 12 (July/Aug. 1988).

Hatt, Michael. "Making a Man of Him: Masculinity and the Black Body in Mid-Nineteenth Century American Sculpture." *Oxford Art Journal* 15, no. 1 (1992): 21–35.

Heartney, Eleanor. "David Salle: Impersonal Effects." *Art in America* 76 (June 1988): 120–29, 175.

Honour, Hugh. *The Image of the Black in Western Art, vol. 4, From the American Revolution to World War One*. Houston: Menil Foundation, 1989–90.

Hooven, F. Valentine. *Tom of Finland*. New York: St. Martin's Press, 1994.

Jones, Amelia. *Postmodernism and the En-Gendering of Marcel Duchamp*. New York: Cambridge University Press, 1994.

Kent, Sarah, and Jacqueline Morreau. *Women's Images of Men*. London: Pandora, 1985.

Lindner, Ines, Sigrid Schade, Silke Wenk, and Gabriele Werner, eds. *A Changing Perspective: The Construction of Masculinity and Femininity in Art and Art History*. Berlin: Dietrich Reimer, 1989.

Linker, Kate, guest curator. *Difference: On Representation and Sexuality*. New York: The New Museum of Contemporary Art, 1984.

Lippard, Lucy. "Out of the Safety Zone (David Wojnarowicz)." *Art in America* 78 (Dec 1990): 130–139, 182, 186.

Lucie-Smith, Edward, ed. *The Male Nude: A Modern View*. Oxford: Phaidon, 1985.

Martin, Fred. "To Be a Man: Searching the Met for Images of Maleness." *Artweek* 22 (4 April 1991): 3.

Mattick, Paul. "Beautiful and Sublime: Gender Totemism in the Construction of Art." *The Journal of Aesthetics and Art Criticism* 48 (Fall 1990): 292–303.

McElroy, Guy. *Facing History: The Black Image in American Art 1710–1940*. San Francisco: Bedford Arts Publishers, 1990.

Melosh, Barbara. *Engendering Culture: Manhood and Womanhood in New Deal Public Art and Theater*. Washington, D.C.: Smithsonian Institution Press, 1991.

Mercer, Kobena. "Engendered Species (Black Masculinity as Seen by Danny Tisdale and Keith Piper)." *Artforum* 30 (summer 1992): 74–77.

Meyer, James. "Some Gay Themes in the 1987 Whitney Biennial." *Arts Magazine* 62 (Oct. 1987): 25–7.

Modleski, Tania. *Feminism Without Women: Culture and Criticism in a 'Postfeminist' Age*. New York: Routledge, 1990.

Nochlin, Linda. *Women, Art, and Power: And Other Essays*. New York: Harper & Row, 1988.

Nordstrom, Robert. "A Book of his Own: Male Visual Diaries: Woodland Pattern Book Center, Milwaukee." *New Art Examiner* 15 (Mar. 1988): 54.

Outram, Dorinda. *The Body and the French Revolution: Sex, Class, and Political Culture.* New Haven: Yale University Press, 1989.

Owens, Craig. *Beyond Recognition: Representation, Power, and Culture.* Edited by Scott Bryson et al. Berkeley: University of California Press, 1992.

Perry, Gill, and Michael Rossington, eds. *Femininity and Masculinity in Eighteenth-century Art and Culture.* Manchester: Manchester University Press, 1994.

Piper, Keith. *Step into the Arena: Notes on Black Masculinity and the Contest of Territory.* Esplanade, Rochdale, Lancashire: Rochdale Art Gallery, 1991.

Pollock, Griselda. *Trouble in the Archives.* Bloomington: Indiana University Press, 1992.

Posner, David. "Caravaggio's Early Homoerotic Works." *Art Quarterly* 24 (1971): 301–26.

Potts, Alex. "Images of Ideal Manhood in the French Revolution." *History Workshop Journal* 30 (fall 1990): 1–20.

Raven, Arlene, Cassandra Langer, and Joanna Frueh, eds. *Feminist Art Criticism: An Anthology.* Ann Arbor: UMI Research Press, 1988.

Rankin, Aimee. "Difference and Deference: Theorizing the Representation of Sexuality at the New Museum, New York." *Art-Network* 16 (winter 1985): 14–19.

Reed, David. "Repression and Exaggeration: The Art of Tom of Finland." *Christopher Street* 4 (Apr. 1980): 16–21.

Rose, Matthew. "David Wojnarowicz: An Interview." *Arts Magazine* 62 (May 1988): 60–65.

Saslow, James M. "Closets in the Museum." In *Lavender Culture* by Karla Jay and Allen Young. New York: Jove, 1978.

_____. *Ganymede in the Renaissance: Homosexuality in Art and Society.* New Haven: Yale University Press, 1986.

_____. "The Tenderest Lover: Saint Sebastian in Renaissance Painting: A Proposed Iconology for Northern Italian Art, 1450–1550." *Gai Saber* 1 (spring 1977): 58–66.

Sokolowski, Thomas W. *The Sailor 1930–45: The Image of an American Demigod.* Norfolk, Va.: Chrysler Museum, 1983.

Solkin, David H. "Great Pictures of Great Men: Reynolds, Male Portraiture, and the Power of Art." *Oxford Art Journal* 9, no. 2 (1986): 42–49.

Solomon-Godeau, Abigail. "Male Trouble: A Crisis in Representation." *Art History* 16 (June 1993): 286–312.

Sprinkle, Annie. "Hard-Core Heaven: Unsafe Sex with Jeff Koons." *Arts Magazine* 80 (Mar. 1992): 46–48.

Stanley, Nick. *Out in Art.* London: Gay Men's Press, 1986.

Stephenson, Andrew. *Visualizing Masculinities.* London: Tate Gallery, 1992.

Wallace, Brian, ed. *Art After Modernism: Rethinking Representation.* New York: The New Museum of Contemporary Art, 1984.

Wallace, Michele. "Defacing History." *Art in America* 78 (Dec. 1990): 120–129, 184–86.

Walters, Margaret. *The Male Nude: A New Perspective.* Harmondsworth, Eng.: Penguin, 1979.

Weinberg, Jonathan. "Demuth and Difference." *Art in America* 76 (1988).

_____. "It's in the Can: Jaspar Johns and the Anal Society." *Genders* (spring 1988): 41–56.

The Arts and Literature

Photography

Adams, Brooks. "Photography: Lee Friedlander and David Salle: Truth or Dare?" *Art in America* 80 (Jan. 1992): 67–69.

Arndt, Thomas Frederick. *Men in America*. Washington, D.C.: National Museum of American Art, 1994.

Barnes, Lawrence, ed. *The Male Nude in Photography*. Waitsfield, Vt.: Crossroads Press, 1980.

Barthes, Roland. *Camera Lucida: Reflections on Photography*, trans. by Richard Howard. New York: Farrar, Straus & Giroux, 1981.

Brettle, Jane, and Sally Rice, eds. *Public Bodies/Private States: New Views on Photography, Representation, and Gender*. Manchester: Manchester University Press, 1993.

Bright, Deborah. "Of Mother Nature and Marlboro Men: An Inquiry into the Cultural Meanings of Landscape Photography." In *The Contest of Meaning*, ed. by Richard Bolton. Cambridge: MIT Press, 1989.

Butler, Judith. "The Force of Fantasy: Feminism, Mapplethorpe, and Discursive Excess." *differences* 2 (1990).

Cooper, Emmanuel. *Fully Exposed: The Male Nude in Photography*. London: Unwin Hyman, 1989.

Crimp, Douglas. "The Boys in My Bedroom." *Art in America* 78 (Feb. 1990): 47–49.

_____. "Photographs at the End of Modernism." In *On the Museum's Ruins*. Cambridge: MIT Press, 1993.

_____. "Portraits of People with AIDS." In *Cultural Studies*, ed. by Lawrence Grossberg, Cary Nelson, and Paula Treichler. New York: Routledge, 1991.

Crump, James, ed. "The Kinsey Institute and Erotic Photography." Special issue. *History of Photography* 18 (spring 1994).

Davis, Melody. *The Male Nude in Contemporary Photography*. Philadelphia: Temple University Press, 1991.

Derbyshire, Philip. "On Posing Male." *Creative Camera* 241 (Jan. 1985): 18–20.

Doan, William, and Craig Dietz, eds. *Photoflexion: A History of Bodybuilding Photography*. New York: St. Martin's Press, 1984.

Ellenzweig, Allen. *The Homoerotic Photograph: Male Images from Durieu/Delacroix to Mapplethorpe*. New York: Columbia University Press, 1992.

Foster, Alasdair. *Behold the Man: The Male Nude in Photography*. Edinburgh: Sills Gallery, 1988.

Gloeden, Wilhelm von. *Photographs of the Classic Male Nude*, ed. by Jean-Claude Lemagny. New York: Camera/Graphic Press, 1977.

Goldberg, Vicki. "Lee Friedlander: Dispassionate Voyeur." *Aperture* 125 (fall 1991): 72–74.

Grundberg, Andy, et al. "Photography's Lost Generation: The Impact of AIDS." Six articles. *American Photographer* 4 (Mar./Apr. 1993): 52–91.

Hendricks, Gordon. *The Photographs of Thomas Eakins*. New York: Grossman, 1972.

Howard, Richard, and Ingrid Sischy, eds. *Robert Mapplethorpe*. New York: Whitney Museum of American Art, 1990.

Hujar, Peter. "Peter Hujar: Nudes." *Aperture* 114 (spring 1989): 27–29.

Jarman, Derek. *Derek Jarman: Queer*. Manchester, Eng.: Manchester City Art Galleries, 1992.

Jordan, Chris. "Chris Jordan: Jeffrey—Man About Town." *Creative Camera* 245 (May 1985): 34–36.

Jussim, Estelle. *Slave to Beauty*. Boston: David R. Godine, 1981.

Kenny, Lorraine. "Traveling Theory: The Cultural Politics of Race and Representation (Interview with Kobena Mercer)." *Afterimage* 18 (Sept. 1990): 7–9.

Klein-Davis, Jennie. "Jump-Starting Masculinity: Queer Artists Expand an Arrested Development." *Afterimage* 21 (Oct. 1993): 4.

Koch, Stephen. "Guilt, Grace, and Robert Mapplethorpe." *Art in America* 74 (Nov. 1986): 144–51.

Kuspit, Donald. "David Salle: Photographic Symptoms." *Aperture* 125 (fall 1991): 74–76.

Labb, Alan. "Erections and Reflections." *San Francisco Camerawork* 18 (summer/fall 1991): 27–32.

Lifson, Ben, and Abigail Solomon-Godeau. "Photophilia." *October* 16 (spring 1981): 111.

Lord, Catherine. "History, Their Story, and (Male) Hysteria." *Afterimage* 18 (summer 1990): 9–10.

Love, Kate. "The Invisible Man: Notes on the Representation of Male Sexuality." *Performance Magazine* 53 (Apr./May 1988): 23–4.

Lynes, George Platt. *George Platt Lynes Photographs 1931–1955*. Pasadena: Twelvetrees Press, 1981.

Malanga, Gerard, ed. *Scopophilia: The Love of Looking*. New York: Alfred van der Marck Editions, 1985.

Mannisto, Glen. "1950s Male Nude Photography (Bookbeat Gallery, Oak Park, Mich.)." *New Art Examiner* 19 (May 1992): 35–36.

Mapplethorpe, Robert. *The Black Book*. New York: St. Martin's Press, 1986.

Mapplethorpe, Robert. *Robert Mapplethorpe*, edited by Arthur Danto. Munich: Schirmer/Mosel, 1992.

Mercer, Kobena. "Looking for Trouble." In *The Lesbian and Gay Studies Reader*, ed. by Henry Abelove, Michele Aina Barale, and

David M. Halperin. New York: Routledge, 1993.

_____. "Skin Head Sex Thing: Racial Difference in the Homoerotic Imaginary." In *How Do I Look?: Queer Film and Video*, ed. by Bad Object Choices. Seattle: Bay Press, 1989.

Metz, Christian. "Photography and Fetish." *October* 34 (fall 1985): 81–90.

Meyer, Richard. "Robert Mapplethorpe and the Discipline of Photography." In *The Lesbian and Gay Studies Reader*, ed. by Henry Abelove, Michele Aina Barale, and David M. Halperin. New York: Routledge, 1993.

Morrison, Paul. "Coffee Table Sex: Robert Mapplethorpe and the Sadomasochism of Everyday Life." *Genders* 11 (fall 1991): 17–36.

Muschamp, Herbert. "On Our Own: Kristen Bjorn, the Best Known Photographer of Gay Male Porn of Our Time." *Aperture* 121 (fall 1990): 71–72.

Richardson, Nan. "Men's Lives." *Aperture* 108 (fall 1987): 74–76.

Smith, Todd D. "Gay Male Pornography and the East: Re-orienting the Orient." *History of Photography* 18 (spring 1994): 13–21.

Sokolowski, Thomas W. "Iconophobics Anonymous: The Human Body, Pornography, and Homosexuality." *Artforum* 28 (summer 1990): 114–19.

Squiers, Carol, ed. *The Critical Image: Essays on Contemporary Photography*. Seattle: Bay Press, 1990.

Sramek, Peter. "Peter Sramek: The Male Image." *Creative Camera* 241 (Jan. 1985): 14–17.

Vance, Carol S. "Photography, Pornography and Sexual Politics." *Aperture* 121 (fall 1990): 52–65.

The Arts and Literature

Waugh, Tom. "Emerging from the Underground: Gay Male Visual Culture During the Fifties." In "Images of Sexuality," Special issue of *Parallelogramme* 12, no. 1 (1986).

_____. "A Heritage of Pornography." *The Body Politic* 90 (1983): 29–33.

_____. "Photography, Passion and Power." *The Body Politic* 101 (Mar. 1984): 29–33.

Weaver, Mike. "Mapplethorpe's Human Geometry: A Whole Other Realm." *Aperture* 101 (winter 1985): 41–51.

Weber, Bruce. *Bruce Weber*. New York: Knopf, 1989.

Weiermair, Peter. *The Hidden Image: Photographs of the Male Nude in the Nineteenth and Twentieth Centuries*. Cambridge: MIT Press, 1988.

Weiley, Susan. "Prince of Darkness, Angel of Light." *Artnews* 87 (Dec. 1988): 106–11.

Winston, Leyland, ed. *Physique: A Pictorial History of the Athletic Model Guild*. San Francisco: Gay Sunshine Press, 1982.

Film

Ames, Christopher. "Restoring the Black Man's Lethal Weapon: Race and Sexuality in Contemporary Cop Films." *Journal of Popular Film and Television* 20 (fall 1992): 52–60.

Bad Object-Choices, ed. *How Do I Look?: Queer Film and Video*. Seattle: Bay Press, 1989.

Becquer, M. "Snap!thology and Other Discursive Practices in 'Tongues Untied'." *Wide Angle* 13, no.2 (1991): 6–17.

Bell-Metereau, Rebecca Louise. *Hollywood Androgyny*. New York: Columbia University Press, 1993.

Bingham, Dennis. "Warren Beatty and the Elusive Male Body in Hollywood Cinema." *Critical Quarterly* 36 (spring 1994): 149–76.

Bogle, Donald. *Toms, Coons, Mulattoes, Mammies, and Bucks: An Interpretive History of Blacks in American Films*. New York: Continuum, 1990.

Bruce, Bryan. "Rosa von Praunheim in Theory and Practice." *CineAction!* 9 (1987): 25–31.

Byars, Jackie. *All That Hollywood Allows: Re-reading Gender in 1950's Melodrama*. Chapel Hill: University of North Carolina Press, 1991.

Carr, C. "Ice Pick Envy: Reclaiming our 'Basic' Rights." *Village Voice* 37 (Apr. 28, 1992): 35–36.

Caughie, John, and Annette Kuhn, eds. *The Sexual Subject: A Screen Reader in Sexuality*. London: Routledge, 1992.

Clover, Carol J. "Her Body, Himself: Gender in the Slasher Film." *Representations* 20 (1987): 187–228.

_____. *Men, Women, and Chain Saws: Gender in the Modern Horror Film*. Princeton, N.J.: Princeton University Press, 1992.

Cohan, Steven. "Cary Grant in the Fifties: Indiscretions of the Bachelor's Masquerade." *Screen* 33 (winter 1992): 394–412.

Cohan, Steven, and Ina Rae Hark, eds. *Screening the Male: Exploring Masculinities in Hollywood Cinema.* New York: Routledge, 1993.

Cohen, Jessica. "Neomacho (A New Kind of Hollywood Hero Emerges)." *American Film* 16 (June 1991): 36–39.

Conlon, James. "Making Love, Not War: The Soldier Male in 'Top Gun' and 'Coming Home'." *Journal of Popular Film and Television* 18 (spring 1990): 18–27.

Cook, Pam. "Masculinity in Crisis?: Identification in 'Raging Bull'." *Screen* 23 (Sept./Oct. 1982): 39–46.

Cooper, S. "Sex/Knowledge/Power in the Detective Genre." *Film Quarterly* 42, no.3 (1989): 23–31.

Corber, Robert J. *In the Name of National Security: Hitchcock, Homophobia, and the Political Construction of Gender in Postwar America.* Durham: Duke University Press, 1993.

Cowan, Gloria, and Margaret O'Brien. "Gender and Survival vs Death in Slasher Films: A Content Analysis." *Sex Roles* 23 (Aug. 1990): 187–96.

Creed, Barbara. "Phallic Panic: Male Hysteria and 'Dead Ringers'." *Screen* 31 (summer 1990): 125–46.

De Lauretis, Teresa. *Alice Doesn't: Feminism, Semiotics, Cinema.* Bloomington: Indiana University Press, 1984.

_____. *Technologies of Gender: Essays on Theory, Film, and Fiction.* Bloomington: Indiana University Press, 1987.

Deming, Robert. "The Return of the Unrepressed: Male Desire, Gender, and Genre." *Quarterly Review of Film and Video* 14, no. 1–2 (1992): 125–47.

Diawara, Manthia. "The Absent One: The Avant-garde and the Black Imaginary in 'Looking for Langston'." *Wide Angle* 13, no. 3/4 (1991): 96–109.

Diawara, Manthia, ed. *Black American Cinema.* New York: Routledge, 1993.

Dieckmann, Katherine. "Obscure Objects of Desire: The Films of Pedro Almodovar." *Aperture* 121 (fall 1990): 74–76.

Dittmar, Linda, and Gene Michaud, eds. *From Hanoi to Hollywood: The Vietnam War in American Film.* New Brunswick, N.J.: Rutgers University Press, 1990.

Dyer, Richard. *Heavenly Bodies: Film Stars and Society.* London: Macmillan, 1986.

_____. "Homosexuality and Film Noir." *Jump Cut* 16 (1977): 18–21.

_____. *The Matter of Images: Essays on Representation.* New York: Routledge, 1993.

_____. *Now You See It: Studies on Lesbian and Gay Film.* New York: Routledge, 1990.

_____. *Only Entertainment.* New York: Routledge, 1992.

_____. "Pasolini and Homosexuality." In *Piero Paolo Pasolini*, ed. by Paul Willemen. London: British Film Institute, 1977.

_____ ed. *Gays and Film.* New York: Zoetrope, 1984.

Dyson, Michael Eric. "The Politics of Black Masculinity and the Ghetto in Black Film." In *The Subversive Imagination: Artists, Society, and Responsibility*, ed. by Carol Becker. New York: Routledge, 1994.

Edelman, Lee. "Plasticity, Paternity, Perversity: Freud's Falcon, Huston's Freud." *American Imago* 51 (spring 1994): 69–104.

Ellis, Trey. "The Gay Subtext in 'Beverly Hills Cop': Did Hollywood Set Out to Undo Eddie Murphy?" *Black Film Review* 3 (spring 1987): 15–17.

Finch, M. "Melodrama and 'Maurice': Homo is Where the Het Is." *Screen* 29, no.3 (1988): 72–80.

Fletcher, John. "Versions of Masquerade." *Screen* 29 (summer 1988): 43–69.

The Arts and Literature

Flitterman-Lewis, Sandy. "Surrealist Cinema: Politics, History, and the Language of Dreams." *American Imago* 50, no. 4 (1993): 441–56.

Fried, Debra. "The Men in 'The Women'." In *Women in Film*, ed. by Janet Todd. New York: Holmes and Meier, 1988.

Friedman, Lester D., ed. *Unspeakable Images: Ethnicity and the American Cinema.* Ubana: University of Illinois Press, 1991.

Gabbard, Krin. "Signifyin(g) the Phallus: 'Mo' Better Blues' and Representations of the Jazz Trumpet." *Cinema Journal* 32 (fall 1992): 43–62.

Glass, Fred. "Totally Recalling Arnold: Sex and Violence in the New Bad Future." *Film Quarterly* 44 (fall 1990): 2–13.

Gever, Martha, Pratibha Parmar, and John Greyson, eds. *Queer Looks: Perspectives on Lesbian and Gay Film and Video.* Toronto: Between the Lines, 1993.

Goldsby, Jackie. "Queens of Language ('Paris is Burning')." *Afterimage* 18 (May 1991): 10–11.

Green, I. "Malefunction: A Contribution to the Debate on Masculinity in the Cinema." *Screen* 25 (July–Oct. 1984): 36–48.

Guerrero, Ed. *Framing Blackness: The African American Image in Film.* Philadelphia: Temple University Press, 1993.

Hadleigh, Boze. *The Lavender Screen: The Gay and Lesbian Films: Their Stars, Makers, Characters, and Critics.* Secaucus, N.J.: Carol Pub. Group, 1993.

Handler, Kristin. "Sexing 'The Crying Game': Difference, Identity, Ethics." *Film Quarterly* 47 (spring 1994): 31–42.

Hansen, Miriam. "Pleasure, Ambivalence, Identification: Valentino and Female Spectatorship." *Cinema Journal* 25 (summer 1986): 6–32.

Harper, P. B. "'The Subversive Edge': 'Paris is Burning', Social Critique, and the Limits of Subjective Agency." *Diacritics* 24, no. 2/3 (1994): 90+.

Harries, Dan M. "Camping with Lady Divine: Star Persona and Parody." *Quarterly Review of Film and Video* 12 (May 1990): 13–22.

Hepworth, John. "Hitchcock's Homophobia." *Christopher Street* 64 (May 1982): 42–49.

Holmlund, Christine. "Sexuality and Power in Male Doppelganger Cinema: The Case of Clint Eastwood's 'Tightrope'." *Cinema Journal* 26 (fall 1986): 31–42.

hooks, bell. "Male Heroes and Female Sex Objects: Sexism in Spike Lee's 'Malcolm X'." *Cineaste* 19, no. 4 (1992): 13–15.

_____. "Seduction and Betrayal: 'The Crying Game' Meets 'The Bodyguard'." In *Outlaw Culture: Resisting Representations.* New York: Routledge, 1994.

Jeffords, Susan. *Hard Bodies: Hollywood Masculinity in the Reagan Era.* New Brunswick, N.J.: Rutgers University Press, 1994.

_____. "Masculinity as Excess in Vietnam Films: The Father Son Dynamic of American Culture." *Genre* 21, no. 4 (1988): 487–515.

Jenkins, Henry, and Kristine Brunovska Karnick, eds. *Classical Hollywood Comedy.* New York: Routledge, 1994.

Jones, A. "'She Was Bad News': Male Paranoia and the Contemporary New Woman." *Camera Obscura* 25/26 (Jan.–May 1991): 296–320.

Jones, Jacqui. "The Construction of Black Sexuality." In *Black American Cinema*, ed. by Manthia Diawara. New York: Routledge, 1993.

Julien, Isaac, and Kobena Mercer, eds. "The Last 'Special Issue' on Race?" *Screen* 29 (fall 1988).

Kirkham, Pat, and Janet Thumin. *You Tarzan: Masculinity, Movies, and Men.* New York: St. Martin's Press, 1993.

Koch, Gertrud. "The Body's Shadow Realm." *October* 50 (fall 1989): 3–29.

Krutnik, Frank. "Desire, Transgression and James M. Cain." *Screen* 23 (May/June 1982): 31–44.

_____. *In a Lonely Street: Film Noir, Genre, Masculinity.* New York: Routledge, 1991.

Kuhn, Annette. *The Power of the Image: Essays on Representation and Sexuality.* London: Routledge and Kegan Paul, 1985.

Leab, Daniel J. *From Sambo to Superspade: The Black Experience in Motion Pictures.* Boston: Houghton Mifflin, 1975.

Lehman, Peter. *Running Scared: Masculinity and the Representation of the Male Body.* Philadelphia: Temple University Press, 1993.

MacBean, James Roy. "Between Kitsch and Fascism: Notes on Fassbinder, Pasolini, (Homo)sexual Politics, the Exotic, the Erotic, and Other Consuming Passions." *Cineaste* 13, no. 4 (1984): 12–19.

Marks, Laura U. "Nice Gun You Got There: John Greyson's Critique of Masculinity." *Parachute* 66 (Apr.–June 1992): 27–32.

Maynard, Richard A. *The Black Man on Film: Racial Stereotyping.* Rochelle Park, N.J.: Hayden Books, 1974.

McCullough, J. "Imagining Mr. Average." *CineAction!* no. 17 (summer 1989): 43–55.

Mellen, Joan. *Big Bad Wolves: Masculinity in American Film.* London: Elm Tree Books, 1978.

Miller, D. A. "Anal 'Rope'." In *Inside/Out: Lesbian Theories, Gay Theories,* ed. by Diana Fuss. New York: Routledge, 1991.

Miller, Randall M., ed. *The Kaleidoscopic Lens: How Hollywood Views Ethnic Groups.* New York: James Ozer, 1980.

Modleski, Tania. "A Father is Being Beaten: Male Feminism and the War Film." *Discourse* 10 (spring/summer 1988): 62–77.

_____. *The Women Who Knew Too Much: Hitchcock and Feminist Theory.* New York: Routledge, 1988.

Moon, Michael. "Flaming Closets." *October* 51 (winter 1989): 19–54.

Mulvey, Laura. *Visual and Other Pleasures.* Bloomington: Indiana University Press, 1989.

Neibaur, James L. *Tough Guy: The American Movie Macho.* Jefferson, N.C.: McFarland, 1989.

Nichols, Bill. *Ideology and the Image: Social Representation in the Cinema and Other Media.* Bloomington: Indian University Press, 1981.

_____. "Sons at the Brink of Manhood: Utopian Movements in Male Subjectivity." *East-West Film Journal* 4, no.1 (1981): 27–43.

Noriega, Chon A., ed. *Chicanos and Film: Essays on Chicano Representation and Resistance.* New York: Garland, 1992.

O'Connor, John. *The Hollywood Indian: Stereotypes of Native Americans in Film.* Trenton: New Jersey State Museum, 1980.

Oehling, Richard A. "Hollywood and the Image of the Oriental." *Film and Film History* 7 (May 1978).

O'Pray, Michael. "Derek Jarman's Cinema: Eros and Thanatos." *Afterimage* 12 (1985): 6–15.

_____. "Fatal Knowledge." *Sight and Sound* 2 (Mar. 1992): 10–1.

_____. "Movies, Mania and Masculinity: A Counter-Cinema of Sexuality." *Screen* 23 (Nov.–Dec. 1982): 63–70.

Pappas, N.A. "'Sea of Love' Among Men." *Film Criticism* 14, no.3 (1990): 14–26.

Parish, James Robert. *Gays and Lesbians in Mainstream Cinema.* Jefferson, N.C.: McFarland, 1993.

Pfeil, Fred. "From Pillar to Postmodern: Race, Class, and Gender in the Male Rampage Film." *Socialist Review* 23, no. 2 (1993): 123.

Pines, Jim. *Blacks in Films: A Survey of Racial Themes and Images in the American Film.* London: Studio Vista, 1975.

The Arts and Literature

Penley, Constance, and Sharon Willis, eds. *Male Trouble*. Minneapolis: University of Minnesota Press, 1993.

Place, Vanessa. "The Politics of Denial: Race, Gender, and Sexuality as Seen in 'The Bodyguard' and 'The Crying Game'." *Film Comment* 29 (May/June 1993): 84–86.

Reyes, L. "Hollywood's Buddy Movies." *Hollywood Studio* 20, no.5 (1987): 26–33.

Rich, B. Ruby, et al. "New Queer Cinema." *Sight and Sound* 2 (Sept. 1992): 30–9.

Ringer, Jeffrey R. *Queer Words, Queer Images: Communication and the Construction of Homosexuality*. New York: New York University Press, 1994.

Rodowick, D. N. *The Difficulty of Difference: Psychoanalysis, Sexual Difference, and Film Theory*. New York: Routledge, 1991.

Rose, Jacqueline. *Sexuality in the Field of Vision*. London: Verso, 1986.

Russo, Vito. *The Celluloid Closet: Homosexuality in the Movies*. New York: Harper & Row, 1987.

Selig, Michael. "From Play to Film: Strange Snow, Jacknife, and Masculine Identity in the Hollywood Vietnam Film." *Literature/Film Quarterly* 20, no. 3 (1992): 173–80.

Silverman, Kaja. "Fassbinder and Lacan: A Reconsideration of Gaze, Look, and Image." *Camera Obscura* 19 (Jan. 1989): 55–84.

_____. *Male Subjectivity at the Margins*. New York: Routledge, 1992.

Sklar, Robert. *City Boys: Cagney, Bogart, Garfield*. Princeton, N.J.: Princeton University Press, 1992.

Smith, Paul. *Clint Eastwood: A Cultural Production*. Minneapolis: University of Minnesota Press, 1993.

Snead, James A., Colin MacCabe, and Cornel West. *White Screens, Black Images: Hollywood from the Dark Side*. New York: Routledge, 1994.

Stam, Robert, and Louise Spence. "Colonialism, Racism and Representation." *Screen* 24 (July/Aug 1983): 2–20.

Straayer, Chris. "Redressing the 'Natural': The Temporary Transvestite Film." *Wide Angle* 14 (Jan. 1992): 36–55.

_____. "The She-man: Postmodern Bi-Sexed Performance in Film and Video." *Screen* 31 (fall 1990): 262–80.

Studlar, Gaylyn. "Discourses of Gender and Ethnicity: The Construction and De(con)struction of Rudolph Valentino as Other." *Film Criticism* 13, no. 2 (1989): 18–35.

Studlar, Gaylyn, and David Desser, eds. *Reflections in a Male Eye: John Huston and the American Experience*. Washington, D.C.: Smithsonian Institution Press, 1993.

Tartaglia, Jerry. "The Gay Sensibility in American Avant-Garde Film." *Millennium Film Journal* no. 4–5 (1979): 53–58.

Tasker, Yvonne. *Spectacular Bodies: Gender, Genre and the Action Cinema*. New York: Routledge, 1993.

Taubin, Amy. "The Men's Room (Quentin Tarantino)." *Sight and Sound* 4 (Dec. 1992): 2–4.

_____. "Soul to Soul (Interview with Isaac Julien)." *Sight and Sound* 1 (Aug. 1991): 14–17.

Thomas, D. "Film Noir: How Hollywood Deals with the Deviant Male." *CineAction* 13/14 (summer 1988): 18–28.

Thorburn, Adam. "Dark Secrets in 'The Prince of Tides'." *The Humanist* 52 (May 1992): 8–11.

Tompkins, Jane. "Language and Landscape: An Ontology for the Western." *Artforum* 28 (Feb. 1990): 94–99.

Treut, Monica. "Man to Man." *Sight and Sound* 4 (May 1994): 69.

Trinh, T. Minh-ha. *When the Moon Waxes Red: Representation, Gender, and Cultural Politics.* New York: Routledge, 1991.

Tyler, Parker. *Screening the Sexes: Homosexuality in the Movies.* New York: Holt, Rinehart & Winston, 1972.

Valentino, L. "Hollywood Hunks: Then." *Hollywood Studio* 21, no.10 (1988): 6–9.

Watney, Simon. "Hollywood's Homosexual World." *Screen* 23 (Sept./Oct. 1982): 107–121.

Waugh, Tom. "Homoerotic Representation in the Stag Film, 1920–40: Imagining an Audience." *Wide Angle* 14, no.2 (1992): 4–19.

_____. "Lesbian and Gay Documentary: Minority Self-Imaging, Oppositional Film Practice, and the Question of Image Ethics." In *Image Ethics: The Moral Rights of Subjects in Photographs, Film, and Television*, ed. by Larry Gross, John Stuart Katz, and Jay Ruby. New York: Oxford University Press, 1988.

Williams, Linda. "Fetishism and the Visual Pleasure of Hard-core: Marx, Freud, and the Money Shot." *Quarterly Review of Film and Video* 11 (Aug. 1989): 23–42.

Williamson, Judith. *Deadline at Dawn: Film Criticism, 1980–1990.* London: M. Boyars, 1993.

Willoquet-Maricondi, Paula. "Full-Metal-Jacketing, or Masculinity in the Making." *Cinema Journal* 33 (winter 1994): 5–21.

Woll, Allen L. *The Latin Image in American Film.* Los Angeles: UCLA Latin American Center Publications, 1977.

Woll, Allen L., and Randall M. Miller, eds. *Ethnic and Racial Images in American Film and Television: Historical Essays and Bibliography.* New York: Garland, 1987.

Wong, Eugene Franklin. *On Visual Media Racism: Asians in American Motion Pictures.* New York: Arno, 1978.

Zizek, Slavoj. "Looking Awry: The Status of the Gaze qua Object in Relation to Pornography, Nostalgia, and Montage." *October* 50 (fall 1989): 31–55.

Mass Media/Popular Culture

Avicolli, Tommi. "Images of Gays in Rock Music." In *Lavender Culture* by Karla Jay and Allen Young. New York: Jove, 1978.

Armstrong, Edward G. "The Rhetoric of Violence in Rap and Country Music." *Sociological Inquiry* 63 (winter 1993): 64–83.

Barth, Jack. "Pee Wee T-V." *Film Comment* 22 (Nov./Dec. 1986): 79.

Bruce, Bryan. "Pee Wee Herman: The Homosexual Subtext." *CineAction!* 9 (summer 1987): 6.

Burston, Paul, and Colin Richardson, eds. *A Queer Romance: Lesbians, Gay Men, and Popular Culture.* New York: Routledge, 1994.

Core, Philip. *Camp: The Lie That Tells the Truth.* New York: Delilah, 1984.

Courtney, Alice E., and Thomas W. Whipple. *Sex Stereotyping in Advertising.* Lexington, Ma.: Lexington, 1983.

Craig, Steve, ed. *Men. Masculinity, and the Media.* Newbury Park, Calif.: Sage, 1992.

Deming, Robert. "The Return of the Unrepressed: Male Desire, Gender and Genre (The Male Viewer/Spectator of Television)." *Quarterly Review of Film and Video* 14 (July 1992): 125–47.

Doty, Alexander. *Making Things Perfectly Queer: Interpreting Mass Culture.* Minneapolis: University of Minnesota Press, 1993.

Doty, Alexander, and Cory Creekmur, eds. *Out in Culture: Gay, Lesbian, and Queer Essays on Popular Culture.* Durham, N.C.: Duke University Press, 1994.

Dyson, Michael Eric. *Reflecting Black: African-American Cultural Criticism.* Minneapolis: University of Minnesota Press, 1993.

Easthope, Anthony. *What a Man's Gotta Do: The Masculine Myth in Popular Culture.* New York: Routledge, 1992.

The Arts and Literature

Emerson, Ken. "The Village People: America's Male Ideal?" *Rolling Stone* no. 275 (Oct. 5, 1978): 26–27.

Farrell, Warren. "Masculine Images in Advertising." In *Liberated Man, Beyond Masculinity: Freeing Men in Their Relationships with Women*, ed. by Warren Farrell. New York: Random House, 1974.

Fejes, F. "Images of Men in Media Research." *Critical Studies in Mass Communication* 6, no. 2 (1989): 215–21.

Foltz, K. "In Ads, Men's Image Becomes Softer." *New York Times* 139 (Mar. 26, 1990): D12.

Fung, Richard. "Looking for My Penis: The Eroticized Asian in Gay Video Porn." In *How Do I Look?: Queer Film and Video*, ed. by Bad Object Choices. Seattle: Bay Press, 1989.

Garber, Marjorie, ed. *Media Spectacles*. New York: Routledge, 1993.

George, N. "Video Blaculinity." *Village Voice* 35 (Dec. 25, 1990): 28.

Gertler, T. "The Pee–wee Perplex." *Rolling Stone* (Feb. 12, 1987): 37–40, 100, 102–103.

Goffman, Erving. *Gender Advertisements*. Cambridge: Harvard University Press, 1979.

Gross, Larry. "Sexual Minorities and the Mass Media." In *Remote Control: Television, Audiences, and Cultural Power*, ed. by Gabrielle Kreutzner and Eve–Maria Worth. New York: Routledge, 1989.

Hadleigh, Boze. *The Vinyl Closet: Gays in the Music World*. San Francisco: Los Hombres, 1991.

Hanke, R. "Hegemonic Masculinity in 'thirtysomething'." *Critical Studies in Mass Communication* 7, no. 3 (1990): 231–48.

Healey, Murray. "The Mark of a Man: Masculine Identities and the Art of Macho Drag (Marky Mark)." *Critical Quarterly* 36 (spring 1994): 86–93.

Hebdige, Dick. *Hiding in the Light: On Images and Things*. London: Routledge, 1988.

Herman, Pee-wee. Interviewed by Margy Rochlin. In *Interview* 17 (July 1987): 45–50.

Hoffman, Randi. "Real Men: Currently Ads are Defining a New Male Image: Neither Alan Alda nor the Marlboro Man." *Art Direction* 38 (Oct. 1986): 54–56.

Kanner, B. "Big Boys Don't Cry." *New York* 23 (May 21, 1990): 20–21.

King, Scott Benjamin. "Sonny's Virtues: The Gender Negotiations of 'Miami Vice'." *Screen* 31 (fall 1990): 281–95.

Kirk, Kris. *The Vinyl Closet*. London: Gay Men's Press, 1986.

Kolbe, Richard H., and Carl D. Langefeld. "Appraising Gender Role Portrayals in TV Commercials." *Sex Roles* 28 (Apr. 1993): 393–417.

Laermer, Richard. "The Televised Gay: How We're Pictured on the Tube." *Advocate* no. 413 (Feb. 5, 1985): 20–25.

Landers, T. "Bodies and Anti-bodies: A Crisis in Representation." *The Independent* 11 (Jan./Feb. 1988): 18–24.

Levine, Judith. "The Man in the Mirror." *Columbia Journalism Review* 32 (Mar./Apr. 1994): 27–31.

McArthur, Leslie Zebrowitz, and Beth Gabrielle Resko. "The Portrayal of Men and Women in American TV Commercials." *Journal of Social Psychology* (Dec. 1975): 209–220.

Miller, T. "Swimming in Masculinity." *Metro* 78 (summer 1988/89): 40–41.

Modleski, Tania. "The Incredible Shrinking He[r]man: Male Regression, the Male Body, and Film." *differences* 2 (summer 1990): 65.

Mort, Frank. "Boy's Own?: Masculinity, Style, and Popular Culture." In *Male Order: Unwrapping Masculinity*, ed. by Rowena Chapman and Jonathan Rutherford. London: Lawrence & Wishart, 1988.

Pearce, Frank. "How to be Immoral and Ill, Dangerous and Pathetic, All at the Same Time: Mass Media and Homosexuality." In *The Manufacture of News*, ed. by Stanley Cohen and Jock Young. London: Constable, 1973.

Pfeil, Fred. "Rock Incorporated: Plugging in to Axl and Bruce." *Michigan Quarterly Review* 32 (fall 1993): 535–71.

Pines, Jim, ed. *Black and White in Color: Black People in British Television Since 1936*. London: British Film Institute, 1992.

Rensin, David. "Can't Stop the Music." *Playboy* 27 (July 1982): 106–107.

Riggs, Marlon T. "Black Macho Revisited: Reflections of a Snap Queen." *The Independent* 14 (Apr. 1991): 32–34.

Robinson, Douglas. *No Less a Man: Masculist Art in a Feminist Age.* Bowling Green, Oh.: Bowling Green State University Popular Press, 1994.

Ross, A. "Masculinity and 'Miami Vice': Selling In." *Oxford Literary Review* 8, no. 1–2 (1986): 143–54.

Signorelli, Michelangelo. *Queer in America: Sex, the Media, and the Closets of Power.* New York: Random House, 1993.

Simels, Steven. *Gender Chameleons: Androgyny in Rock and Roll.* New York: Arbor House, 1985.

Starr, M. E. "The Marlboro-man: Cigarette-smoking and Masculinity in America." *Journal of Popular Culture* 17, no. 4 (1984).

Straayer, Chris. "Sexuality and Video Narrative." *Afterimage* 16 (May 1989): 8–11.

Studer, Wayne Malcolm. *Rock on the Wild Side: Gay Male Images in Popular Music of the Rock Era.* San Francisco: Leylend Pub., 1994.

Sullivan, Andrew. "Flogging Underwear: The New Raunchiness of American Advertising." *Communication Arts Magazine* 30 (May/June 1988): 76–82.

Trujillo, N. "Hegemonic Masculinity on the Mound: Media Representations of Nolan Ryan and American Sports Culture." *Critical Studies in Mass Communication* 8 (Sept. 1991): 290–308.

Tyler, C.A. "The Supreme Sacrifice? TV and the Renee Richards Story." *differences* 1, no. 3 (1989): 160–186.

Walser, Robert. *Running with the Devil: Power, Gender, and Madness in Heavy Metal Music.* Hanover, N.H.: University Press of New England, 1993.

Walters, Barry. "Triumph of the Twerp." *The Village Voice* (Sept. 23, 1986): 43–44.

Watney, Simon. *Policing Desire: Pornography, AIDS, and the Media.* Minneapolis: University of Minnesota Press, 1987.

White, Philip G., and James Gillett. "Reading the Muscular Body: A Critical Decoding of Advertisements in 'Flex Magazine'." *Sociology of Sport Journal* 11 (Mar. 1994): 18–39.

Williamson, Judith. *Decoding Advertisements: Ideology and Meaning in Advertising.* London: Boyars, 1984.

Winning, Rob. "Pee Wee Herman Un-Mascs Our Cultural Myths About Masculinity." *Journal of American Culture* 11 (summer 1988): 57–63.

Wolf, Michelle Andrea, and Alfred P. Kielwasser, eds. *Gay People, Sex, and the Media.* New York: Haworth, 1991.

Yeoman, Barry. *Moral Judgements Before the News: An Historical Survey of the Treatment of Lesbian and Gay Issues by the Straight Print News Media, 1897–1982.* Lafayette, La.: B. Yeoman, 1982.

Zizek, Slovoj. *Looking Awry: An Introduction to Jacques Lacan Through Popular Culture.* Cambridge: MIT Press, 1991.

The Arts and Literature

Gender/Cultural Studies

Barratt, Barnaby B., and Barrie Ruth Strauss. "Toward Postmodern Masculinities." *American Imago* 51 (spring 1994): 37–68.

Breen, Dana, ed. *The Gender Conundrum: Contemporary Psychoanalytic Perspectives on Femininity and Masculinity.* New York: Routledge, 1993.

Brittan, Arthur. *Masculinity and Power.* Oxford: Basil Blackwell, 1989.

Brod, Harry. "Pornography and the Alienation of Male Sexuality." *Social Theory and Practice* 14 (fall 1988): 265–84.

Brod, Harry, ed. *The Making of Masculinities: The New Men's Studies.* Boston: Allen & Unwin, 1987.

_____, ed. *Theorizing Masculinities.* Thousand Oaks, Calif.: Sage, 1994.

Brown, Ian. *Man Medium Rare: Sex, Guns, and Other Perversions of Masculinity.* New York: Dutton, 1994.

Butler, Judith. *Bodies That Matter: On the Discursive Limits of Sex.* New York: Routledge, 1993.

_____. *Gender Trouble: Feminism and the Subversion of Identity.* New York: Routledge, 1990.

_____. *Subjects of Desire: Hegelian Reflections in Twentieth-Century France.* New York: Columbia University, 1987.

Carnes, Mark C., and Clyde Griffin. *Meanings for Manhood: Constructions of Masculinity in Victorian America.* Chicago: University of Chicago Press, 1990.

Chapman, Rowena, and Jonathan Rutherford, eds. *Male Order: Unwrapping Masculinity.* London: Lawrence & Wishart, 1988.

Clatterbaugh, Kenneth C. *Contemporary Perspectives on Masculinity: Men, Women, and Politics in US Society.* Boulder: Westview, 1990.

Cohen, Ed. *Talk on the Wilde Side: Toward a Genealogy of a Discourse on Male Sexualities.* New York: Routledge, 1993.

Collier, Richard. *Masculinity, Law, and the Family.* New York: Routledge, 1994.

Cornwall, Andrea, and Nancy Lindisfarne, eds. *Dislocating Masculinity: Comparative Ethnographies.* London: Routledge, 1994.

Deleuze, Gilles, and Felix Guattari. *Anti-Oedipus: Capitalism and Schizophrenia.* New York: Viking, 1977.

D'Emilio, John, and Estelle B. Freeman. *Intimate Matters: A History of Sexuality in America.* New York: Perennial Library, 1988.

Di Stefano, Christine. *Configurations of Masculinity: A Feminist Perspective on Modern Political Theory.* Ithaca, N.Y.: Cornell University Press, 1991.

Dollimore, Jonathan. "Homophobia and Sexual Difference." Special issue, "Sexual Difference." *Oxford Literary Review* 8, no. 1–2 (1986).

Doty, William G. *Myths of Masculinity.* New York: Crossroad, 1993.

Dunning, Eric. "Sport as a Male Preserve: Notes on the Social Sources of Masculine Identity and Its Transformations." In *Quest for Excitement: Sport and Leisure in the Civilizing Process*, ed. by Norbert Elias and Eric Dunning. Oxford: Basil Blackwell, 1986.

Ehrenreich, Barbara. "A Feminist's View of the New Man." *New York Times Magazine* 13 (May 20, 1984).

_____. *The Hearts of Men: American Dreams and the Flight from Commitment.* New York: Doubleday, 1983.

Fee, Dwight. "Masculinities, Identity, and the Politics of Essentialism: A Social Constructionist Critique of the Men's Movement." *Feminism and Psychology* 2 (June 1992): 171–76.

Ferguson, Russell, ed. *Out There: Marginalization and Contemporary Cultures.* New York: New Museum of Contemporary Culture, and Cambridge: MIT Press, 1990.

Fogel, Gerald I., Frederick M. Lane, and Robert S. Liebert, eds. *The Psychology of Men: New Psychoanalytic Perspectives.* New York: Basic, 1986.

Foucault, Michel. *The History of Sexuality,* 3 vols., trans. by Robert Hurley. New York: Pantheon, 1978–86.

Frosh, Stephen. *Sexual Difference: Masculinity and Psychoanalysis.* New York: Routledge, 1994.

Fuss, Diana J. *Essentially Speaking: Feminism, Nature, and Difference.* New York: Routledge, 1989.

Fussell, Paul. *The Boy Scout Handbook and Other Observations.* New York: Oxford University Press, 1982.

Gallop, Jane. *Reading Lacan.* Ithaca: Cornell University Press, 1985.

Garber, Marjorie. *Vested Interests: Cross-dressing and Cultural Anxiety.* New York: Routledge, 1992.

Gerzon, Mark. *A Choice of Heroes: The Changing Faces of American Manhood.* Boston: Houghton Mifflin, 1992.

Gilbert, Richard K. "Revisiting the Psychology of Men: Robert Bly and the Mythopoetic Movement." *Journal of Psychology* 32 (spring 1992): 41–67.

Gillett, James, and Philip G. White. "Male Bodybuilding and the Reassertion of Hegemonic Masculinity: A Critical Feminist Perspective." *Play and Culture* 5 (Nov. 1992): 358–69.

Gilmore, David D. *Manhood in the Making: Cultural Concepts of Masculinity.* New Haven: Yale University Press, 1990.

Green, Martin Burgess. *The Adventurous Male: Chapters in the History of the White Male Mind.* University Park: Pennsylvania State University Press, 1993.

Griswold, Robert L. *Fatherhood in America: A History.* New York: Basic, 1993.

Haddad, Tony, ed. *Men and Masculinities: A Critical Anthology.* Toronto: Canadian Scholar's Press, 1993.

Harding, Christopher, ed. *Wingspan: Inside the Men's Movement.* New York: St. Martin's, 1992.

Hartsock, N.C.M. "Gender and Sexuality: Masculinity, Violence, and Domination." *Humanities in Society* 7, no. 1–2 (1984).

Hearn, Jeff. *The Gender of Oppression: Men, Masculinity, and the Critique of Marxism.* Brighton, Sussex: Wheatsheaf, 1987.

_____. *Men in the Public Eye: The Construction and Deconstruction of Public Men and Public Patriarchies.* New York: Routledge, 1992.

_____. "The Politics of Essentialism and the Analysis of the 'Men's Movement(s)'." *Feminism and Psychology* 3 (Oct. 1993): 405–409.

Hearn, Jeff, and David Morgan, eds. *Men, Masculinities, and Social Theory.* London: Unwin Hyman, 1990.

Hertz, Neil. "Medusa's Head: Male Hysteria Under Political Pressure." *Representations* 4 (fall 1983): 27–54.

Heath, Stephen. *The Sexual Fix.* New York: Macmillan, 1982.

Higonnet, Margaret, et al, eds. *Behind the Lines: Gender and the Two World Wars.* New Haven: Yale University Press, 1987.

Horrocks, Roger. *Masculinity in Crisis: Myths, Fantasies, and Realities.* New York: St. Martin's, 1994.

Jackson, David. *Unmasking Masculinity: A Critical Autobiography.* Boston: Unwin Hyman, 1990.

Jansen, Sue Curry, and Don Sabo. "The Sport/War Metaphor: Hegemonic Masculinity, the Persian Gulf War, and the New World Order." *Sociology of Sport Journal* 11 (Mar. 1994): 1–17.

Jardine, Alice, and Paul Smith. *Men in Feminism.* New York: Methuen, 1987.

General

Jeffords, Susan. *The Remasculinization of America: Gender and the Vietnam War.* Bloomington: Indiana University Press, 1989.

_____, ed. *Seeing Through the Media: The Persian Gulf War.* New Brunswick, N.J.: Rutgers University Press, 1994.

Jordanova, Ludmilla. *Sexual Visions: Images of Gender in Science and Medicine Between the Eighteenth and Twentieth Centuries.* Madison: University of Wisconsin Press, 1989.

Kaufman, Michael. *Cracking the Armor: Power, Pain, and the Lives of Men.* Toronto: Penguin, 1994.

Kaufman, Michael, ed. *Beyond Patriarchy: Essays by Men on Pleasure, Power, and Change.* New York: Oxford University Press, 1987.

Kidd, B. "Sports and Masculinity." *Queens Quarterly* 94, no. 1 (1987): 116–31.

Kilmartin, Christopher T. *The Masculine Self.* New York: Macmillan, 1994.

Kimmel, Michael. *Gender and Desire.* New York: Basic, 1989.

_____. "Invisible Masculinity." *Society* 30 (Sept. 1993): 28–35.

_____. "Reading Men: Men, Masculinity, and Publishing." *Contemporary Sociology* 21 (Mar. 1992): 162–70.

Kimmel, Michael, ed. *Changing Men: New Directions in Research on Men and Masculinity.* Newbury Park, Calif.: Sage, 1987.

Kimmel, Michael, and Michael Messner. *Men's Lives.* New York: Macmillan, 1989.

Kimmel, Michael, and Thomas E. Mosmiller, eds. *Against the Tide: Pro-feminist Men in the United States, 1776–1990: A Documentary History.* Boston: Beacon, 1992.

Klein, Alan M. *Little Big Men: Bodybuilding Subculture and Gender Construction.* Albany: State University of New York Press, 1993.

_____. "Managing Deviance: Hustling, Homophobia, and the Bodybuilding Subculture." *Deviant Behavior* 10, no.1 (1989): 11–27.

Klein, Fritz, and Timothy J. Wolf, eds. *Bisexualities: Theory and Research.* New York: Haworth, 1985.

Kopay, David, and Perry Deane Young. *The David Kopay Story: An Extraordinary Self-Revelation.* New York: Arbor House, 1977.

Kupers, Terry Allen. *Revisioning Men's Lives: Gender, Intimacy, and Power.* New York: Guilford, 1993.

Lacan, Jacques. *Ecrits: A Selection,* trans. by Alan Sheridan. New York: Norton, 1977.

MacLeod, David. *Building Character in the American Boy: The Boy Scouts, the YMCA, and their Forerunners, 1870–1920.* Madison: University of Wisconsin Press, 1983.

Mangan, J.A., and James Walvin, eds. *Manliness and Morality: Middle-class Masculinity in Britain and America, 1800–1940.* Manchester: Manchester University Press, 1987.

May, Larry, Robert A. Strikwerda, and Patrick D. Hopkins, eds. *Rethinking Masculinity: Philosophical Explorations in Light of Feminism.* Lanham, Md.: Littlefield Adams, 1992.

Messerschmidt, James W. *Masculinities and Crime: Critique and Reconceptualization of Theory.* Lanham, Md.: Rowan & Littlefield, 1993.

Messner, Michael A. "Boyhood, Organized Sports, and the Construction of Masculinities." *Journal of Contemporary Ethnography* 18 (Jan. 1990): 416–44.

_____. *Power at Play: Sports and the Problem of Masculinity.* Boston: Beacon, 1992.

_____. *Sex, Violence, and Power in Sports.* Freedom, Calif.: Crossing, 1994.

_____. "White Men Misbehaving: Feminism, Afrocentrism, and the Promise of a Critical Standpoint." *Journal of Sport and Social Issues* 16 (Dec. 1992): 136–44.

Messner, Michael A., and Don F. Sabo, eds. *Sport, Men, and the Gender Order: Critical Feminist Perspectives.* Champaign, Ill.: Human Kinetics, 1990.

Mitchell, Juliet, and Jacqueline Rose, eds. *Feminine Sexuality: Jacques Lacan and the Ecole Freudienne.* New York: W. W. Norton, 1982.

Moi, Toril. "Representation of Patriarchy: Sexuality and Epistemology in Freud's Dora." In *Dora's Case: Freud, Hysteria, Feminism,* ed. by Charles Bernheimer and Claire Kahane. New York: Columbia University Press, 1985.

Money, John. *Gay, Straight, and In-Between: The Sexology of Erotic Orientation.* New York: Oxford University Press, 1988.

Monick, Eugene. *Castration and Male Rage: The Phallic Wound.* Toronto: Inner City, 1991.

Moon, Brian. "Theorizing Violence in the Discourse of Masculinities." *South Atlantic Review* 25 (July 1992): 194–204.

Morgan, D.H.J. *Discovering Men.* New York: Routledge, 1992.

Morgan, David. *It Will Make a Man of You.* Manchester: Manchester University Press, 1987.

Mosher, Donald L. "Macho Men, Machismo, and Sexuality." *Annual Review of Sex Research* 2 (1991): 199–247.

Mosher, Donald L., and Silvan S. Tomkins. "Scripting the Macho Man: Hypermasculine Socialization and Enculturation." *The Journal of Sex Research* 25 (Feb. 1988): 60–84.

Newburn, Tim, and Elizabeth Anne Stanko, eds. *Just Boys Doing Business?: Men, Masculinities and Crime.* New York: Routledge, 1994.

Nye, Robert A. *Masculinity and Male Codes of Honor in Modern France.* New York: Oxford University Press, 1993.

Pittman, Frank S. *Man Enough: Fathers, Sons, and the Search for Masculinity.* New York: G. P. Putnam's Sons, 1993.

Pleck, Elizabeth H., and Joseph H. Pleck, eds. *The American Man.* Englewood Cliffs, N.J.: Prentice-Hall, 1980.

Pleck, Joseph. *The Myth of Masculinity.* Cambridge: MIT Press, 1983.

Porter, David, ed. *Between Men and Feminism.* New York: Routledge, 1992.

Pugh, David G. *Sons of Liberty: The Masculine Mind in Nineteenth Century America.* Westport, Conn.: Greenwood, 1983.

Raphael, Ray. *The Men from the Boys: Rites of Passage in Male America.* Lincoln: University of Nebraska Press, 1988.

Reynaud, Emmanuel. *Holy Virility: The Social Construction of Masculinity.* London: Pluto, 1983.

Rogers, Barbara. *Men Only: An Investigation Into Men's Organizations.* London: Pandora, 1988.

Roper, Michael, and John Tosh, eds. *Manful Assertions: Masculinities in Britain since 1800.* London: Routledge, 1991.

Ross, John Munder. *The Male Paradox.* New York: Simon & Schuster, 1992.

_____. *What Men Want: Mothers, Fathers, and Manhood.* Cambridge: Harvard University Press, 1994.

Rotundo, E. Anthony. *American Manhood: Transformations in Masculinity from the Revolution to the Modern Era.* New York: Basic, 1993.

Rowan, John. *The Horned God: Feminism and Men as Wounding and Healing.* London: Routledge & Kegan Paul, 1987.

Rutherford, Jonathan. *Men's Silences: Predicaments in Masculinity.* New York: Routledge, 1992.

General

Sabo, Donald F., and Ross Runfola, eds. *Jock: Sports and Male Identity.* Englewood Cliffs, N.J.: Prentice-Hall, 1980.

Segal, Lynne. *Slow Motion: Changing Masculinities, Changing Men.* New Brunswick, N.J.: Rutgers University Press, 1990.

Seidler, Victor J. *Rediscovering Masculinity: Reason, Language, and Sexuality.* New York: Routledge, 1989.

_____. *Unreasonable Men: Masculinity and Social Theory.* New York: Routledge, 1994.

Seidler, Victor J., ed. *Men, Sex, and Relationships: Writings from 'Achilles Heel'.* New York: Routledge, 1992.

Silverman, Kaja. "The Lacanian Phallus." *differences: A Journal of Feminist Studies* 4, no. 1 (1992): 84–115.

Simpson, Mark. *Male Impersonators: Men Performing Masculinity.* New York: Routledge, 1994.

Smith-Rosenberg, Carol. *Disorderly Conduct: Visions of Gender in Victorian America.* New York: Oxford University Press, 1985.

Snitow, Ann, Christine Stansell, and Sharon Thompson, eds. *Powers of Desire: The Politics of Sexuality.* New York: Monthly Review Press, 1983.

Talamini, John T. *Boys Will be Girls: The Hidden World of the Heterosexual Male Transvestite.* Washington, D.C.: University Presses of America, 1982.

Thornton, Margaret. "Hegemonic Masculinity and the Academy." *International Journal of the Sociology of Law* 17 (May 1989): 115–30.

Threadgold, Terry, and Anne Cranny-Francis, eds. *Feminine, Masculine and Representation.* Sydney: Allen & Unwin, 1990.

Turner, James Grantham, ed. *Sexuality and Gender in Early Modern Europe: Institutions, Texts, Images.* Cambridge: Cambridge University Press, 1993.

Walczek, Yvette. *He and She: Men in the Eighties.* London: Routledge, 1988.

Weeks, Jeffrey. *Against Nature: Essays on History, Sexuality and Identity.* London: Rivers Oram, 1991.

_____. *Sex, Politics, and Society: The Regulation of Sexuality Since 1800.* London: Longman, 1989.

_____. *Sexuality and its Discontents: Meanings, Myths, and Modern Sexualities.* London: Routledge & Kegan Paul, 1985.

Wetherell, Margaret, and Christine Griffin. "Feminist Psychology and the Study of Men and Masculinity." *Feminism and Psychology* 1 (Oct. 1991): 361–91.

Whitehead, Tony L., and Barbara V. Reid, eds. *Gender Constructs and Social Issues.* Urbana: University of Illinois Press, 1992.

Wyly, James. *The Phallic Quest: Priapus and Masculine Inflation.* Toronto: Inner City, 1989.

Gay & Lesbian/Queer Studies

Abelove, Henry, Michele Aina Barale, and David M. Halperin, eds. *The Lesbian and Gay Studies Reader.* New York: Routledge, 1993.

Altman, Dennis, ed. *Homosexuality: Which Homosexuality?* Amsterdam: An Dekker/Schorer, 1989.

Beam, Joseph, ed. *In the Life: A Black Gay Anthology.* Boston: Allyson, 1986.

Bell, Alan P., and Martin S. Weinberg, eds. *Homosexualities: A Study of Diversity Among Men and Women.* New York: Simon & Schuster, 1978.

Bergman, David, ed. *Camp Grounds: Style and Homosexuality.* Amherst: University of Massachusetts Press, 1993.

Bersani, Leo. "Is the Rectum a Grave?" *October* 43 (1987): 197–222.

Berube, Alan. *Coming Out Under Fire: The History of Gay Men and Women in World War Two.* New York: Penguin, 1991.

Boswell, John. *Christianity, Social Tolerance, and Homosexuality: Gay People in Western Europe from the Beginning of the Christian Era to the Fourteenth Century.* Chicago: University of Chicago Press, 1980.

_____. *Same-sex Unions in Pre-modern Europe.* New York: Random House, 1994.

Bray, Alan. *Homosexuality in Renaissance England.* London: Gay Men's Press, 1988.

Bronski, Michael. *Culture Clash: The Making of Gay Sensibility.* Boston: South End, 1984.

Chauncy, George Jr. *Gay New York: Gender, Urban Culture, and the Makings of the Gay Male World, 1890–1940.* New York: Basic, 1994.

Connell, R. W. "A Very Straight Gay: Masculinity, Homosexual Experience, and the Dynamics of Gender." *American Sociological Review* 57 (Dec. 1992): 735–51.

Crimp, Douglas. *AIDS: Cultural Analysis, Cultural Activism.* Cambridge: MIT Press, 1988.

De Lauretis, Teresa, ed. *Queer Theory: Lesbian and Gay Sexualities.* Bloomington: Indiana University Press, 1991.

D'Emilio, John. *Sexual Politics, Sexual Communities: The Making of a Homosexual Minority in the United States, 1940–1970.* Chicago: University of Chicago Press, 1983.

Duberman, Martin Bauml, ed. *About Time: Exploring the Gay Past.* New York: Seahorse, 1986.

Duberman, Martin Bauml, Martha Vicinus, and George Chauncy Jr., eds. *Hidden From History: Reclaiming the Gay and Lesbian Past.* New York: New American Library, 1989.

Dynes, Wayne. *Homosexuality: A Research Guide.* New York: Garland, 1987.

Dynes, Wayne, Warren Johansson, William A. Percy, and Stephen Donaldson, eds. *Encyclopedia of Homosexuality.* New York: Garland, 1990.

Edwards, Tim. *Erotics and Politics: Gay Male Sexuality, Masculinity, and Feminism.* London: Routledge, 1994.

Epstein, Steven. "Gay Politics, Ethnic Identity: The Limits of Social Construction." *Socialist Review* 17 (May/Aug. 1987): 9–54.

Fone, Byrne R.S. *A Road to Stonewall: Male Homosexuality and Homophobia in England and America, 1750–1969.* New York: Twayne, 1994.

Greenberg, David F. *The Construction of Homosexuality.* Chicago: University of Chicago Press, 1988.

Halperin, David. *One Hundred Years of Homosexuality: And Other Essays on Greek Love.* New York: Routledge, 1990.

Hemphill, Essex. *Ceremonies: Prose and Poetry.* New York: Penguin, 1992.

Hocquenghem, Guy. *Homosexual Desire,* trans. by Daniella Dangoor. London: Allison & Busby, 1978.

General

Icard, Larry. "Black Gay Men and Conflicting Social Identities: Sexual Orientation versus Racial Identity." *Journal of Social Work and Human Sexuality* 4 (1985–86): 83–93.

Katz, Jonathan. *Gay American History: Lesbians and Gay Men in the U.S.A.: A Documentary.* New York: Crowell, 1976.

_____. *Gay/Lesbian Almanac: A New Documentary.* New York: Harper & Row, 1983.

Kleinberg, Seymour. *Alienated Affection: Being Gay in America.* New York: St. Martin's, 1980.

Koestenbaum, Wayne. *The Queen's Throat: Opera, Homosexuality, and the Mystery of Desire.* London: Gay Men's Press, 1993.

Lewes, Kenneth. *The Psychoanalytic Theory of Male Homosexuality.* New York: Simon & Schuster, 1988.

Miller, Neil. *In Search of Gay America.* New York: Harper & Row, 1989.

_____. *Out in the World: Gay and Lesbian Life from Buenos Aires to Bangkok.* New York: Vintage, 1992.

Monette, Paul. *Becoming a Man: Half a Life's Story.* New York: Harcourt Brace Jovanovich, 1992.

Plummer, Kenneth, ed. *The Making of the Modern Homosexual.* London: Hutchison, 1981.

_____, ed. *Modern Homosexualities: Fragments of Lesbian and Gay Experience.* New York: Routledge, 1992.

Porter, Kevin, and Jeffrey Weeks, eds. *Between the Acts: Lives of Homosexual Men, 1885–1967.* London: Routledge, 1991.

Preston, John. *My Life as a Pornographer and Other Indecent Acts.* New York: Masquerade, 1993.

Pronger, Brian. *The Arena of Masculinity: Sports, Homosexuality, and the Meaning of Sex.* London: Gay Men's Press, 1990.

Rist, Darrell Yates. *Heartlands: A Gay Man's Odyssey Across America.* New York: Penguin, 1992.

Sedgewick, Eve Kosofsky. *Tendencies.* Durham, N.C.: Duke University Press, 1993.

Siegel, Stanley. *Uncharted Lives: The Psychological Journey of Gay Men.* New York: Dutton, 1994.

Signorelli, Michelangelo. "Clone Wars." *Outweek* 28 (Nov. 1990): 39–45.

Sinfield, Alan. *The Wilde Century: Effeminacy, Oscar Wilde, and the Queer Movement.* New York: Columbia University Press, 1994.

Steakley, James D. *The Homosexual Emancipation Movement in Germany.* New York: Arno, 1975.

Thompson, Mark, ed. *Leatherfolk: Radical Sex, Politics, and Practice.* Boston: Allyson, 1991.

Weeks, Jeffrey. *Coming Out: Homosexual Politics in Britain.* New York: Quartet, 1977.

Williams, Walter. *The Spirit and the Flesh: Sexual Diversity in American Indian Culture.* Boston: Beacon, 1986.

Winkler, John J. *Constraints of Desire: The Anthropology of Sex and Gender in Ancient Greece.* New York: Routledge, 1989.

Wooden, Wayne S., Harvey Kawasaki, and Raymond Mayeda. "Identity Maintenance of Japanese-American Gays." *Alternative Lifestyles* 6 (1983): 236–43.

Race/Ethnicity

Boskin, Joseph. *Sambo: The Rise and Demise of an American Jester.* New York: Oxford University Press, 1986.

Brod, Harry, ed. *A Mensch Among Men: Explorations in Jewish Masculinity.* Freedom, Calif.: Crossing, 1988.

De La Cancela, Victor. "Labor Pains: Puerto Rican Males in Transition." *Centro de Estudios Puertorriquenos Bulletin* 2 (fall 1988): 40–55.

Duneier, Mitchell. *Slim's Table: Race, Respectability, and Masculinity.* Chicago: University of Chicago Press, 1992.

Harriss, Shanette M. "Black Male Masculinity and Same-sex Friendships." *Western Journal of Black Studies* 16 (summer 1992): 74–81.

Hoch, Paul. *White Hero, Black Beast: Racism, Sexism, and the Mask of Masculinity.* London: Pluto, 1979.

hooks, bell. *Black Looks: Race and Representation.* Boston: South End, 1992.

_____. *Talking Back: Thinking Feminist, Thinking Black.* Boston: South End, 1989.

_____. *Yearning: Race, Gender, and Cultural Politics.* Boston: South End, 1990.

Hunter, Andrea G., and James E. Davis. "Constructing Gender: An Exploration of Afro-American Men's Conceptualization of Manhood." *Gender and Society* 6 (Sept. 1992): 464–79.

"Jewishness and Masculinity." Special Issue. *Changing Men* 18 (summer/fall 1987). Madison: Feminist Men's Publications, 1987.

Mercer, Kobena. "Fear of a Black Penis." *Artforum* 32 (Apr. 1994): 80–1, 122.

Mercer, Kobena, and Isaac Julien. "Race, Sexual Politics, and Black Masculinity: A Dossier." In *Male Order: Unwrapping Masculinity*, ed. by Rowena Chapman and Jonathan Rutherford. London: Lawrence & Wishart, 1988.

Powell, Kevin. "Looking for a Man: African American Males' Search for Masculinity." *Essence* 25 (Aug. 1994): 36.

Roberts, George W. "Brother to Brother: African American Modes of Relating Among Men." *Journal of Black Studies* 24 (June 1994): 379–90.

Staples, Robert. *Black Masculinity: The Black Man's Role in American Society.* San Francisco: Black Scholar, 1982.

Wallace, Michele. *Black Macho and the Myth of the Superwoman.* New York: Dial, 1979.

General

Harry Brod is an Assistant Professor of Philosophy at the University of Delaware. He has edited *The Making of Masculinities: The New Men's Studies; A Mensch Among Men: Explorations in Jewish Masculinity;* and most recently (with Michael Kaufman), *Theorizing Masculinities.* He is the author of *Hegel's Philosophy of Politics* and is a spokesperson for the National Organization for Men Against Sexism.

Steven Cohan is a Professor of English at Syracuse University. He is the coauthor of *Telling Stories: A Theoretical Analysis of Narrative Fiction* (Routledge, 1988), coeditor of *Screening the Male: Exploring Masculinities in Hollywood Cinema* (Routledge, 1993), and has written on film in *Camera Obscura* and *Screen.* At present he is writing a book on American masculinity and the movies of the fifties.

bell hooks is a Distinguished Professor of English at City College, New York. She is the author of *Sisters of Yam: Black Women and Self-Recovery* (South End, 1993), *Black Looks: Race and Representation* (South End, 1992) and *Yearning: Race, Gender, and Cultural Politics* (South End, 1990). She is a noted feminist theorist and cultural critic.

Michael Leininger is the Architecture Librarian for the MIT Libraries and a past president of the Association of Architecture School Librarians.

Glenn Ligon is an artist who lives and works in Brooklyn, New York. His work has been shown in the *1991* and *1993 Biennial Exhibitions* at the Whitney Museum of American Art, in *Double Take: Collective Memory and Current Art* (1992) at the Hayward Gallery, London, and in *Dark O'Clock* (1994) at the Museu de Arte Moderna, São Paulo, Brazil.

Andrew Perchuk is a former Curator and Deputy Director of the Alternative Museum, New York. He has written for numerous art publications and institutions, including the Whitney Museum of American Art, Hallwalls, and Art in General. He is a regular contributor to *Artforum* magazine and is working on his Ph.D. in art history at the University of Southern California, Los Angeles.

Helaine Posner is Curator at the MIT List Visual Arts Center, Cambridge, Massachusetts. She is curator of the exhibition and coauthor of the catalogue *Corporal Politics* (Beacon, 1992). She has organized numerous exhibitions of contemporary art, including *Leon Golub and Nancy Spero: War and Memory* (with Katy Kline); *Per Kirkeby: Paintings and Drawings;* and *Ann Hamilton: aleph,* among others.

Simon Watney is a writer and critic. He is the author of *Practices of Freedom: Selected Writings on HIV/AIDS* (Duke University Press, 1994). He is Director of the London-based Red Hot AIDS Charitable Trust, a funding initiative that supports community-based HIV/AIDS education around the world.

Photography

Matthew Barney:
Video stills courtesy Barbara Gladstone Gallery, New York

Tina Barney:
Photograph of *John's Den* courtesy Janet Borden Inc.
Photograph of *Card Game* courtesy Janet Borden, Inc.
Photograph of *The Boys* courtesy Museum of Fine Arts, Boston

Clegg & Guttmann:
Photograph of *The Financiers* courtesy of the artists

Graham Durward:
Photograph of *Snow Drift* courtesy Sandra Gering Gallery

Lyle Ashton Harris:
Photograph of *Alexandra and Lyle* by Olson Color Expansions
Photographs of *Brotherhood, Crossroads and Etcetera*
by Olson Color Expansions

Dale Kistemaker:
Photographs of installation courtesy of the artist

Mary Kelly:
Photograph of installation by Klaus Ottmann
Photographs of details by Ray Barrie

Glenn Ligon:
Photographs of photo-essay by Charles Mayer

Donald Moffett:
Photographs of *Choke* and *Glory* by Geoffrey Clements
Photograph of *Sutured Snowman* by Ellen Page Wilson

Keith Piper:
Video Stills courtesy World Wide Video Centre, The Hague

Charles Ray:
Photograph of *Self-Portrait* courtesy Feature Gallery

Michael Yue Tong:
Photographs of *Red Sky at Morning* courtesy of the artist

Design
Kohn Cruikshank Inc, Boston

Printing and binding
through Palace Press International, San Francisco
in Hong Kong